The Places in Between

'An extraordinary journey across one of the world's
most unsettled countries – the accumulations of meetings
and slowly changing landscapes, the tragedy of war and the
humour of its survivors, the sight of men throwing open
their doors and the occasional boys flinging stones – all this
casts light on a part of the world about which we have
heard a great deal and about which we know little'
Sunday Times

'Stewart has a Mughal miniature-painter's gift:
to render observed reality with the extreme clarity
possible on a small scale'
Guardian

'Unlike most anything written about Afghanistan in
the years since the invasion . . . By turns harrowing and
hilarious . . . captures a part of Afghanistan that has eluded
many journalists and writers. Using walking as meditation,
he turns the pedestrian into the profound'
Far Eastern Economic Review

'A unique fascinating journey'
Herald

'Journeys like this are extremely rare in the
21st century . . . *The Places in Between* goes straight in
the highest echelons of travel literature'
Wanderlust

RORY STEWART

The Places in Between

PICADOR

First published 2004 by Picador

This edition published 2005 by Picador
Pan Macmillan, 20 New Wharf Road, London N1 9RR
Basingstoke and Oxford
Associated companies throughout the world
www.panmacmillan.com

ISBN 0 330 48634 9

1 3 5 7 9 8 6 4 2

A CIP catalogue record for this book is available from
the British Library.

Typeset by Intype Libra Ltd
Printed and bound in Great Britain by
Mackays of Chatham plc, Chatham, Kent

This book is dedicated to the people of Iran, Afghanistan, Pakistan, India and Nepal, who showed me the way, fed me, protected me, housed me and made this walk possible. They were not all saints, though some of them were. A number were greedy, idle, stupid, hypocritical, insensitive, mendacious, ignorant and cruel. Some of them had robbed or killed others; many of them threatened me and begged from me. But never in twenty-one months of travel did they attempt to kidnap or kill me. I was alone and a stranger, walking in very remote areas; I represented a culture that many of them hated and I was carrying enough money to save or at least transform their lives. In more than five hundred village houses, I was indulged, fed, nursed, and protected by people poorer, hungrier, sicker and more vulnerable than myself. Almost every group I met: Sunni Kurds, Shia Hazara, Punjabi Christians, Sikhs, Brahmins of Kedarnath, Garwhal Dalits and Newari Buddhists, gave me hospitality without any thought of reward.

I owe this journey and my life to them.

Contents

Preface

I'm not good at explaining why I walked across Afghanistan. Perhaps I did it because it was an adventure. But it was the most interesting part of my journey across Asia. The Taliban had banned posters and films, but I arrived six weeks after their departure and saw the Herat arcade hung with posters of the Hindi film star Hrithik Roshan, standing on a cliff at sunset, his bouffant hair ruffled by the evening breeze. In the courtyard where Al-Qaeda men had gathered to chat in Urdu, students were waiting to practise their English on war reporters. I found *Man in the Iron Mask* amongst a pile of DVDs on a handcart. It had been touched up for the Afghan market so that Leonardo Di Caprio, as Louis XIV in seventeenth-century dress, brandished a Browning 9mm. Herat, which had been a great medieval market for China, Turkey and Persia, was now selling Chinese alarm clocks, Turkish sunglasses and Iranian apple juice.

It was the beginning of 2002. I had just spent sixteen months walking twenty to twenty-five miles a day across Iran, Pakistan, India and Nepal. I had wanted to walk every step of the way without using a vehicle and I had intended to cross Afghanistan a year earlier. But in December 2000 the Iranian government took my visa away. They may have discovered that I had been a British diplomat and become suspicious of my motives. The Taliban then refused to allow me into Afghanistan and the Government of Pakistan excluded me from Baluchistan. As a result, I had to leave a gap between Iran and the next stage of my journey, which started in

Multan in Pakistan and continued in an unbroken line to Eastern Nepal.

Just before Christmas 2001, I reached a town in eastern Nepal and heard that the Taliban had fallen. I decided to return by vehicle to Afghanistan and walk from Herat to Kabul and thus connect my walk in Iran with my walk in Pakistan. I chose to walk from Herat to Kabul in a straight line through the central mountains. The normal dog-leg through Kandahar was flatter, easier and free of snow. But it was also longer and controlled in parts by the Taliban.

The country had been at war for twenty-five years; the new government had been in place for only two weeks; there was no electricity between Herat and Kabul, no television and no T-shirts. Villages combined medieval etiquette with new political ideologies. In many houses the only piece of foreign technology was a Kalashnikov, and the only global brand was Islam. All that had made Afghanistan seem backward, peripheral and irrelevant now made it the centre of the world's attention.

Introduction

The country is quite covered by darkness, so that
people outside it cannot see anything in it; and no one
dares go in for fear of the darkness. Nevertheless men
who live in the country round about say that they can
sometimes hear the voices of men, and horses neigh-
ing, and cocks crowing, and thereby that some kind
of folks live there, but they do not know what kind of
folk they are.

– *The Travels of Sir John Mandeville,*
c.1360, Chapter 28

The New Civil Service

I watched two men enter the lobby of the Hotel Mowafaq.

Most Afghans seemed to glide up the centre of the lobby staircase with their shawls trailing behind them like Venetian cloaks. But these men wore western jackets, walked quietly and stayed close to the banister. I felt a hand on my shoulder. It was the hotel manager.

'Follow them.' He had never spoken to me before.

'I'm sorry, no,' I said. 'I am busy.'

'Now. They are from the government.'

I followed him to a room on a floor which I didn't know existed and he told me to take off my shoes and enter alone in my socks. The two men were seated on a heavy black-wood sofa, beside an aluminium spittoon. They were still wearing their shoes. I smiled. They did not. There were lace curtains across the windows and there was no electricity in the city, so it was dark in the room.

'*Chi kar mikonid?*' What are you doing? asked the man in the black suit and collarless Iranian shirt. I expected him to stand in the normal way, shake hands and wish me peace. He remained seated.

'*Salaam aleikum,*' Peace be with you, I said and sat down.

'*Waleikum a-salaam. Chi kar mikonid?*' he repeated quietly, leaning back and running his fat manicured hand along the purple velveteen arm of the sofa. His bouffant hair and goatee beard were neatly trimmed. I felt conscious of not having shaved in eight weeks.

'I have explained what I am doing many times to His

Excellency, Yuzufi, in the Foreign Ministry,' I said. 'I was told to meet him again now. I am late.'

A pulse was beating strongly in my neck. I knew it would be visible. I tried to breathe more slowly. Neither of us spoke. After a little while, I looked away.

The thinner man drew out a small new radio, said something into it and straightened his stiff jacket over his traditional shirt. I didn't need to see the shoulder holster. I had already guessed that they were members of the Security Service. They did not care what I said or what I thought of them. They had watched people through hidden cameras in bedrooms, in torture cells and on execution grounds. They knew that, however I presented myself, I could be reduced. But why had they decided to question me? In the silence, I heard a car reversing in the courtyard and then the first slow notes of the call to prayer.

'Let's go,' said the man in the black suit. He told me to walk in front. On the stairs, I passed a waiter to whom I had spoken. He turned away. I was led to a small Japanese car, parked on the dirt forecourt. The paintwork of the car was new and it had been washed recently. They told me to sit in the back. There was nothing in the pockets or on the floor of the car. It looked as though it had just come from the factory. Without saying anything, they turned on to the main boulevard.

It was January 2002. The American-led coalition was ending its bombardment of the Tora Bora complex; Usama Bin Laden and Mullah Muhammad Omar had apparently escaped; operations in Gardez were beginning. The new government, which had taken over from the Taliban, had been in place for two weeks. The laws banning television and female education had been dropped. Political prisoners had been released, refugees were returning home. Some women were coming out without veils. The UN and the US military were running the basic infrastructure and food supplies. There was no frontier guard and I had entered the country without a visa. The Afghan government seemed to me hardly to exist. Yet these men were apparently already well established.

The car turned into the Foreign Ministry, and the gate guards saluted and stood back. As I walked up the stairs, I felt that I was walking unnaturally quickly and that the men had noticed this. A secretary showed us straight into Mr Yuzufi's office without knocking. For a moment Yuzufi stared at us and did not move from his desk, then he stood, straightened his baggy pinstriped jacket, and showed the others to the most senior position in the room. The two men walked slowly down the linoleum floor. They looked at the furniture, which Yuzufi had managed to assemble since he had inherited an empty office: the splintered desk, the four mismatched filing cabinets in different olive greens and the stove, which made the room smell strongly of petrol.

The week I had known Yuzufi comprised half his career in the Foreign Ministry. A fortnight earlier he had been in Pakistan. The day before he had given me tea and a boiled sweet, told me he admired my journey, laughed at a photograph of my father in his kilt and discussed Persian poetry. This time he did not greet me but instead sat in a chair facing me and asked, 'What has happened?'

Before I could reply the man with the goatee cut in, 'What is this foreigner doing here?'

'These men are from the Security Service,' said Yuzufi.

I nodded. I noticed that Yuzufi had clasped his hands together and that his hands, like mine, were trembling slightly.

'I will translate to make sure you understand what they are asking,' continued Yuzufi. 'Tell them your intentions. Exactly as you told me.'

I looked into the eyes of the man on my left. 'I am planning to walk across Afghanistan. From Herat to Kabul. On foot.' I was not breathing enough to complete my phrases.

I was surprised they didn't interrupt. 'I am following in the footsteps of Babur, the first emperor of Mughal India. I want to get away from the roads. Journalists, aid workers and tourists mostly travel by car but I . . .'

'There are no tourists,' said the man in the stiff jacket, who had not yet spoken. 'You are the first tourist in Afghanistan. It is midwinter: there are three metres of snow on the high passes, there are wolves and this is a war. You will die, I can guarantee. Do you want to die?'

'Thank you very much for your advice. I note those three points.' I guessed from his tone that such advice was intended as an order. 'But I have spoken to the Cabinet,' I said, misrepresenting a brief meeting with the young secretary to the Minister of Social Welfare. 'I must do this journey.'

'Do it in a year's time,' said the man in the black suit.

He had taken from Yuzufi the tattered evidence of my walk across South Asia and was examining it: the clipping from the newspaper in western Nepal, 'Mr Stewart is a pilgrim for peace'; the letter from the Conservator, Second Circle, Forestry Department, Himachal Pradesh, India: 'Mr Stewart, a Scot, is interested in the environment'; from a District Officer in the Punjab and a Secretary of the Interior in a Himalayan state and a Chief Engineer of the Pakistan Department of Irrigation requesting 'All Executive Engineers (XENs) on the Lower Bari Doab to assist Mr Stewart, who will be undertaking a journey on foot to research the history of the canal system'.

'I have explained this,' I added, 'to His Excellency the Emir's son, the Minister of Social Welfare, when he also gave me a letter of introduction.'

'From His Excellency Mir Wais?'

'Here.' I handed over the sheet of headed paper which I had received from the Minister's secretary. 'Mr Stewart is a medieval antiquary interested in the anthropology of Herat'.

'But it is not signed.'

'Mr Yuzufi lost the signed copy.'

Yuzufi, who was staring at the ground, nodded slightly.

The two men talked together for a few minutes. I did not try to follow what they were saying. I noticed, however, that they were using Iranian not Afghan Persian words in their conversation. That and their clothes and their manner made me think they had spent a great deal of time with the Iranian intelligence services. I had been questioned by the Iranians, who seemed to suspect me of being a spy. I did not want to be questioned by them again.

The man in the stiff jacket said, 'We will allow him to walk to Chaghcharan. But our gunmen will accompany him all the way.' Chaghcharan was halfway between Herat and Kabul and about a fortnight into my journey.

The villagers with whom I was hoping to stay would be terrified by a secret police escort. This was presumably the point. But why were they letting me do the journey at all rather than expelling me? I wondered if they were looking for money. 'Thank you so much for your concern for my security,' I said, 'but I am quite happy to take the risk. I have walked alone across the other Asian countries without any problems.'

'You will take the escort,' said Yuzufi, interrupting for the first time, 'that is non-negotiable.'

'But I have introductions to the local commanders. I will be much safer with them than with Heratis.'

'You will go with our men,' he repeated.

'I cannot afford to pay for an escort. I have no money.'

'We were not expecting any money,' said the man in the stiff jacket.

'This is non-negotiable,' repeated Yuzufi. His broad knee was now jigging up and down. 'If you refuse this you will be expelled from the country. They want to know how many of their gunmen you are taking.'

'If it is compulsory, one.'

'Two . . . with weapons,' said the man in the dark suit, 'and you will leave tomorrow.'

The two men stood up and left the room. They said good-bye to Yuzufi but not to me.

Tanks into Sticks

Back outside Yuzufi's office, I bought some jam-rings from a glass box in a pastry shop. The men who had just interviewed me were not new to their jobs. The reactions of the hotel staff implied that they were already well known in Herat. They had probably worked for the KGB-trained KHAD. But I was disturbed that they were already functioning so effectively within the two-week-old administration and I wondered how they had found me. I ate all thirty biscuits quickly, dropping crumbs on my shawl, walking in the dust below the kerb. My boots kicked over the tracks of donkeys, tyres and other men's shoes. I was worried that these men would never allow me to walk. I felt trapped. I wanted to be moving again and to see the places between Herat and Kabul.

Herat that morning looked like a provincial Iranian shanty town. Everything had been constructed hurriedly and recently. On the flat roofs of half-finished shopping arcades, bare girders clustered like dead insect legs, and the walls were the same colour as the sand-drifts by the kerb. This was the architecture of political Islam, representing its combination of Marxism and puritan theology with drab Soviet brick. The men were dressed mostly in dirt-speckled black or faded brown like provincial Iranians. I did not like the city. To fill time I went to the bazaar to get a walking stick.

I had owned the ideal walking stick in Pakistan. It was five feet long and made of polished bamboo with an iron top and bottom; I had walked with it for nine months but had not brought it into Afghanistan. It was called a *dang* and Jats,

a farming caste from the Punjab, used to carry them, partly
for self-protection, until the middle of the twentieth century.
Many people still had their grandfathers' sticks in their
houses. Young men in both the Pakistani and Indian Punjab
liked to play with my stick, spinning it around their body,
taking the handle and bringing the base down in an accelerating arc on the head of an imaginary opponent. One man told
me that his great-grandfather had killed the last lion in the
Punjab with his *dang*. I liked walking with my *dang*: striking
the ground on every fourth step gave a rhythm to my movement. It was useful when I was climbing and it took the
weight off my left knee. But no one else carried them now
except the riot police. The Punjabi word '*dang*' had an archaic
flavour and people laughed when I used it.

There were Afghan students sitting in the Herat Friday
Mosque. They were seated near a giant medieval bronze
cauldron, staring at the jagged Ghorid script on the colon-
nade.

I asked one of the students where I could buy a heavy
walking stick.

He giggled. 'Like an old man?'

'Like an old man.'

'But you are young. Why do you need a stick?'

'Because I am walking to Kabul.'

'Take a bus.' They all laughed.

'Or a plane . . .' said another. They laughed more.

'So you've no idea where I could buy a walking stick.'

'Nowhere here. We have cars in Afghanistan.'

'Where do your old men get their walking sticks?'

'They make them.'

*

I continued beneath the remaining vaulted sections of the old
covered bazaar, which Robert Byron watched being demol-
ished in 1933. I wasn't sure what to call the stick. It certainly

seemed a waste of time to use the Punjabi word *dang*, in a place where people spoke Persian. But whatever word I used, people denied ever having heard of anything like it, so I asked where I could find a broom-handle and was directed to a wheelwright's store. Against his shop wall, surrounded by baskets of henna and dried apricots, were dozens of pine poles. They were much heavier than the bamboo that I had carried in the Punjab, but there was no bamboo to be found in the bazaar. I chose one that was five feet long, reasonably straight and well balanced in the centre.

Now I needed the iron. I followed a cloud of dark smoke down the main street and found a blacksmith with scorch-marked cheeks working a bright red furnace. In south Asia, a blacksmith would have been a low-caste man, an untouchable. But this man, Haji Ramzun, had visited Mecca, and here at his dark forge was a respected pilgrim, powerful among his peers. I explained my walk and what I wanted done to the pole. He offered to stick a section of rusty pipe to the bottom and a large nut to the top, paint them both sky blue and charge me for six days' work. I walked on.

I turned off Piaz Furushi, which meant 'Onion Street' but sold rugs and gold, and entered a courtyard. A donkey lay asleep in the centre of the square. Five men were sitting on rugs eating their lunch. I sketched the design of the stick and one of the men, Wakil Arna, said he could help. He led me towards the anvil, fixed to the rough wooden planks of his shed. A crowd of young boys gathered around to watch him. He took a sheet of green metal that he had salvaged from a Russian armoured personnel carrier, and cut off a triangular piece on a small guillotine. Then he bent this into a cone and welded the seam; plunged it in water; pierced a hole; forced the piece over the wood; hammered a nail through the hole and cut off the nail head. He worked quickly and in silence. Then he paused. The point was sharp and it was more a spear than a stick.

I explained that in Pakistan my stick had a round top not a pointed one. He shrugged. I asked if he had any metal balls.

'No.'

'Does anyone else?'

'Hussein might,' said one of the older spectators.

There was much chattering and then everyone looked at me.

'Well?' I asked.

'We have no ball,' said Wakil Ama.

'How about Hussein?' I suggested.

Wakil Ama shrugged again as though he hadn't thought of it before. 'Hussein might.'

'Can someone lead me there? I'll go there now.'

Wakil Ama shouted at a young boy, telling him to guide me. The boy ran off, giggling, forcing me to run behind him. We raced through a dark covered arch into a large courtyard, down another street and stopped at a junk shop. On the pavement was a battered tin tray containing two iron nuts, the face of a cheap alarm clock, some metal cubes, a shell case from an anti-aircraft round and a lead ball.

We returned to the forge. Wakil Ama took the ball, grunted and welded it to the point of the stick. Then he plunged it in water and wound another strip of tank metal around the base. The metal was dull and sharp barnacles of welding slip hung on all the seams, but I now had a strong, well-balanced stick, weighing about three pounds. Wakil Ama smiled at the result. He only accepted payment reluctantly, leaving me to choose the amount. Then he offered me some tea.

As I walked out an old man with a bushy white beard looked at the stick.

'You're carrying it for the wolves, I presume,' he said.

'And the humans.'

He nodded.

'What do you call this type of stick?' I asked.

'A *dang*,' he said.

Whether on the Shores of Asia

I had told the Security Service that I was crossing Afghanistan in the footsteps of Babur, the first Emperor of Mughal India, but this was misleading. Initially I had decided to walk the central route from Herat to Kabul because it was shorter and because the Taliban were still fighting on the main southern route. I was starting in January because I did not want to wait five months for the snow to clear. It was only after I had made my decision that I discovered that Babur had also travelled the central route on foot in January and recorded the journey in his diary.

I wasn't keen to read Babur's diary. I did not like medieval texts, with their references to faded theologies and forgotten viziers. I wanted to focus on modern Afghanistan, not its history, and I couldn't see the relevance of a man who was a contemporary of the Aztecs.

The beginning of Babur's diary was as bad as I had anticipated:

> Ush is situated to the South-East of Andejan, but more to the east and distant from Andejan four farsangs by the road . . . The mother of Yunus Khan was either the daughter or the granddaughter of Sheikh Nur-ed-din Beg, who was one of the Amirs of Kipchak and had been brought forward by Taimur Beg.

As I kept reading, however, the geography and the genealogy faded and a narrative emerged. Babur was born in 1480 as the prince of a poor, remote kingdom in Uzbekistan. By the time he was twenty-three he had lost all his land in Central Asia and was hiding in the mountains with a few followers, most of whom were on foot and armed only with clubs, but at twenty-six he had recovered and conquered Kabul. That year he visited Herat, then the most civilized city in the Islamic world. He returned from Herat to Kabul on the central route, almost dying in the snow on the way. Then he pressed east to conquer Delhi and found the Mughal dynasty. He died as the ruler of one of the largest and wealthiest empires in the world.

He tells this adventure story with impressive modesty. What he did was very dangerous, but he never draws attention to this. Instead, he focuses on the people that he meets and uses portraits of individuals to suggest a whole society. He pays more attention to his contemporary world than to legends or ancient history and he is a careful observer. He mentions hangovers and agricultural techniques, poetry and economics, pederasty and garden design with the sense of humour and experience of a man who has fought, travelled and governed. He does not embroider anecdotes to make them neater, funnier, more personal or more symbolic. Unlike most travel writers, he is honest.

At times, it seems that the only thing missing from his story is himself. He never explains what drives him to live this extraordinary life and take these kinds of risks. He does not describe his emotions, and as a result he can appear distant and the episodes of his life sometimes seem repetitive. Confronted by dead bodies or people trying to kill him, his prose becomes increasingly dispassionate and impersonal. But this restraint only emphasizes the extraordinary nature of his experiences. This is his attempt to defend Akhsi at the age of twenty-one:

My horse was wounded by an arrow. He bolted and sprung aside throwing me on the ground in the middle of the enemy. I got to my feet and fired a single shot and my attendant Kahil, who was on a bad horse, dismounted and handed it to me. At that moment Qasim's son arrived. He was wounded. He said that my brother had fled. I said to Ibrahim Beg, 'What is to be done now?' Perhaps because he was slightly wounded or because he was frightened he didn't give me a very distinct answer . . . A man shot an arrow at me, which struck me under the arm, piercing and breaking two plates of my Kalmuk armour. I shot an arrow back at him and then struck a passing horseman on his temples with the point of my sword. He bent over as if ready to fall from his horse but he caught himself on the wall of the lane, kept his seat and escaped . . . I had about twenty arrows left. I wondered whether to dismount and keep my ground as long as my arrows lasted but I decided to head for the hill.

Babur is tolerant and kind to his friends, but tough, ambitious and hard on himself. His admiration for courage, religion and intelligence is implicit in even the shortest passages of his diaries. This is his description of his old companion on his Afghan journey, who was called Qasim, 'the Divider':

He had distinguished himself by his gallant use of his scimitar. He was a pious, religious, faithful Muslim and carefully abstained from all doubtful meats. His judgements and talents were uncommonly good. He was facetious. He could neither read nor write but he had an ingenious and elegant turn of wit.

Babur does not attempt to conceal his own impoverished origins, his defeats, embarrassments and unrequited love. He is aware of his absurdities, his self-delusion and his weaknesses without entirely forgiving himself. He boasts of his poetry, but not of his courage or resourcefulness. He is sceptical of authority and religion, and takes little for granted about the world or himself.

Although the diaries changed my view of fifteenth-century Asia, they had little relevance to modern Afghanistan. Babur was a medieval man. His world view was formed by his being a direct royal descendant of Genghis Khan and Tamurlaine, by his contact with fifteenth-century Persian culture and Islam and by his never having travelled west of Herat. The flamboyant culture that he describes in Herat in 1504 has no equivalent in the modern city, with its shabby cement walls, illegal DVDs and atmosphere of provincial convention:

> *Herat was a refined city, in which every means of heightening pleasure and gaiety was possessed in perfection; in which all the incentives and apparatus of enjoyment were combined with an invitation to indulgence . . . Hussein Mirza [the ruler] dressed in gay-coloured red and green wool. On festival days he put on a small turban tied in three folds, broad and showy and having placed a plume nodding over it went in this style to prayers . . . He had a turn for poetry and composed a divan . . . He was fond as a child of keeping butting rams and of amusing himself with flying pigeons and cock-fighting . . . He was addicted to wine and debauchery. He created a court, which abounded with eminent men of unrivalled accomplishments, each of whom made it his aim and ambition to carry to the highest perfection the art to which he devoted himself.*
>
> *There were kebabs of fowl, and of goose, and indeed dishes of every kind . . . When the wine began to take effect, a man began to dance, and he danced excessively well . . . then another sang but in a dreadfully loud, rough, disagreeable tone . . . the cup-bearers in waiting began to supply all who were of the party with pure wine, which they quaffed as if it had been the water of life.*[1]

Almost every activity that Babur describes, gambling, dancing, colourful clothing, debauchery, singing and alcohol, was illegal

---

1. Babur describes scores of men in Herat and their painting, theology, dancing and poetry and most of all drinking. Some of them were unusual people; see, for example, *'the mullah who left a Persian prosody which omits many useful and difficult subjects and writes about obvious subjects in the minutest detail and was remarkable for the force with which he could deliver a blow with his fist'*.

under the Taliban and remained illegal or discouraged under Ismail Khan's new government.

*

Babur decided to leave Herat after only twenty days in the city, despite his cousins' pleas that he should defend them against an Uzbek warlord. Babur claims that he left because his winter quarters were inadequate, but since he was staying in the palace of the wealthiest and most cultivated man in the city, this is unlikely. It is more likely that he and his illiterate chancellor Qasim, with their provincial origins, felt intimidated by the sophisticated court society. Qasim had only narrowly prevented Babur from committing an important faux pas in the audience chamber, and from drinking alcohol for the first time. Qasim may have wanted to take his protégé away before he was further corrupted or humiliated. Their new kingdom of Kabul was, however, also under threat, and Babur was often restless. Whatever the determining factor, Babur must have felt strongly about leaving the city because it was the middle of winter and that is a very bad time to travel along the central route.

Part One

Herat . . . The policeman at the cross-roads with a whistling fit to scare the Chicago underworld

— Robert Byron, *The Road to Oxiana*, 1933

Herat . . . The police directing a thin trickle of automobiles with whistles and ill-tempered gestures like referees

— Eric Newby, *A Short Walk in the Hindu Kush*, 1952

Herat . . . A small lonely policeman in the centre of a vast deserted square, directing two donkeys and a bicycle with a majesty and ferocity more appropriate to the Champs Elysées

— Peter Levi, *The Light Garden of the Angel King*, 1970

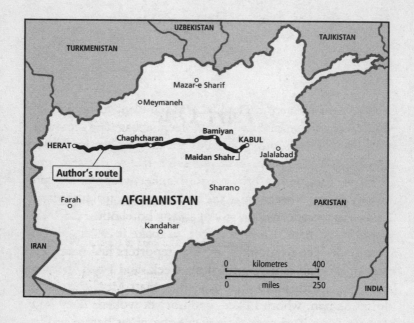

Chicago and Paris

On my last morning in Herat, I was reluctant to get out of bed. It was cold despite my Nepali sleeping bag, and I knew it would be colder in the mountains ahead. I put on my walking clothes: a long *shalwar kemis* shirt, baggy trousers and a Chitrali cap, with a brown *patu* blanket wrapped around my shoulders. I went into the dining room for breakfast. Foreigners were forbidden to stay in any hotel other than the Mowafaq, perhaps, I now thought, to make it easier for the Security Service to monitor us. War reporters had occupied most of the tables in the previous week, and I had spent a lot of time with them. I noticed that Matt McAllester and Moises Saman, whom I liked, had not yet woken. They had been drinking Turkmen champagne the night before in the UN bar to celebrate Moises's birthday.

Television France 2 had brought their own cafetière and a packet of Lavazza coffee and sent to the bazaar for fresh juice. The day before, I had heard them talking about Chinese motifs on a shrine, the similarity between the minarets and factory chimneys and the soldiers that chased them from the Bala Hissar fort. Now they were discussing whether to visit the hand-blown glass shop or the refugee camp. One of them was pointing out of the window at the traffic policeman. These things had attracted the attention of foreigners in Herat for seventy years. I had read five different travel writers on the traffic policemen. Their peaked hats and whistles struck visitors as particularly incongruous amongst the tumult of the Afghan bazaar. I wanted to write about them myself.

I sat with the British beside Alex, the *Telegraph* correspondent, whom I had met in Jakarta, and Vaughan Smith, who had
been a Grenadier Guards' officer before he became a freelance
cameraman. He had been filming in Afghanistan for a decade.

'Are you leaving this morning?' asked Vaughan.

'I hope so.'

'And you are really going to walk to Kabul through Ghor?'
'Yes.'

Vaughan smiled. 'Good luck,' he said and gave me his fried
eggs. I ate six eggs to stock up on protein. Then I took up
my stick and pack, said goodbye and walked into the street. A
strong, cold wind was blowing the sand into the air and I had
to squint.

On the street corner, I watched men unloading tablecloths
from China and Iranian flip-flops marked 'Nike by Ralph
Lauren'. The goods had been imported on a truck from
Tabriz. It had come through the fog of diesel fumes down the
multi-lane highway, which the Iranian government still called
the Silk Road. This was the route that Alexander the Great
took in pursuit of a Persian rival. From Herat, the Persian
had fled on up the central route into the mountains and
Alexander, instead of following him, had taken the safer
Kandahar route to Kabul. I watched a fruit wrapper from
Isfahan, flying in Alexander's footsteps. I followed the Persian,
passing a man with a prosthetic leg, whom I had met before.

'*Shoma Ghor miravid?*' (Are you going to the province of
Ghor?) he shouted.

'Yes.'

'*Shoma be ghabr miravid*' (You are going to your grave), he
replied. I shook his hand and walked on as he repeated the
pun to himself '*Ghor miyayid . . . ghabr miyayid*' and laughed.

Huma

When I reached his office, Yuzufi stood, smiled, fastened his double-breasted jacket very slowly and came round his large desk to embrace me. As I sat down, a dozen people came fast through the door without knocking. I recognized them from the hotel: *Wall Street Journal*, *Guardian*, *Deutsche Allgemeine Zeitung*, but none of them acknowledged me. Their train was formed by young Kabuli translators in pleated leather jackets and baggy trousers. As they approached his desk, they were speaking over the top of each other in English: 'Can we see him?' 'Can we make an appointment to see him?' 'But His Excellency said . . .', 'There is no higher authority', 'With no letter?' 'What happens if?' And as though it were a comic opera, Yuzufi's deep bass voice broke in, in harmony: 'It is not known . . . Worry not . . . All will be fine . . .'

The journalists were demanding access to a Taliban prisoner. Yuzufi was promising to look into it. This overture had been rehearsed many times. Some of the journalists had been in town for a fortnight without getting inside the jail. Now, confronted by Yuzufi's patient obfuscation, they snapped at their translators who, being far from Kabul, were almost as confused as the journalists themselves. Finally, while Yuzufi was still talking, they all wheeled around and flowed out without saying goodbye, leaving only me and the row of peasants by the door.

Yuzufi smiled. He was meant to be searching for the letters of introduction, which I had acquired with trouble in Kabul. I waited for him to say that he had found them again. He didn't. Instead, he said, 'I was thinking about you last night, Rory. You are like a medieval walking dervish.'

He compared me with Attar, who lived in the twelfth century under the dynasty of Ghor. When Genghis Khan invaded, Attar was killed for making a joke and Rumi, whom Attar had held as a baby, walked to Turkey to found the whirling dervishes.

'What you will see on your walk,' he continued, 'is that we are one country today just as we were in the twelfth century under the Ghorids, in Attar's day.'

I smiled. Whereas the new governor was learning the jargon of a post-modern state, Yuzufi had an older view of an Afghanistan with a single national identity, natural frontiers, and ambassadors and a culture defined by medieval poetry. The Security Service saw my walk only as a journey to the edge of Ismail Khan's terrain. The Hazara area was as foreign to them as Iran. But for Yuzufi my walk was a journey across a single country. Perhaps this was why he was one of the only people who thought the walk was possible.

'I,' Yuzufi sighed, 'would love to come with you, but I am like the birds that refused to join the sacred quest.' Then he quoted some poetry, which may have been Attar's description of the birds' excuses for staying at home:

> The owl loves its nest in the ruins,
> The Huma revels in making kings,
> The falcon will not leave the King's hand,
> And the wagtail pleads weakness.[2]

---

2. The mythical Huma bird never alights on the ground but is perpetually in flight. Its diet is bones. The female drops her eggs from the sky and her chick hatches as the egg plummets, escaping before it hits the ground. Anyone over whom the Huma flies will become king. It is part of the myths of both Persia and India and is celebrated by the Hindu poets as well as by Muslim Sufis such as Attar and Rumi. There were once two giant golden Huma on the walls of the lost Ghorid capital of the

Finally a soldier marched in and, holding his right hand to his chest, said, '*Salaam aleikum. Chetor hastid? Jan-e-shoma jur ast? Khub hastid? Sahat-e-shoma khub ast? Be khair hastid? Jur hastid? Khane kheirat ast? Zinde bashi.*'

Which in Dari, the Afghan dialect of Persian, means, 'Peace be with you. How are you? Is your soul healthy? Are you well? Are you well? Are you healthy? Are you fine? Is your household flourishing? Long life to you.' Or: 'Hello.'

He was a small man in his mid-forties with bandy legs, a wispy chestnut-brown beard and pinched purple cheeks. In his webbing pouch I could see a military radio, his link to headquarters; a pen, suggesting he was literate; a packet of pills showing he could afford antibiotics and a roll of pink toilet paper, a more subtle status indicator.

Yuzufi did not stand up to greet him but he moved three files on his heavy wooden desk and replied with his nine greetings. Against the far wall of the office four Afghan villagers were sitting uncomfortably straight on plastic chairs, their rubber galoshes planted squarely on the linoleum. Beneath frayed *shalwar* pyjama trousers, their narrow brown ankles were covered with white hairline cracks and scars. They had been waiting for hours to speak to Yuzufi.

'I am Seyyed Qasim,' continued the soldier, emphasizing the title '*Seyyed*', meaning descendant of the prophet, 'from the Department for Intelligence and Security.'

'Indeed. *Seyyed* Qasim, I am His Excellency Yuzufi,' Seyyed Yuzufi replied. 'This is His Excellency Rory, our only tourist, standing by, ready for you to walk with him.'

My escort did not glance in my direction.

'*Salaam aleikum,*' I said.

'*Waleikum a-salaam,*' the small man replied and turned

Turquoise Mountain. Even Babur quotes a poem about the Huma, written by one of his courtiers . . .

back to Yuzufi. 'Well, Your Excellency, we have a Land Cruiser outside.'

'Please understand,' I interrupted, 'I am walking to Chaghcharan.'

'To Chaghcharan? No.' Seyyed Qasim stood straight and made firm statements but he did not seem comfortable in this office. He kept looking around the room. His eyes were small and blue, his eyelids puffy.

'Not just to Chaghcharan,' said Yuzufi, 'to Kabul.'

'He will be killed. What is this foreigner trying to do?'

'I am a professor of history,' I said.

Qasim squinted at my shabby clothes and frowned.

The door swung open and a younger soldier marched in and saluted. He was about six feet tall: nearly seven inches taller than Qasim and much broader in the shoulders. Unusually for an Afghan who came from a rural area, he had shaved off his beard, leaving a drooping moustache, which gave him the air of a Mexican bandit. Visible in his webbing were five spare magazines, three grenades, a packet of cigarettes and again a bundle of pink toilet paper in his chest-pouch. Qasim introduced him as Abdul Haq.

Yuzufi, who had been skimming two files, now looked up and spoke to them at length. Turning to me he added, 'I have told these two that you have met His Excellency the Emir, Ismail Khan, and that he wished you luck on your journey. They are to do what you instruct and you will record their bad behaviour. Your walk starts now.' He stood up from behind his desk and gravely enfolded my hand. 'Record me in your book. As the Persian poet says: "Man's life is brief and transitory, Literature endures forever."'

He smiled. 'Good luck Marco Polo.'

Fare Forward

We walked back down the corridor and pushed through the crowds that were still waiting to present petitions to the governor. When we reached the street, rather than turning west to the hotel, we turned east towards the desert and the mountains. The sun had come out, casting a harsh clear light over the sand-caked brick and sharpening the shadows of tired men pushing handcarts. As we walked, I adjusted the straps of my pack and wondered what I had forgotten to buy and, therefore, would not be able to get in the next two months. I felt the familiar unevenness in the inner sole of my left boot, stretched my toes and paced out. My companions were only carrying automatic rifles and sleeping bags, and had no food or warm clothing.

I felt a little ludicrous in my Afghan clothes, shrugging my shoulders under the weight of the pack. Qasim, the older man, was wearing neatly pressed camouflage trousers, made for someone much larger. He had gathered the loose waist in pleats beneath his belt, but the thigh pockets fell down almost to his mid-calf. Although he was the senior man, Qasim seemed much less comfortable than Abdul Haq. He kept his red, pockmarked face down, with his pale eyes flickering nervously, as though he were waiting for something to erupt from the pavement. Abdul Haq had an upright stance and looked very tall beside Qasim. He took two paces for every three of Qasim's.

Nobody on the street even glanced at us and neither Qasim nor Abdul Haq looked at me. They didn't speak

English. I guessed that they had only an uncertain idea of the walk ahead, that they had not dealt with a foreigner before and that they were relatively junior. Since their uniforms looked as though they had just been unpacked from a new American consignment, I also assumed they were new to their jobs. But they handled their weapons comfortably. We walked side by side, or almost, for the street was crowded, and Abdul Haq stopped a couple of times to adjust the circular magazine on his Kalashnikov. The sand on the rough asphalt became thicker and the crowds thinned.

I looked into the blank eyes of a crow which was sitting on a wall. Beneath it an antique shop had placed its wares on a tray. Beside a nineteenth-century Gardener teapot and two Lee Enfields with splintering stocks were a tile from the Musalla complex, a Gandharan head of a Buddha and a mythical bird made from clay: objects from Babur's Herat and the civilizations of Bamiyan and Ghor baldly presented on a dusty road for a trinket hunter. I doubted whether the seller cared any more for them than the crow. We passed biscuit shops and pharmacists and dust-caked fruit in boxes and, lastly, the last petrol station.

Finally, Abdul Haq looked at me with his dark eyes and asked, 'You're not a journalist, are you?'

'No.'

'A pity, otherwise you could write a story about us.'

* * *

At the edge of the city, we sat on a table in the street for lunch. There was a choice of eggs, bread and yoghurt. I had had enough eggs for the day. Qasim pulled his small legs up underneath him, carefully took my bowl of yoghurt, stuck his small finger in, and licked it before handing the bowl to me. It appeared that he was showing his concern for his guest by checking for poison. Poisoning was common in medieval courts. Babur once disembowelled a cook for it. Qasim's gesture, however, was a piece of conventional manners. He was not expecting me to be poisoned. I thanked him and smiled. For the first time, he smiled back.

Opposite our food stall were elaborate medieval mud towers, built to house pigeons because their droppings fertilized the vineyards. The Taliban had burnt the vineyards and banned the keeping of birds. The ornate balconies of the towers were crumbling and pigeonless. In the past, the pigeons were kept for pleasure too. Like Hussein Mirza, the fifteenth-century ruler of Herat, Babur's father had pigeons that were trained to tumble or somersault in the air. When his city was being invaded and he was on the verge of defeat, he went up to his pigeon tower, which lay on a cliff. Babur writes that the land slipped, the cliff collapsed and '*the pigeons and my father took flight to the next world*'.

After lunch, we walked on. At the outskirts of town, we passed one of the traditional junctions for the Silk Road, where the caravan route turned north to China or south to India: the route taken by the hippies in the 1970s. We continued east. I was just beginning to feel that I had left Herat and started on my journey. Then a jeep clattered up and stopped beside us. It was David from the *LA Times*, who had run out of stories and wanted to know if he could interview me.

I liked David. He had allowed me to use his satellite phone to say goodbye to my parents. This was a privilege, for there would be no phone in the next six weeks of walking. Now he asked me questions about why I was doing the walk. My answers didn't really satisfy him.

I told him that Afghanistan was the missing section of my walk, the place in between the deserts and the Himalayas, between Persian, Hellenic and Hindu culture, between Islam and Buddhism, between mystical and militant Islam. I wanted to see where these cultures merged into one another or touched the global world.

I talked about how I had been walking one afternoon in

Scotland and thought: why don't I just keep going. There was, I said, a magic in leaving a line of footprints stretching behind me across Asia.

He asked me whether I didn't think what I was doing was dangerous. I paused. I had never found a way to answer that question without sounding awkward, insincere or ludicrous. 'Surely you can understand,' I said, 'the stillness of that man, Qasim. The Prussian blue sky – this air. It feels like a gift. Everything,' I said, warming to my theme, 'suddenly makes sense. I feel I have been preparing for this all my life.'

But he wrote none of this down. Instead, while Loomis, his photographer, shot pictures of me from a ditch, he apparently scribbled, '20–27 miles a day every day – living on bread – "the hunger belt." Babur loses men and horses in the snow. One change of clothes. Thin with a wispy beard.' When Loomis gave me a plastic-wrapped handwarmer, I tried to explain that the physical side didn't matter to me, that it was more a way of looking at Afghanistan and being by myself.

Loomis nodded. 'Have you read *Into the Wild* . . . that book about the wealthy young American who headed off into the Alaskan wilderness to find himself and then died on his own in the snow . . . It's a great piece of journalism.'

*

They left me and we continued. Abdul Haq pushed his baseball cap onto the back of his head, smoothed down his long Mexican moustache, shrugged to throw his American camouflage jacket back on his shoulders, and moved five yards in front of me, leaning so far forward that he was forced to walk quickly just to stay on his feet. A cloud of apricot sand billowed around his boots. It mingled with the grey smoke that trailed from the cigarette, which he hid by his thigh in the traditional pose of a soldier smoking on duty. Beside me, Qasim took smaller, pedantic steps in keeping with his size, bringing his heel down sharply on the edge of the road.

Our shadows lengthened on the gravel floor: Abdul Haq's the largest, Qasim's the smallest, mine with a hunchback formed by my pack. The desert grew around us and the three of us diminished in size. I kept thinking of David's article as a distorted obituary, and it took some time for my muscles to warm and to settle me into the familiar rhythm of another day's walk. When I caught up with him, Abdul Haq flashed a smile, stuck the barrel of his rifle into the sand and performed a miniature pole vault, shouting 'Allah-u-Akbar' (God is Great) as he landed. Qasim scowled at the younger man. I wondered how much control he had over his deputy.

I was used, apart from my weeks in the Maoist areas of western Nepal, to walking in relatively peaceful areas. Although I walked about forty kilometres every day, I met few people and the scenery, at five kilometres an hour, changed very slowly. I was accustomed to concentrating on details: on the great shisham trees in the Punjab, on leopard tracks in the lowland jungle and on the pale green *brahma* flowers of the Himalayas. I recorded all the objects in village guest rooms. I examined battery-chicken farms and truck stops in Iran; in Nepal I watched men ploughing with white oxen, flails striking the threshing floor and the clouds of chaff flung into the sun. I recorded people's experiences as manual labourers in Saudi Arabia and their conspiracy theories about America. I tried to uncover traces of ancient history along the Indian–Nepali border, following a line of battered stones carved with cavalry and the sun god, which was, I thought, an ancient imperial Malla footpath.[3]

Suddenly there was an explosion, the ground trembled under our feet and acrid black smoke rolled from the field on our left. I had not imagined how loud a landmine could be.

3. The Malla were a medieval Nepali dynasty who conquered much of the Indian Himalayas. I walked from Gangotri, through Kedarnath and Joshimath to Jumla in Nepal, along their routes.

The others didn't turn their heads. I was not used to such things.

We were in a gravel desert stretching bare to low hills on either side. There were no trees to deliver variety of height and colour. The gravel and sand would not alter with the seasons. In the Iranian desert, there would have been marks in the soil made by the plough, vertical lines formed by pylons, drab eagles on electricity wires and scraps of plastic bag. Because of the drought and the poverty, even such bland signs of human occupation were missing in Afghanistan.

*

But the road was flat, the day was cool, my feet were comfortable and my pack didn't feel too heavy. The pace of my legs began to transform the rhythm of my breathing and of my thinking although I still felt unusually nervous. I wondered whether after fifteen months of walking across Asia, my luck was running out. I had promised my mother that this would be my last journey and that if I made it safely to Kabul, I would stop walking and come home.

I began to take longer and faster strides, half racing along the dirt track. My anxiety faded and I enjoyed the movement of my muscles, revelling in it, remembering that in forty days it might be over. I had left the offices and interviews in Herat behind and I was once again pushing myself east. I watched the pebbles flashing past beneath me and felt that with the strike of each carefully placed heel step I was marking Afghanistan. I wanted to touch as much as possible of the country with my feet. I remembered why I had once thought of walking right around the world.

After two hours, we arrived at a bazaar, Herat Sha'ede, consisting of a short line of mud shops on either side of the mud road, eight kilometres outside Herat.

'Here,' said Qasim, 'is our night's halt.'

'But there are three hours of daylight left. We can do another fifteen kilometres.'

'Ahead is only the desert. We must stop here for the night. We can cross the desert tomorrow.'

I was concerned that at this pace I wouldn't reach Kabul in six months. But I had no sketch-map with which to contradict him and I didn't want to start an argument on the first day, so I reluctantly agreed. Qasim handed his sleeping bag to Abdul Haq, tugged a crease out of his camouflage jacket, and turned towards a mud house. I followed him. We took off our boots on the threshold, stooped beneath the arch and entered a dark room. I could just make out twenty men in camouflage uniform, sitting on the carpet. They all stood to greet Qasim. I pushed clumsily through the crowd with my pack, laid it in the corner, and then went through the formal greetings; '*Salaam aleikum. Chetor hastid? Be khair hastid? Bakheir hastid . . .*' and sat and drank tea with them. It was an infuri-atingly short day and I hoped I would be able to get rid of my companions soon.

When they began to chat to each other, I took Qasim aside and put two hundred dollars into his hand, asking him to use it for our food. This was six months' wages for some Afghans, but I wanted to keep Qasim on my side. I told him I would give him some more as soon as he let me continue alone. He said nothing, but he folded the two hundred dollar bills and put them in his breast pocket. Then a squinting, dark-faced man with a patchy beard pushed into the room. He was even smaller than Qasim and was introduced to me as Qasim's brother-in-law Aziz. Qasim told me that Aziz wanted to walk with us. We were now apparently going to be a group of four.

These Boots

Half an hour later, Qasim suggested that I go with him to see the bazaar. He wanted to buy some boots. I followed him down the street into a small hut. A pair of white suede boots with fur tops stood on rough planks nailed to the sagging mud walls. Qasim asked the shopkeeper to reach for them and sat on the floor, struggling to get his feet into them. They went well with his camouflage trousers, he thought, but they were too small even for his tiny feet. He and the shopkeeper then rummaged amongst the pills, salt, rice, cigarettes and batteries and found a pair in red leatherette. They were very big. In exchange, Qasim gave the shopkeeper his pair of battered combat boots. The shopkeeper seemed to have got a bad deal. Combat boots were everywhere, supplied free by the CIA. I assumed, however, that the shopkeeper could count on calling on Qasim and his contacts for something later. I was more worried for Qasim. The new boots seemed guaranteed to shred his feet.

Qasim was delighted. He stepped, hand in hand with the shopkeeper, over the tray of onions and into the sunlit street, roaring 'Salaam aleikum' (Peace be with you) at some passing men. The men shouted, 'And also with you.' They hugged, kissed, and, still holding hands, began a lengthy patter of formal greetings. They had apparently forgotten about me. I was left alone in the shop front, looking at the street.

The landscape reminded me of a Victorian print of the Orient. To the north, beyond the crumbling mud buildings, flocks of sheep moved on a gravel desert that wrinkled grey and green under a deep blue sky. To the east, my destination, I saw the distant snow-peaks of the Paropamisus, half dissolved under a paler light. Men in black turbans with thick white beards walked very slowly down the street of the bazaar, rosary beads trailing from their hands and their ankle-length coat sleeves teased by a flurry of pale dust. The low sun glinted on tiny mirrors in the prayer caps of two young men wrestling on the roadside, and on the Iranian wafer biscuits beside them. A white pickup raced across the uneven track, with a large card fixed to the windscreen reading 'Shipped for Mr Shafiq, Kabul for the UAE, Free of Duty'. On the open back stood a man in a black turban holding a mounted Russian anti-aircraft gun.

I stepped out of the shadows into the street. A crowd was watching an argument between a policeman and a bus driver, who was shouting that under the new government even policemen should pay for a ride. The matter was settled without money; they shook hands and parted suddenly laughing. Perhaps because the bazaar was full of strangers no one seemed to look at me in my Afghan clothes. I wandered on slowly with the sun on my face in the late afternoon heat.

The air was very clean and the desert floor was pristine. I looked along the gentle lines of the shop fronts. The clear light was absorbed and warmed in the baked mud of the walls. I was pleased to be in the place. But these things were also signs of poverty. There would have been more cement and plastic in this bazaar thirty years ago, before the war. Even this desert was new: it had appeared out of the fields with the recent drought. I wandered down the womanless street, listening to the rich roar of the unemployed mullahs and the illiterate gunmen discussing cousin-marriage. No one was buying anything; everything, it seemed, was bartered or given. Everyone knew each other. Two young men were talking to each other about me, where England was and about what a foreigner ate and carried and enjoyed. It was an easy rolling chain of speculation and it didn't require my participation.

'He may be tougher than he looks,' one of them said as I passed, 'but I don't think he understands what he is doing.' They smiled at me and I grinned back.

*

After half an hour, Qasim and Abdul Haq reappeared with another soldier and suggested we should visit the garden outside the bazaar. I followed them. Herat had been overcast and cold, but here the sun was warm. About a kilometre away, we turned towards a cemetery up an avenue of cypresses, which hid us from the village. The men were all carrying their rifles and Qasim's new friend was for some reason holding a naked bayonet. I was still trying to understand Afghanistan, as I did other countries, in terms of its scenery, history and architecture. But this was a country at war and I was not in control of the gunmen beside me. I still could not believe that the Security Service had any interest in protecting me for free. Nor could I believe that if they thought I was a spy they would let me walk across the province. It was possible that they had simply told Qasim and Abdul Haq to take me outside the city and kill me. No one would notice in the middle of a war. I felt that it would have been ludicrous to be killed only eight kilometres into my journey and not for the first time I worried that when I was killed people would think I was foolhardy.

But they weren't thinking of killing me. They only wanted to show me other people's graves. They left me and climbed onto the roof of an abandoned building to smoke. They were smoking cannabis.

'This is the shrine and mausoleum of Saint Ulya,' Qasim shouted down. 'He was a very important man; he was "Ten-Feet-Tall".' It was a fittingly large grave. I returned to looking at the landscape. There was a mud wall in front of me, two hundred feet long, with a gate. I entered and continued down a dark tunnel for about thirty feet until a courtyard opened out on my left. From the sunken floor, surfaces of mud billowed twenty feet into the air, forming steps and roofs, walls and courtyards. I watched the play of shade and refracted sunlight on curving ramparts, wooden struts, granite keystones and beehive domes. At one of the miniature windows a pair of young eyes, above a veil, appeared and disappeared. The floor was scattered with grain-husks from the autumn harvest and there were soot stains above the doorframes. I climbed some stairs onto the roof and found a lean-to of dead branches that served as a kitchen, containing two faded machine-made rugs, a hurricane lamp, and a tea towel depicting a mosque.

'That is all that the family possesses,' Qasim shouted up, appearing with the others, 'one hundred people live in this building.' I could not understand this medieval tenement block: a village in a single building with circular stairs, half-stories and abortive tunnels.

'They are very poor,' I said.

'*Jang-e bist-o-se saal bud ab nist. Mardom-e-karia gharib . . .*' he replied. I did not need him to complete the phrase because I had heard it word for word, from men in Herat and Kabul. 'There has been war for twenty-three years. There is no water. The villagers are poor, illiterate, mad and dangerous. Afghanistan is destroyed.' In this standard analysis, Islam and ethnicity did not feature and violence was the product of mad rural illiterates. It suggested that a little education, money and counselling might restore a golden age that existed before Afghanistan was 'destroyed'. But I was not sure how the exact words of the slogan had become so fixed or what part the media had played in it all. It told me nothing about this community.

We walked back into the garden. Beyond the avenue were stunted patterns of formal box and faded roses, and in the centre a dry concrete pool. Despite twenty-four years of war and the last four years of drought, the grass was green and mown. I still expected Afghanistan to look like some apocalyptic wasteland, with untended fields and a shattered society held to ransom by the dangerous and the traumatized. I had not anticipated the smiling warmth of the bazaar or the peace and beauty of this elaborate garden, on the edge of the gravel sands.

When Babur visited, Herat was planted with many gardens.

> In Herat I saw the garden of Ali Sher Beg, the public pleasure grounds at Gazergah, the Raven-garden, the new Garden, Zobeideh's garden, the White garden and the City garden.

Babur pursued a passionate interest in creating watered paradises in the arid soil of his kingdom in Kabul. This is his entry from 1504:

> In the mountains [west of Kabul], the ground is richly diversified by different kinds of tulips. I once directed them to be counted and they brought in thirty-two or thirty-three different sorts of tulips. There is one species which has a scent in some degree like a rose . . . On the outside of the garden are large and beautiful spreading plane trees, under the shadow of which there are agreeable spots finely sheltered. On the two sides of the fountain, there are a number of oak trees. In front of this fountain there are many spots covered with flowering Arhwan trees [the Judas tree]. I directed this fountain to be built round with stone . . . At a time when the Arhwan flowers begin to blow, I do not know there is any place in the world to be compared to it.

*

The slender shadows of the thorns fell like a jagged Kufic script over the new mud wall. Out of sight, beyond the wall, the desert into which we would walk stretched unbroken. We stood up and Abdul Haq picked a pink flower and put it in my cap. There was a large full moon to the east, the air had stilled enough for the snow to be visible, pure on the upper slopes, and a low orange sun was descending dust-muffled to the west. I, with a tiny pink flower in my cap, strode with the three armed men down the avenue of cypresses towards the sunset.

A rare flock of pigeon-doves dipped amongst the fruit trees, perhaps the kind that Babur's father kept to tumble. Abdul Haq unslung his barrel-chambered Kalashnikov and handed it to me. It was heavy.

'Go ahead,' he said, smoothing his drooping moustache with his right hand.

'What?'

'Kill the bird.' He pointed at the last dove, descending, wings folded, towards the empty pool.

'No, thank you.'

'Don't worry. Go ahead. It's the government's ammunition, not mine.'

Part Two

Heraut . . . stands in a fertile plain, which is watered
by a river [the Hari Rud] crowded with villages and
covered with fields of corn. The inhabitants of the
country around Heraut are for the most part Tajiks
. . . a mild, sober, industrious people.

– Mountstuart Elphinstone,
The Kingdom of Kaubul, and its Dependencies, 1815

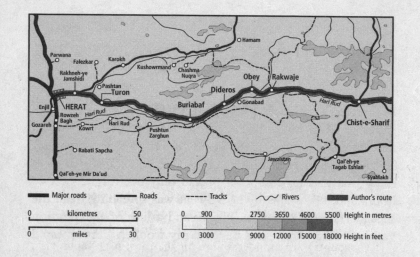

Day 1 – Herat-Sha'ede

Day 2 – Turon

Day 3 – Buriabaf

Day 4 – Dideros

Day 5 – Rakwaje

Day 6 – Chist-e-Sharif

Qasim

We stayed that night in the house of the village headman Haji Mumtaz. The next morning, after a breakfast of dry *nan* bread and sweet tea, we began again. Abdul Haq was walking with his long, gangling stride, shouting into the static roar of a radio that had no reception. It had only been light for two hours and it was already hot. Sweat was spreading from the shoulder straps of my backpack, and a line of perspiration gathered on my forehead beneath my woollen Chitrali cap. I shifted the heavy stick from one hand to the other and hoped the pain in my left knee was going to pass. Behind me Qasim was shouting at Aziz. They were both limping slightly, probably from blisters, and Aziz was coughing. He adjusted his black and white scarf around his neck. Qasim looked at me, smiled and snapped at Aziz again. I couldn't understand what he was saying but I noticed that Aziz, although the smallest and apparently weakest of them, had been given their sleeping bags and Qasim's rifle to carry.

I still knew very little about my companions, but I had learnt something about Qasim's status the previous night when Haji Mumtaz met us at his courtyard gate and invited us to stay. We accepted. He asked us to enter ahead of him. We refused; he pleaded; we tried to push him; he struggled, smiling. Finally, it was Qasim who went first, followed by Haji Mumtaz, Abdul Haq, Aziz and myself in that order. We were led to the threshold of a small mud building, where we wrestled again:

'Please, you are my host.'

'Please, you are my guest.'

Again, Qasim entered first. There were red carpets from Iran on the floor and some mattresses piled in the corner, but no furniture or decorations. Three men stood to greet us:

'No, no – please sit down . . . don't stand for us.'

'Of course we must – have my seat. But I insist.'

We arranged ourselves on the floor with Qasim seated furthest from the door and then, after a short pause, one of the strangers turned to Qasim, placed his hand on his chest, and said:

'*Salaam Aleikum, Manda na Bashi*, Peace be with you, May you not be tired. I hope your family is well. Long life to you.'

Qasim replied, speaking at the same time, 'And also with you . . . may your health be good . . . may you be strong . . . I hope your house is well.'

When Qasim had finished, the man turned to Abdul Haq: 'Peace be with you . . .' he said, '*Manda na Bashi.*' And Abdul Haq replied in kind. After the man had greeted each of us in this fashion, we in turn went round the room saying the same things, one by one. Our host picked up the teapot.

'No, no,' said Abdul Haq. 'I will pour it.'

'I insist – you are my guest.'

Abdul Haq grabbed the handle; Haji Mumtaz took it back off him.

This was a ritual which I had gone through almost every night as I walked across Iran. This village had been part of an empire centred in Persia for most of the previous two thousand years. In both Iran and Afghanistan, the order in which men enter, sit, greet, drink, wash and eat defines their status, their manners and their view of their companions. If a warlord had been with us he would have been expected, as the most senior man, to enter first, sit in the place furthest from the door, have his hands washed by others, be served, eat and drink first.[4] People would have stood to greet him and he would not normally have stood to greet others. But we were not warlords and the best way for us was to refuse honours: not least because no one else's status was clear. Status depended not only on age, ancestry, wealth and profession, but also on whether a man was a guest, whether a third person was present and whether he knew the others well.

Qasim had not struggled very much before taking the most senior position in every case. He probably thought he deserved it as a descendant of the Prophet, the oldest guest and the most senior civil servant present. But he could have made more of an effort to hold back. Our host, Haji Mumtaz, showed his manners by ostentatiously deferring to Qasim. The more he did so, the more we were reminded that he had done the pilgrimage to Mecca, was the village headman and twenty years older and much richer than Qasim, his pushy guest.

Abdul Haq sat himself at a junior position, folding his long legs beneath him, with a natural easy smile. Aziz's poverty was evident from his scrawny frame, ill-kept beard and poorly fitting clothes. He was only walking with us because he had married Qasim's sister. He moved to the bottom of the room with a defensive scowl. Only I deferred to Aziz, but then I was very low down the scale: visibly young, shabbily dressed,

---

4. In fact, Ismail Khan was very keen to refuse formal deference. He would not allow people to bow to him. Ritual was even more complex in the sixteenth century, when status was also measured by how far a man advanced up a room. This is Babur describing being presented at court in Herat:

As soon as I entered the Hall of State I bowed, and then without stopping, advanced to meet the ruler, who rose up rather tardily to come to meet me. Qasim Beg, who was keenly alive to my honour and regarded my consequence as his own, laid hold of my girdle and gave me a tug; I instantly understood him and advancing more deliberately we embraced at the spot that had been arranged.

travelling on foot and, although they might not know this, not a Muslim. But perhaps because I was a foreign guest and had letters from the Emir, I was promoted after a long debate and made to sit beside Mumtaz. When other senior men from the village entered, we all stood up in their honour. But when the servants brought the food, I was the only one to look up. Servants, like women and children, were socially invisible.

Qasim leaned against the wall, his arm draped over his knee, and pushed his over-large *pakul* cap back on his head. He looked at me with his blue watery eyes, and I thought his smile indicated a sympathy between us that recognized our very different lives, our difficulties in communication and our shared experience of the journey. He was old enough to be my father, and it seemed that there was something paternal in his weather-beaten face.

'Your Excellency Rory,' said Qasim, lingering thoughtfully over the name. 'Where are you from?'

'Scotland,' I said. There was a pause.

'What do you do, Haji Mumtaz?' I asked.

All I understood from his reply was 'in three metres of snow on the road to Chaghcharan'.

Having walked across Iran I spoke some Persian and they were speaking Dari, which is a dialect of Persian, spoken across northern Afghanistan. But I had been speaking Urdu and Nepali for a year and I was struggling to resurrect my Persian. I guessed his trucks were probably stuck in the snow. 'Three metres is a great deal,' I said vaguely.

'Haji Mumtaz has a deal of respect for me,' interrupted Qasim. 'This is because he is a religious man – and he knows that I am a Seyyed – Seyyed Qasim.'

'Indeed,' said Mumtaz.

'Of course, Qasim, you are a Seyyed,' I said, 'a descendant of Muhammad.'

'Of the Prophet, Peace Be Upon Him.'

'OftheProphetpeacebeuponhim,' I added quickly.

There was another pause. Qasim laid his hand on my knee as though he knew me better than he did, and sniffed. 'I am a very poor man; Afghanistan is a very poor country. We have no money. Haji Mumtaz has no money. I have no money.' I didn't believe him; it looked like a prosperous house.

A servant laid a cloth between us on the bright carpet and unfolded it, revealing thick roundels of *nan* bread. The conversation stopped. Bowls of soup and plates of rice were brought in. There were pieces of boiled and salted mutton hidden in the mounds of rice. The meat was very tender. No one spoke during dinner and we ate quickly with our hands. No one dropped any food except for me, who dribbled rice grains onto the carpet.

When the seniors had finished they passed the leftovers down to the men at the bottom of the room, all of whom were younger and thinner than Haji Mumtaz. Aziz, who had already eaten the equivalent of three large plates of rice, continued until he had picked every remaining grain off the two platters, and burped in appreciation. Trays of walnuts and apples and oranges were laid out, more tea was produced and, after an entirely silent meal, the conversation began again.

In the Kurdish areas of Iran in winter, there had been no vegetables, meat or fruit, and I usually ate unleavened bread for breakfast and bread and white goat's cheese for lunch and supper. In Pakistani and northern Indian villages I relied on bread and lentil curry. In Nepal, they ate at ten or eleven in the morning and again in the evening, which did not fit with my schedule so I carried cheap biscuits and ate rice and lentils, sometimes with black millet bread in the evening. This Afghan dinner had been an impressive feast in a poor and hungry country.

'Where is our guest from, Commander Seyyed?' asked Mumtaz.

'From Ukraine,' said Qasim confidently.

'He is a communist then, Commander Seyyed?'

Qasim paused.

'No, I am not,' I said, also in Persian.

'No, he is not,' repeated Qasim.

'Is he a Muslim?'

'Yes,' said Qasim. I was not. Qasim was simply saying the first thing that came into his head. He didn't want to admit that he knew very little about me and next to nothing about my country. For the sake of his status, he wanted to show that he was not simply in charge of a young foreigner in shabby clothes, but instead responsible for an interesting and important man. I also suspected that, like many villagers in Iran, Qasim took pleasure from making people believe preposterous stories.

When Mumtaz was called outside, I said to Qasim, 'I'm not from the Ukraine – I'm from Scotland. The Ukraine was part of the Soviet Union. He will think I am a Russian.'

'He will not. Even I don't know where Ukraine is.'

Mumtaz re-entered. 'Does he speak Russian, Commander Seyyed?' he asked.

'Yes, very well,' said Qasim. I didn't.

'What is he doing?'

'We are travelling with him because the Emir has instructed us to look after him. We are walking all the way to Chaghcharan.'

'Excuse me, Haji Mumtaz,' I interrupted, 'what are the villages ahead where we will be able to stop for the night?'

'I know,' said Qasim, 'I'll tell you in the morning.'

'And you, Haji Mumtaz,' I persisted, 'how do you see the route ahead?'

'Well I suppose Sha'ede, Turon, Mawar Bazaar, Saray-e-Pul, Obey.'

They were presumably Tajik Sunni villages, but I had no idea what to expect.

'Look at this,' said Qasim to Haji Mumtaz. He turned over

his foot, revealing a purple and black pus-filled blister on his heel. We had been walking less than three hours. I hoped his new boots were going to be better than his old ones.

'Are you sure you will make it?' asked Mumtaz.

'We will, of course. We are Mujahidin, but him . . . I don't know . . .'

'I think I'll be all right,' I interjected, 'I have done a lot of walking.'

'In Iraq and India and Russia and Japan,' Qasim said impatiently, making up countries, 'everywhere walking.'

'And what is his job?'

Qasim paused. So did I.

'I am a historian,' I said.

'He works for the United Nations,' said Qasim.

'Is he a doctor?'

'Yes.'

'No,' I said.

'Well,' said Mumtaz, 'I've got a pain in my chest, what can you give me?'

'I'll see,' I said, opening my pack.

Qasim shouted the question at me again as if he were translating rather than merely repeating. 'Haji Mumtaz has a pain in his chest; what can you give him?' He treated me as though I were some exotic animal, whom he had been selected to exercise for the Emir – a Barbary ape being danced down the Silk Road. He enjoyed talking about me in his loud dominating voice, and he was pleased when I performed tricks for his friends and produced money or medicine. But he was not so keen on my tendency to speak for myself. Through all this, Abdul Haq remained silent, smiling to himself and occasionally shifting position to stretch his long legs.

'He speaks Dari; do you speak English?' Mumtaz asked Qasim.

'Yes,' he replied.

When I had handed over the anti-spasmodic pills, Haji

Mumtaz's sons distributed the mattresses and blankets, which were stacked in the corner of the room, so that we could lie down on the floor to sleep. Haji Mumtaz and his two sons also lay down with us to do us honour as guests. I was tired, but found it difficult to sleep. Abdul Haq left his transistor radio on all night. There was no reception and all he got was a loud static hiss, but it showed everyone that he owned a radio.

Impersonal Pronoun

On our second day together, leaving Haji Mumtaz's, I quickened my pace after half an hour and soon passed Abdul Haq, walking towards the rising sun. Nothing was visible in the dawn haze except a hint of mountains. I could neither see nor hear my companions. I was leaning forward against the weight of my pack, blinking the sweat out of my eyes. A gravel desert was opening up on every side. With each pace, I stretched further into my stride, jabbing with the metal-tipped staff through the ice beside the track. My feet beat out a steady muffled rhythm on the soil. My thoughts participated in each step, never getting ahead of me. It had snowed in the hills. A stream, swollen with melt-water, broke out of its ice shell and the dark blue flood pushed the ice blades out over the arid soil. I found it difficult to believe I had been allowed to do the walk. Despite my anxieties about the route and my companions I felt that I had been given a great gift. For two hours I was entirely absorbed in walking, feeling confident, elated and free. Then the belt of my pack was chafing against my hips and perhaps because I had taken no exercise for a month I was a little tired.

I slowed to allow the others to catch up and we walked in a line of four for some time. Abdul Haq was holding his dusty weapon by the barrel and resting it on his shoulder. I was learning that Abdul Haq's rifle was his favourite possession, narrowly beating his hand grenades. I had watched him use it as a comic prop, a walking stick and a source for impromptu firework displays when he was bored. There was no wind.

The gravel and sand under our feet was firm and we were walking quickly, all squinting slightly because of the bright sun. We didn't talk but we walked almost in step.

A small figure on the horizon grew steadily larger. It was an old man riding a donkey. When he reached us, we saw that the animal was so small that the old man's oversize gum boots dragged along the sand. I smiled at him. Aziz asked him angrily where he was going. The old man answered placidly and rode on and when I turned, he was again a miniature detail vanishing into an expanse of sand. I watched our own shadows moving. Qasim's small steps were smaller than before. He was walking in his new red leatherette boots half on tiptoe. I guessed that his blisters were getting worse.

For some time we had been able to see a hamlet ahead of us in the heat haze. We reached it, walked through to a small roadside truck stall and sat down. We had been walking for four hours and I was pleased to take off my pack. The stall served us a stew of beef and rice, and tea, which came steaming from the samovar, thick with limescale.

The others had met a friend and showed no intention of getting up again. Leaning back, in a corner, with a small pot of tea in front of me, I took out my Iranian school exercise book, which had a class timetable on the back and a picture of seagulls on the front cover, and wrote in my diary that I could think of nothing better than the morning's walk. But my sense that I was on an adventure seemed self-indulgent in the context of the war. I found it difficult to write about the risk of being killed. I wrote 'one' instead of 'I', as though I were shying away from myself. '. . . Strangely walking makes one feel one has had a fuller life . . .'

As I wrote this convoluted prose, Abdul Haq and Qasim were passing round painkillers for blisters. I was pleased when Qasim stood, cocked his head from side to side to stretch his neck and said we should go. I wanted to walk more before I wrote again.

Babur's decision to take this road into the mountains was one he lived to regret and perhaps as a result he blamed his old chancellor, Qasim, for it.

> We had consulted what was the best route to Kabul: I and some others proposed that, as it was winter, we should go by the way of Kandahar because though rather the longer road, it might be travelled without risk or trouble, while the hill road was difficult and dangerous. Qasim Beg, saying that that road was far about and this [the central route through Chaghcharan] direct, behaved very perversely; and in the end we resolved on attempting the short road.

Not surprisingly, given the season and circumstances of his departure, many of his courtiers refused to accompany him. Some returned later by alternative routes; others, perhaps drawn by the entertainments of the city, never left Herat:

> Several of my followers stayed behind in Herat . . . including Sidim who took service with the ruler. Sidim was a man of valour in war . . . He had a polished manner and address and his style of conversation and of telling a story was particularly agreeable. He was lively witty and humorous His great fault was that he was addicted to pederasty . . . [Two years later] Sidim was put to death and thrown into the river Helmand.

Babur's group was not well equipped. He was not carrying supplies and relied on villages to provide him with water, food and animal fodder along the way. Sometimes he paid for fodder, but he largely relied on traditions of hospitality. Although he often lived in a tent, on this occasion he appears to have left his tents in Bamiyan. Later in the journey, his men were forced to sleep sitting upright on their horses and he lay uncovered in a snowdrift, until the scouts found a cave. His horror at that one night implies that the rest of the time he slept like me in village houses.

The land through which he was travelling was then ruled by the prime minister of Herat, a man called Zulnun Arghun. There were administrative centres along the way at Obey and Chaghcharan, and large settlements at Yakawlang and Bamiyan, but there was not much in the places in between. Little had changed in that respect for five hundred years. It was still a very isolated area and Obey, Chaghcharan, Yakawlang and Bamiyan were still almost the only places on the route where I knew that I could find some semblance of government. The stretch from Obey to Chaghcharan was sparsely inhabited by semi-nomadic Tajik peoples called Aimaq and the stretch from Chaghcharan through Bamiyan by the Hazara. Then as now, the region contained four different ethnic groups (Tajik, Aimaq, Hazara and Pushtu), two main languages (Dari and Pushtu), and two different sects of Islam (Shia and Sunni).Its mountain landscape preserved traces of lost cultures, religions and dynasties.[5]

5. Babur may have faced greater linguistic problems. Although everyone then, as now, spoke dialects of Persian, the differences between dialects were probably more dramatic. Babur says that there were seven languages spoken in Kabul at his time, some of which have vanished or are now confined to very small communities.

A Tajik Village

Two hours into our afternoon walk we stopped to rest in a village. I sat with Qasim and Aziz beside an old man, leaning our backs against the mosque wall. Abdul Haq was pacing in the desert, trying to talk to headquarters on the radio. His call-sign, which he kept shouting, was 'Ansari' – the name of an eleventh-century Sufi saint who is buried in Herat. The old man beside us was entirely still. He sat on his heels with his knees up, draped in loose clothes, a blanket and a turban. His hands, immobile on his knees, were dark from the sun and swollen from work in the winter fields. Only his eyes moved. He looked at Abdul Haq, registering how young he was and how tall, and examining his American clothes, clean-shaven chin and Chinese baseball cap. Every man left in this village had a beard and turban.

Many of the village houses were empty. Most of the men, if they had not taken their families to the refugee camps, were working in Iran. There was no electricity to power a television. There was no clinic and no school for the children. There were no women visible in the streets. The only public building that mattered was the mosque behind us. And it was not a new Iranian model with cement walls, bathroom tiles and a bright aluminium dome. It was made of mud brick. This was the kind of village in which Abdul Haq had grown up.

'What are you doing here?' barked Abdul Haq.

'Waiting for afternoon prayer,' said the old man.

'I am *Abdul Haq* from the Security Service,' he said, rolling the syllables and stressing them as though he were speaking an exaggerated Arabic. The name Abdul Haq literally means 'Servant of Truth' just as Qasim means the 'Divider'.[6] 'My brothers and I are thirsty.' It was curious that Abdul Haq was giving the orders, but Qasim had his eyes closed beside me and seemed too tired to care. The old man stood up and slowly walked back towards his house and returned some time later with a tray. He unfolded a cloth in front of us. It contained some pieces of thick *nan* bread. Then he laid out two pots, one of green and one of black tea, and five glasses.

Silent and gravely polite in his traditional clothes, the old man poured our tea and then leaned back against the mosque wall, staring at Abdul Haq. These men were all that he had seen of the new administration. What impression of the government did he derive from the restless, half-modern, young Abdul Haq with his foreign equipment and muddled past?

Abdul Haq sat down beside us and helped himself to a biscuit. 'There are bad men here,' he whispered to me and taking my hand he added, in a parody of my Persian accent, '*Man haraji hastam*,' I am a foreigner. Then, standing up, he stuck the barrel of his rifle in the sand, performed a pole vault, hopped twice on his left foot and grinned. The old man remained expressionless for a moment and then laughed.

The old villager paid no taxes and received nothing from the state. Government was something that happened in grand, bullet-scarred buildings in Herat and Kabul. There, three weeks after the Taliban had gone, civil servants such as Yuzufi were again performing the ceremonies of fees and triplicate forms in front of sceptical congregations of war reporters needing visas. The Security Service was again putting people in their characterless cars. Outside the cities, there were only Abdul Haq, Qasim and Aziz, who with each

---

6. The first refers to an attribute of God; the second is a name for the Prophet.

ungainly stride were carrying a new culture into rural Afghanistan, like modern Alexander the Greats. And theoretically in control of all of this was the governor of Herat, Ismail Khan.

The Emir of the West

Ismail Khan is an appealing person . . . He's thought-
ful, measured and self-confident . . . I could tell you
what we talked about, but I'm not going to.

– US Secretary of Defence Donald Rumsfeld,
visiting Herat, 29 April 2002

Ismail Khan was the most powerful man in western
Afghanistan. Two days earlier, on my last afternoon in Herat,
I had gone to meet him, hoping that his support would provide some protection against the Security Service. A few bulbs
were still lit in the chandeliers of the gold-columned audience
chamber. In the dark corners, I could see scores of Afghan
villagers sleeping on the floor under pillars of stacked chairs.
They were waiting to petition Ismail Khan.

I joined the foreign journalists in a side room. They
glanced up as I entered but they did not greet me. They
seemed preoccupied. I noticed that most of the war reporters
had grown beards to look like Afghans or because there was
no hot water in their rooms. This was not true of the beautiful female correspondent with Television France Two but
even she seemed worn down. Nothing happened for half
an hour. I chatted with them. It appeared that everyone
had flu and had been waiting for an interview for a week.
They were flanked by their young, leather-jacketed Afghan
interpreters.

These were bright and dedicated reporters. Most of what

the European and American public knew about Afghanistan came from these people. It was not easy for them and the stress and tiredness showed in their expressions. They could not speak an Afghan language, they were afraid to leave their vehicles, the food was unfamiliar, they were sleeping badly, it was three and a half months after September 11th and their editors were pushing for more and more words and demanding to know why they had missed the stories on the 'Secret Hunt for Usama Bin Laden'. A month earlier, four of them had been dragged from their jeep on a road outside Jalalabad and executed. When I passed through the narrow, black-walled gorge shortly after it had happened and saw the lonely spot, I understood why the journalists were no longer prepared to travel on that road. Twelve foreign war reporters had been killed in Afghanistan in the previous two months.

Yuzufi entered buttoning his baggy pinstriped suit. He too seemed tired. A Japanese photographer asked him when the governor was coming.

'Soon,' he said.

Then Yuzufi saw me, smiled and put his hand on my shoulder. 'I'm glad you've come,' he whispered, 'at the end of the press conference I will point to you – then just introduce yourself quickly and tell him about your journey.'

Yuzufi left and then re-entered. Beside him was a portly man with a bushy white beard, who wore a neat black silk turban and baggy grey parka. The room was small and they both had to squeeze past us. It was only when he sat at the head of the table and wished us peace that I realized that this was Governor Ismail Khan. The cameras flashed and the BBC crew cursed because they hadn't switched something on. When the photographs had finished, Ismail Khan stopped smiling and said something to Yuzufi. He was sitting in a low chair, pressed against the end wall. Other governors would have entered through a separate door with a large train of gun-men but he had come in with only Yuzufi. He did not like ceremonial etiquette. He would not allow even his followers to kiss his hands.

Ismail Khan had captured Herat from the Taliban on 13 November 2001, six weeks before I met him. He had started the entire Afghan war with the Russians by killing hundreds of Russian advisers and their families in 1979. For the past twenty-two years he had been fighting the Russians and the Taliban, interrupted by periods spent either as governor of Herat, in jail or in exile in Iran. He had been the governor this time for a fortnight.

It was difficult to assess him. I had met his Security Service, which still tortured opponents with electric crank generators. He was rumoured to receive nearly a million dollars a day in customs revenue and passed none of it to the central government. But his human rights record was better than that of many of the ministers in Kabul and instead of pocketing the customs money he seemed to be spending it on rural development projects. Many Heratis were pleased to have a modest and pious local man running their affairs. Kabul, however, worried that he was trying to create an independent kingdom, supported by Iran. It was said that he had taken the title 'Emir of the West'.

It was important that I should be able to tell people that I had met Ismail Khan. Every person I met in the next month of walking would be defined in some way by their relationship to him. He had appointed the governors of all the neighbouring provinces and the district commanders for two hundred kilometres were all now his allies, even if they had been his enemies in the past. The Security Service were his personal elite.

'If your own interpreters wish to translate that is fine,' said Mr Yuzufi, opening the meeting in English, 'but I will retranslate.' Ismail Khan nodded. He spoke good English but during this meeting he would only speak Dari. He was facing television cameras from BBC, CBS and Television France and journalists from most of the largest international newspapers. This was probably the first time that either he or Yuzufi had spoken to so many foreign journalists at once. Ismail Khan may have wanted the retranslation to give him time to prepare his answers. 'In your questions please,' continued Yuzufi, 'only call His Excellency, "Your Excellency", never "you".'

Ismail Khan must have learned a completely new way of thinking and talking in six weeks. For twenty years, Iranian clerics and American intelligence officers had lectured him on political Islam and anti-Communism and rewarded him for killing Russians or Taliban. But now, American intelligence officers were pressing him on: *international terrorism, narcotics, organized crime and proliferation of weapons of mass destruction*. They were joined by diplomats, the United Nations, the relief and development agencies and uniformed military. These men gave him cash and grain according to World Bank-inspired *Needs Assessment Process* and *Quick Impact Projects for Afghan Reconstruction*. He seemed to impress those that he met.

Yuzufi no longer attempted to find Persian equivalents for this new jargon. English thrust up through the ornate surfaces of his sentences: *'U fekr mikonid ke* Internet broadband access *khub bud.'*

'Please, your question,' Yuzufi pointed to a French journalist, who spoke in English.

'I would like to know if Mister has any military aid from Iran . . .'

Yuzufi interrupted, 'His Excellency not Mister.'

'I would like to say,' said Ismail Khan, 'that before we came there was no furniture here – the Taliban was against furniture. We've bought all this furniture in the last two weeks.'

Ismail Khan disagreed with the Taliban more about furniture than he did about Islam. He believed in the jihad and hated atheist foreigners interfering in Afghanistan. He had encouraged women to return to education but believed they should be well covered and should not speak to men to whom they were not related. He was about to order new 'vice and virtue' squads to raid the arcades which I had seen and burn the DVDs. He had implemented laws forcing women to wear headscarves and forbidding men from wearing neckties. Women who met men to whom they were not related could be forcibly examined in hospitals to determine whether they had recently had sex.[7] But I was not sure how many of the people in the room understood his vision of an Islamic state. He was certainly not going to share his views on women with the woman from Television France Two who had not covered her blonde hair.

'Now, Mr Stewart,' said Yuzufi. I looked up from my notebook, where I had been trying to scribble down what I wanted to say. Before I could speak the woman cut in. 'If I can just interrupt,' she said smiling, 'can we have a private interview?'

Ismail Khan looked at her and then said, 'Of course, why not? Come tomorrow.'

There was a mutter from other journalists whose interview requests had been refused.

'Mr Stewart . . .'

I leaned forward. '*Agha Ismail Khan*,' I said and paused. I wanted to speak in Persian but I felt self-conscious in front of all the interpreters, so I continued in English. 'I am a British writer, focusing on the history and culture of Afghanistan.' Yuzufi nodded encouragement. 'I am planning to walk on

---

7. In Herat under Ismail Khan, people who committed 'vice crimes', such as drinking alcohol, had their heads shaved or were denounced on television. Women could not walk or ride in a car alone with a man who was not a close relative, even a taxi driver. A police task force patrolled Herat city, arresting men and women who were seen together and suspected of being unrelated or unmarried. Men were taken to jail; women and girls were taken to a hospital to undergo forced medical examinations.

foot to Kabul, via Bamiyan, not using a vehicle. I would like to thank His Excellency Yuzufi for his support.' I glanced at Ismail Khan. He was looking at a Koranic inscription on the wall. I skipped a few sentences. 'I am following the route of the Emperor Babur, who did this journey in the winter of 1506. I am hoping that I can show my people what a wonderful place Afghanistan is.'

There was a long pause. I was aware of the journalists staring at me. Ismail Khan turned to Yuzufi, who whispered something. Then the governor looked at me. 'A big journey, which I would like to support. Tell me please if there is anything I can do to help. But . . .' he paused, apparently confused, 'this journey is not possible in the winter. I know this. I have fought in the region at this season.'

I wondered whether I could ask him to tell the Security Service to leave me alone but Yuzufi had raised his hand as though to tell me to stop. 'Thank you,' I said. The governor smiled broadly and the audience was over.

*

Yuzufi insisted I travel in his van back to the hotel because it was after curfew. 'You are very lucky,' he said. 'What the governor said is more important than you know – I will write a note saying you are under his protection. Now you will be stronger with the Security Service.' Yuzufi seemed relieved by how the press conference had gone. I said that I thought his job must be a difficult one.

'Ah, Rory, how you understand me,' he said laughing. 'This morning a woman came in from a New York journal . . .'

'My friend Carlotta from the *New York Times?*'

'Perhaps. She said that it is "the most important newspaper in the world" and I must arrange a private interview with His Excellency. I almost believed her but another woman came here. From CNN. Apparently that is also "the most important in the world". Who can I believe? Now, I have cancelled them both and told them to come to the press conference with . . .' he paused, '*Newsday*, the *Christian Science Monitor*. Have I done correctly?'

Before I could answer three men stepped into the centre of the road in front of us and pointed their automatics at the windscreen. They were the curfew guard. Yuzufi got out of the car to explain who we were and we were allowed slowly forward. 'It must be satisfying to have this much influence,' I said.

'Not for me. Although I admire His Excellency I would like to go to England to study a master's degree and to serve as an ambassador overseas,' said Yuzufi. He looked out of the window. There had been a power cut and Herat was dark. We were stopped again by another group of policemen. Yuzufi paused before speaking to them. 'Nothing changes in Herat,' he said.

Caravanserai, whose portals . . .

Two days later in the desert, Yuzufi, the journalists and Ismail Khan seemed remote. Qasim and Aziz were finding walking increasingly difficult. They were not used to walking eight hours at a stretch. Qasim kept saying that we should travel by bus.

At dusk, we saw a fortified building on the plain to the south and beyond it a village. Since they had no tents I suggested we find somewhere to sleep. Qasim replied that there were bad men in the village and they wouldn't receive us. I said that I'd often walked into villages without an introduction. Abdul Haq shrugged and turned off the footpath, striding across the desert towards the building. For a moment I considered walking in Abdul Haq's footsteps because of mines but I felt embarrassed to let him take the risk alone so I walked beside him.

'Do you understand what I am saying?' Qasim shouted from behind Abdul Haq. 'I have been a Mujahid for twenty-two years. When walking you must stay on the roads not walk in the fields.'

'But this is a short cut,' replied Abdul Haq.

'If you please! We must walk on the road.'

'Don't talk like that,' said Abdul Haq. 'Our guest will lose confidence in us.'

'Don't worry; he can't understand what we are saying.'

Abdul Haq began to goose step across the sand, swinging his right arm in front of his chest and kicking up the dust with his heels. Then he launched into a guerrilla song which opened 'Welcome, Ismail Khan, Welcome, Commander'. For the next ten minutes he chanted his welcome to every comrade he could think of. He had just reached 'Welcome, Qasim, Welcome, Commander' when we arrived at a path and met a man who confirmed we could stay in the building. 'Someone will take you in,' he said. 'It contains thirty families.'

When we reached the building, with its high mud walls and its single corner tower, I realized it was a medieval caravanserai, built to accommodate merchants on the Silk Road. Because caravanserai were built each a day's walk apart I had used them for accommodation when I walked across the Iranian desert between Arak and Isfahan. It was surrounded by a shallow moat. A broad wooden bridge led to a three-arched portico, large enough for a loaded camel. Abdul Haq knocked on the wooden door and while we waited I photographed the three of them. Abdul Haq flashed his broad grin. A dark band of evening shadow was rising fast up the coffee-coloured brick. We were all tired and relieved to have found shelter.

This legacy of the Silk Road was the kind of thing that had appealed to me about an Asian walk when I had the idea five years earlier. There would once have been lapis lazuli here, carried west from the mines of Afghanistan to make the blue in medieval Sienese paintings, and amber cut from tree fossils in the Baltic and brought east for Tibetan necklaces. Even more mysterious objects had moved down such trading routes: diamonds that could make you a king, Buddhist texts on birch-bark scrolls in characters that could no longer be deciphered, Chinese astrolabes to mystify the Vatican. But such things had little to do with modern Afghanistan and I doubted whether the people who lived in this building had a very clear idea of its past.

A delicate-featured boy of eight appeared at the gate and said that there was no one at home. Qasim told him to have a second look. After some minutes he reappeared. The sun had sunk and we were beginning to feel cold. The boy looked at us with his dark, steady eyes and said, 'No. There is no one here.'

Qasim snapped, 'Don't lie, boy. You have been told to say this. I know there are people inside. Look again.' Another child appeared from the caravanserai. He was slightly smaller, with spiky black hair and he was wearing a faded red *shalwar kemis*.

'Tell them I am a *meman* (guest), *mosafer* (traveller),' continued Qasim. 'Muslims cannot refuse hospitality. We're from the government. We have a right to enter.'

The first boy stared at Qasim and then at me and said, 'No. There is no one here.'

There was a pause and suddenly Abdul Haq grabbed the boy by the collar and began to push him through the medieval arch towards the courtyard.

Qasim shouted, 'Stop, don't go in there. This was an Al-Qaeda place. You'll both be shot.'

Abdul Haq bent down, looked into the boy's eyes and then pushed him roughly away. The boy stumbled backwards but did not fall. 'Tell them now that we are going to come in,' said Abdul Haq.

'There is no one here,' said the boy.

Abdul Haq looked at the other two men and then turned and walked with them back across the moat bridge. I followed. When we reached the end of the bridge, Abdul Haq nodded at Aziz, spun, dropped to one knee and brought his rifle to his shoulder, aiming at the boys. Aziz did the same.

The first boy leapt behind the door, the other stood motionless in the archway, and began to cry, waiting for the shot.

I paused and then I stepped towards Abdul Haq. He glanced sideways at me and I laid my hand over the rifle sight, smiled and said, 'No,' gently. The other boy ran out, grabbed his friend and pushed him behind the door. There was a pause.

I dropped my hand. Abdul Haq laughed and we walked off towards the village. I fell back. I did not want to walk alongside these men.

On the outskirts of the village, they found a man squatting behind a wall, possibly hiding from them. He stood up and bowed and seized the hands of Abdul Haq and Qasim, ignoring me. Qasim went through the elaborate chain of greetings and then asked where we could stay.

'Over there.'

'Lead us,' barked Qasim.

'No,' replied the man, turning away, 'I really . . .'

Abdul Haq grabbed his wrist and Aziz pointed his rifle at his chest and the man said, 'Of course, of course, I will come with you.'

We entered the village and saw three old men sitting with their grandchildren on the platform beside the mosque. One white-bearded man advanced with a broad smile. Qasim was becoming aware of how nervous everyone was. He made his greetings particularly polite and lengthy, adding, 'No need to be afraid. We just wondered whether we could find some bread, a place to sleep. We are not asking you to kill a sheep for us.'

'Ah yes,' said the old man. 'Yes. I'm afraid it is such a pity we simply have nothing at all.' He smiled even more broadly. 'Nothing at all.'

'Just a little,' said Qasim, smiling back.

'I'm so sorry,' said the old man. 'I wish I could help.'

'Right,' shouted Abdul Haq. 'That's it. We'll sleep in the desert. This is your Muslim hospitality . . . how you treat guests . . . I see it now. If we wanted to kill you, you'd be dead. Look you idiots. You stupid, old . . . idiots. Look,' he pointed his rifle at them. They all stepped back and the old man stopped smiling. 'Bahh,' he roared, imitating the sound of the weapon and the recoil on his shoulders, 'Bahh, Bahh . . .' And he walked off.

'No, no, please come back,' said the old man, 'stay with us.'

'I would never touch your bread.'

'Please,' shouted the first man. 'Stay with me.'

'I'm never staying in this village. You are men without hospitality and without honour . . .'

'It's just the weapons,' said the old man. 'We were just a little afraid. Can't you understand? Many have been killed in this place.'

Suddenly Qasim stepped in, grabbing the younger man's arm, talking calmly, restraining him, and reasoning with him. Another villager offered his house and we moved towards his door. On the threshold, Abdul Haq pointed at me and shouted, 'Look at this man. This man is a foreigner. Look how disgustingly you have behaved towards him.'

*

Inside, I sat on the floor beside the others. We all put our legs under the low *kursi* table. There was a coal brazier beneath the *kursi* and a thick felt blanket over it, which we pressed down over our knees to keep the heat in. Abdul Haq took off his baseball cap, ruffled his hair and, worried perhaps about revenge from the people he had bullied that afternoon, pulled out his hand grenades and ostentatiously screwed in the firing pins. Qasim stacked up Kalashnikov magazines neatly beside him and removed two bullets that he had hidden in his collar. Aziz curled up in the corner and fell asleep. Our host was silent and kept his eyes on the weapons. I was used to walking alone, observing subtle changes in the landscape and scraps of ancient history. Villagers usually took me into their houses. I did not feel I understood these sudden happenings or such people.

On the wall was a Technicolor poster depicting the Prophet Mohammed's cousin and son-in-law, Ali, who died in the seventh century. This part of Afghanistan had been conquered by the Arabs while Ali was still alive. But it took Islam another four hundred years to spread a week's walk further east to Ghor. The poster made Ali look like a Hollywood sheikh with sparkling pale eyes. It showed that our host was a Shia Muslim. This was a Sunni area. Abdul Haq started to tease him about being a Shia and Qasim joined in, but when he didn't respond they gave up.

After dinner, Qasim told us that he had executed five Taliban in Herat but he seemed a little bored by the story, perhaps because he had told it too often, and he did not tell it well. Abdul Haq said he had been at the shoulder of Ismail Khan when they attacked the city.

'Well you are a big man,' said Qasim and they all laughed.

Then Abdul Haq looked at me, smiled and put his arm around me. 'You are my brother. You would be dead without me. You are, like me, a fighting man,' he said. 'Other people don't like you because you are not Muslim but I don't care. I can see it in your eyes. We are both men of honour. We have had the same lives. We are the same.'

I moved to the corner of the room and began to unpack. I had covered my pack with a plastic rice bag to make it look more like something a villager would carry and this made it difficult to get into the pockets. From one side, I took out a plastic bag containing my small, limp yellow towel and my toothbrush. In the main compartment were warm clothes, a sleeping bag and a yellow MRE ration pack, marked 'From the People of America Not for Resale.' It had probably been dropped from the air as emergency food relief. My friend Peter Jouvenal had bought it in the Kabul bazaar and given it to me in case I was stuck out in the snow. Another pocket contained antibiotics for dysentery and infections, which I had collected from five Asian countries without prescriptions, and some morphine tablets, in case of a broken leg. I laid my sleeping bag in the corner of the room and spread out my white cotton turban as a pillowcase.

Finally, I reached into the damp-proof container, a smaller rice sack wrapped in masking tape, which held my passport, a translation of the Koran and an excerpt from Babur's diary. I took out four photographs to show my host. One was a picture of a white-haired man sitting on a bench. Standing behind him were two women and a girl with Down's syndrome who was smiling more broadly than anyone. It was my father and my three sisters, although the Nepalis had assumed that one of my sisters was my mother. The Iranians had found the second picture of my father in his kilt particularly funny; Hindus had admired his lurcher dog in the third, and a family of Shahsevan Turks had assured me that the two-humped camel on which my mother was sitting in the fourth had been theirs – they would recognize it anywhere. The camel was photographed on the Great Wall of China.

My host glanced at the pictures and then pointed to a photograph of his son on the wall, which had a garland of plastic flowers around the frame. He had been killed by a tank shell seven years earlier.

To a Blind Man's Eye

I lay down reflecting on my first full day of walking: the gravel underfoot, Qasim's lies, our host's dead son, the old man who had scrutinized Abdul Haq, the terrified boy. The abrupt episodes and half-understood conversations were already suggesting a society that was an unpredictable composite of etiquette, humour and extreme brutality. I dozed off, thinking of the stubby shadow of Abdul Haq's Kalashnikov: a weapon designed by Russians, made by Iranians and now used by Afghans on the American side. The weapons were, I thought, the only piece of machinery visible in this room that could connect us to the modern age. Except for the radio. This woke me with a louder burst of static and a hint of a Hindi song. Two hours had passed and Abdul Haq was lying on one arm in the dark, smoking a cigarette. Aziz was coughing. For two weeks I had been away from villages and I had forgotten how little villagers slept, how early they woke and how much noise they made. I went outside to relieve myself. Despite the money that our host had spent on his neat mud buildings and clipped hedges, he had not invested in a latrine. I was usually locked every night in a village house before dark. This was my opportunity to see the night sky and to be away from my companions. There were a few stars and a three-quarter moon and I sensed the silent, invisible desert outside the high courtyard walls. I squatted in the corner.

At dawn we immediately rolled our bedding away for morning prayers, but only our host prayed. We were given sweet tea and bread. As we were eating, five village elders came to apologize for the night before and to escort us to Gawashik. They were led by the District Commander of Pushtun Zargon, a broad-shouldered, middle-aged man with a thick black beard and a large nose. He told me he had visited Pakistan during the war to procure weapons and he repeated some phrases in Urdu to prove it. Qasim and Aziz hobbled beside him, coughing and pulling their checked scarves up around their scraggly beards.[8] I had become used to the way they moved. But beside this large bearded man with his fine silk turban they looked particularly fragile. The commander walked with his arms stiff by his side, so that the green prayer beads in his left hand swung back and forth like a pendulum.

We followed a footpath that led from the young boys' caravanserai towards Buriabaf. It was presumably the old road. The newer 'vehicle' road was two kilometres to our north but perhaps because its upper reaches were blocked by snow, we could not see any vehicles on it. After two hours the black-bearded commander left us. On our right was the Hari Rud River and on either side a line of low rounded shale and lime hills. The gravel stretched flat in front of us for another hundred kilometres across the flood plains to Chist, the ancient base of the Chistiyah dervish and the edge of the province of Ghor. There, I hoped, the others would leave me. I would continue alone into the hills of Ghor and to the source of the Hari Rud River in the Grandfather Mountains and then over the watershed and down the Kabul River to the flat desert and the capital.

The route would take me through four provinces: Herat, Ghor, Bamiyan and Wardak. They represented, very roughly, four different landscapes and four different ethnic groups. I had asked an interpreter in Herat what the differences were and he replied, without hesitation:

---

8. Only Ismail Khan's men wore these scarves, which resembled the Palestinian *keffiyah*.

First, you are with the Tajik of Herat, who are the ancient Persians. Their farms are on the flat plains of the Hari Rud. Second, you will reach the Aimaq, a tent-dwelling tribal people, who live in the hill country of Ghor. There was the centre of the ancient Ghorids who invaded India. Two hundred kilometres further east are the high mountains of Bamiyan. There the Hazara live who are descended from Genghis Khan. They look like Chinese, are dangerous and are Shia Muslims. Finally, after weeks with the Hazara, you will descend again to the valleys and the desert, where you will meet the Pashtun tribe of Wardak. All the other peoples you will meet speak Dari [the Afghan dialect of Persian] but the Wardak do not speak Persian, they speak Pushtu. They support the Taliban.[9]

This central route was unpopular with travellers. Had it been popular, Herat would not have existed. But the caravans wanted to avoid the centre, so they used Herat as a junction, turning either north on to the Silk Roads to China or south on to the Spice Roads to India. In the centre the passes were fourteen thousand feet high and ancient travellers believed that their camels would begin to bleed from the nose because of the altitude.[10] In the winter, temperatures could drop to

---

9. His description, which was to prove more than a little misleading, bears a strong resemblance to that of Mountstuart Elphinstone in 1815. The bold generalizations probably reflected the fact that, like Elphinstone, he had never visited the interior in person.

10. The main pass through to Chaghcharan is called Shotor Khun – camel's blood – for this reason. All the ancient cultures seem to have agreed that the edge of the great Asian mountain massif beyond Herat was an import-ant frontier. The Greeks called its mountains the *Paropamisus* from the Persian word *Uparisena* – peaks over which the eagles cannot fly. Aristotle believed that from these mountains you could see the eastern edge of the earth. Perhaps as a result, when the ruler of Herat, Satibarzanes, fled along the central route, Alexander the Great did not follow him, but instead took what is now known as the hippy trail to Kandahar.

minus forty, blizzards were frequent, navigation difficult and the snow was often nine feet deep. In 1976, Nancy Dupree's impressive guidebook was 'reluctant to recommend this route without the gravest reservations' and the hippy buses continued to take the flatter, warmer route to Kandahar.

The central region, therefore, remained largely unknown. The ancient Persians excluded it from the provinces of their Empire. The medieval Arab geographers mocked it as a backward place and the last pagan region of the Persian-speaking world. Even in the twentieth century, those who did this route did so in mid-summer, prepared carefully and rarely left a single track. As a result they did not see much of the interior. The first foreigner known to have followed the Hari Rud River one hundred and fifty kilometres due east of Herat to the village of Jam was a Frenchman, André Mariq, who did it in 1957. He was rewarded by discovering on the river banks a magnificent minaret, sixty metres tall, previously unknown in the West. The archaeologists who followed him were unable to make much sense of it.

*

'Qasim, what do you do?' I asked. Abdul Haq and Aziz had fallen behind us, Abdul Haq because his radio was not working, Aziz because he could not walk fast. Qasim seemed to have recovered some of his energy.

'I am a commander in the Security Service of Ismail Khan.'

'But what do you do?'

'*Amniat.*' (Security.)

'And why are you walking with me?'

'*Amniat.*'

'Perhaps we should leave each other at Darai-e-Takht. You don't need to go all the way to Chaghcharan. Darai-e-Takht is much closer.'

'We were told to take you to Chaghcharan.'

'Perhaps we can negotiate.'

He said nothing. We walked on a little further.

'I did not tell those people who walked with us that you were a writer,' said Qasim.

'What did you tell them?'

'I told some of them that you were in the United Nations. I told the others that you were an American soldier.'

'That's not a good idea.'

'It's a great idea. Now they are frightened. I told them that your walking stick was a beacon for summoning helicopters.'

Abdul Haq appeared beside us, laughed, raised his rifle to his shoulder and fired a round next to my ear. I called a halt for a drink.

'We don't have time,' said Qasim.

I ignored him, sat down and remembering my Persian manners, offered my bottle to the others before drinking. Aziz drank gratefully and when he had finished unleashed a rattling consumptive cough that concluded with a thick gobbet of phlegm, green from his tobacco. Although I was thirsty I decided not to drink. A little later, Abdul Haq stopped by a broken irrigation ditch to drink from a brackish puddle. Qasim wouldn't drink and I asked him why.

'Because this is the spot where I was ambushed two years ago in the Taliban era.'

'By the Taliban?'

'No, no, two men from Gawashik, looking for money,' said Qasim. 'I was in a jeep and they stepped out from behind that boulder so I shot them both through the windscreen, dragged their corpses back behind the boulder. That's where I also found their motorcycle. I still have it.'

'But I thought road security was good under the Taliban.'

'Yes,' he replied. 'Road security was very good under the Taliban. The Taliban were very good people; Al-Qaeda foreigners were bad but Taliban were good.'

Five hundred yards further on we came to a large stretch

of bare black gravel. There were boulders along the side of the path, painted red. 'That is a minefield,' said Qasim. There was no building in sight. I had been told to expect minefields in strategic areas, near military posts and towns. I could not see any reason why there should have been a minefield here and I would not have stayed on the path without his warning. Qasim said it had been laid by the Russians to prevent the Mujahidin coming onto the road from the hills. I noticed that there were no sheep droppings on this patch, though the droppings were scattered elsewhere right across the plain. This seemed a good clue to where the mines were.

We stopped that afternoon to rest near a dark green Russian armoured personnel carrier and another caravanserai. We had probably completed one farsang or day's stage for a caravan from where we had spent the previous night. There was an old man watching us from the doorway.

'That man is Taliban,' said Abdul Haq, 'you're going to get me killed.' Then he laughed. Abdul Haq didn't worry too much. He even seemed to enjoy the journey. Each of us thought the other would get us both killed. He found that funny. So did I. But I could not grasp the view he took as an Afghan of the history of this featureless landscape. 'That's a Russian APC, isn't it?' I said, as I stood up.

Abdul Haq grunted, 'P sixty-six.'

'What's that building?'

'Nothing,' Abdul Haq replied.

'It's a caravanserai, isn't it?'

'No.'

I walked over to look at it. Abdul Haq was not interested. Instead he pointed to a low mound and said, 'There is the grave of a Taliban. Our group ambushed them here, six months ago, killed five of them.'

'Qasim, were you part of the ambush?'

'No, I participated in an ambush two kilometres further on.'

'I missed that one,' said Abdul Haq.

Abdul Haq's landscape was composed of violent events in the recent past. Despite his laconic manner, his continual clowning and his unpredictable threats, Abdul Haq was an intelligent and literate man. He knew that this was Babur's route and that ahead lay remote mountain regions, which had once contained two ancient civilizations: the Buddhist culture of Bamiyan and the now-lost Islamic capital of the Turquoise Mountain. But he didn't care. These were the kind of things that he heard politicians discussing in their speeches about the historic greatness of Afghanistan.

He saw Afghanistan as a poor, superstitious country, with corrupt leaders and nothing to gain from looking backwards. His sympathies were with baseball caps not caravanserai. When he denied that the building was a caravanserai I do not think he was being ignorant: he was saying that whatever the building had once been, it was nothing any more. He doubted it had ever been much in the first place. He was probably right about that. We were further from the main Silk Road, nearing impassable peaks. The building had probably never attracted many traders and it was unlikely ever to have been filled with precious gems or even the everyday goods that Babur describes being traded in Afghanistan: *slaves, white clothes, sugar-candy, refined and common sugar, drugs and spices*.[11]

As we set off again, Qasim was limping. He seemed suddenly very small and old. Just before dusk there was a village visible on our right.

'Where do you plan to stop tonight?' I asked Qasim.

'At Dideros.'

'How far is that?'

---

11. It had perhaps been built as a status symbol by a local ruler who may have wanted to attract trade or to simply imply by its presence that his kingdom was a more integral part of classical Persian civilization and trade than it had ever been in reality.

'Near.'

'How many hours' walk?'

'Three perhaps.'

'If this road is as dangerous as you say, we cannot walk in the dark. We must sleep here,' I said.

'Are you too weak to walk?' snapped Qasim. His tone was petulant and his voice was more high-pitched than usual. 'This is the desert.'

'There is a village there.'

'We don't know anyone in that village. It would be too dangerous to just walk in.'

It was even more dangerous to walk at night. I said so and turned off. They followed me.

Genealogies

This village, Buriabaf, like most in the valley, was perhaps half a kilometre from the path, in contrast to the Indian subcontinent where houses cling to the edge of the road. Perhaps this was to discourage visitors. A farmer with a rifle on his shoulder directed us to the headman's house. We walked in single file beside a canal flowing with clean water and lined with a double row of bare poplars. The water had picked up the last pale intensity of the evening sky and the reflections of the silver trees trembled in the wind and in the water. There was no one in the street.

We crossed a bridge, turned down a narrow lane and found a dark wooden door. We knocked. The headman appeared. He was a young man with an incomplete beard. Qasim brought his heels together, leaned forward on the balls of his feet in an approximation of a salute and then, after lengthy greetings, said, 'Our car has broken down.'

'Where?'

'In the desert,' said Qasim. 'We are officers of the Security Service.' He produced a bundle of letters from his jacket. The headman summoned another young man from the compound and they gazed at the letters together.

'His Excellency Rory,' continued Qasim, 'gives international financial assistance to villages in Afghanistan.'

The headman glanced sceptically at my faded woollen blanket, stick and pack but he asked us in.

We entered a compound arranged above a sunken courtyard ten feet deep. At one corner there was a ruined circular tower with battlements. Ten men, mostly armed, stood beside it, watching us. Qasim didn't even glance at them. The headman stood back politely at the guest room door and Qasim pushed past with a patronizing smile. Taking our shoes off at the door, we followed, with a sockless Abdul Haq complaining loudly about his feet. It was a small, unfurnished mud room. We sat on the earth.

'Where have you walked from?' asked the headman.

'From Herat,' said Abdul Haq, 'we're shattered.'

'But I thought you said that your car . . .'

'Could you get someone to massage my men?' asked Qasim, changing the subject. He was lying on his back with his feet held up against the wall.

'Of course,' said the headman, summoning one of the boys who were staring at us from the door. He was put to work on Aziz's leg muscles.

'This is a very poor village,' said Qasim loudly to me. 'The headman is a very poor man.' Then he winked at the headman. The headman looked perplexed.

I took out a Steinbeck novel from my pack, hoping to read it. It was the only English book I'd been able to find on sale in Herat. Qasim removed it from me and began to mumble over it.

'I can read English,' Qasim said to the headman, pointing to a phrase 'this says "Ox-kew-lee".' He turned to me and asked, ' "Ox-Kew-Lee," *chi ast*?' (What is Ox-Kew-Lee?)

I looked at the phrase. 'It means "*khosh amadid*" but we normally pronounce it "You're welcome".'

Abdul Haq, perhaps jealous of this learned conversation, took off his Chinese baseball cap and turned on his military radio, which gave its normal static hiss, and barked, '*Ansari, Ansari*' into it.

*

During fifteen months of sleeping in village houses I had seen countless interiors but it was difficult to decipher much from the uniformity of cheap rugs, Koran boxes and family photographs. I rarely had a chance to look properly at a village. I said I'd go for a walk.

'No, you won't,' said Qasim.

The headman and the other villagers looked at me to see if I would accept this order.

'Why not?'

'It's too dangerous for you to go out alone.' Qasim believed I would be shot by a village if I walked out alone.

'I'll be fine,' I said, smiling and standing up.

'Aziz will have to go with you.'

'Aziz is too ill,' I said.

'What can he do if you insist on going for a walk?' asked Qasim.

Aziz staggered to his feet and we walked outside together. Aziz carried a rifle and wore a black bandanna and a checked Arab scarf. He looked like a Palestinian terrorist. He rarely smiled and was always the first to point his rifle at passers-by. When we were with the other two I couldn't get him to speak.

'How are you?' I asked.

'Very sick,' he said. 'I don't know how much further I can continue.' Although his legs and his chest had been getting much worse in the last three days, he was still forced to carry Abdul Haq and Qasim's sleeping bags as well as Qasim's rifle.

Entering the village I had seen little of interest. As in most villages everything was hidden behind high, blank courtyard walls. There were no squares, gardens or restaurants. The only public place was the mosque, and in Sunni areas villagers were unwilling to let me enter the mosque. Now as I walked in the dusk I began to notice how the mud varied from coarse, dove-grey bricks to pink, waxy plaster on the walls, the path and the canal banks. A darkening, cloud-troubled sky framed the silhouettes of towers and domes. One of the thick walls of an old fort had crumbled inwards, revealing an overgrown rose garden in a courtyard, sunk twelve feet below the level of the street and fed by a slender waterfall. Through a half-open gate I could see a mulberry tree. Firelight played around the thick frame of a high window. The deep courtyards and the old arches and windows that rose just a foot above the street had been parts of substantial houses built long before, now folded into the foundations of the village.

'Do you agree with Qasim that this is a poor village?' I asked Aziz.

'No,' said Aziz, 'this is a good village with good water. A rich village. People live well here: avenues, gardens, a big mosque.'

'But Qasim said . . .'

Aziz laughed, 'This is not poor. I am poor.' And he leaned his shoulder against mine.

*

We walked back to the house in silence. A young man was waiting to let us back into the compound, the gate closed behind us and that was all that I ever knew or saw of that village. Perhaps the villagers knew who had first dug the canals and who had built the corner tower. They might have told me who had resisted or collaborated with the Russians or the Taliban. But I was tired and I doubted whether I would be able to learn much in a single evening.

I was generally confused when villagers talked about history. Entering the guest room, I remembered how a Muslim Turkish host in Iranian Kurdistan had talked about his village, a year earlier.

'Goz Hasle is a very old village, God be praised,' the Turk had said. 'My father was born here and my grandfather was born here. We were always here.'

'What does Goz Hasle mean?' I asked.

'It means "cross-wearing girl".'

'So it was a Christian village?'

'No.'

'But then why is it called "cross-wearing girl"?'

'My grandparents did not live alongside Armenian Christians. The Armenians left a very, very long time ago.'

'When?'

'When my father was a child.'

Faced with these contradictions I assumed, perhaps unfairly, that his family had helped the Ottomans drive the Armenians out.

'Where was the Armenian church?'

'I don't know.'

I left it at that. It was only thinking back, months later, that I remembered that my host had kept his horse in a long building with a tall door, a base of neatly dressed masonry and a wooden roof that soared thirty feet high; in the south side was the trace of an arched window.

Every night, in over five hundred villages, I interviewed villagers about their possessions, communities and history and wrote for two hours in my diary. It had become a fixed habit and I was not in control of these conversations. I was often tired and as I interviewed others, I was also defending myself against suspicious questions and trying to be polite to my host.

My notebooks were filled with facts about places that I could rarely find again on maps. I had made sketches of medieval mosques, accounts of previous visitors, lists of people's possessions and their incomes, copies of feudal genealogies and diagrams of arrow-making or weaving. I had recorded claims about recent killings, descriptions of possible Neolithic burial mounds and short biographies. I had speculated on pre-Islamic or pre-Hindu religions, which were suggested by a burial practice or a carving on a stone pillar.

I had looked at the importance of mass-produced imported goods, foreign missionaries and development agencies in remote communities, and the journeys which men had made on pilgrimage or for work in cities. I noticed how religion, language and social practices were becoming homogenized, and how little interest people took in ancient history. I noticed all of this but I was not sure whether writing it down was any more than a cover story to justify the journey to myself.

Lest he returning chide . . .

In the guest room an old man was making a long speech to the villagers. Five young boys were sitting wide-eyed and silent, perhaps too young to understand the sense but observing in awe the modulations in his voice, his whispers, laughs and gestures. Their eyes never shifted. Afghan toddlers never interrupt in the guest room.

'Here he is at last,' said Qasim to the headman, seeing me enter. 'Now's your chance to tell Agha Rory what you want. I have told Agha Rory what a poor village this is. Is there anything you need, headman?'

'A tarmac road.'

'Well, that shouldn't be too difficult should it Rory?' said Qasim.

Before I could reply the headman, thoroughly excited, shouted, 'If you'll excuse me, money for a new mosque.'

Another villager joined in, 'And money for crops, if you please.'

Qasim beamed and nodded and said, 'Keep going. Rory has thousands of dollars to spend.'

'If you please, handpumps . . . more handpumps . . .'

'And a tube well, if you please.'

Silence.

'Well,' I replied, playing my role for Qasim, 'I will present a report on your requirements to Kabul.'

'Why, Agha Qasim, are you accompanying Agha Rory? Are you there to protect him from wolves and bandits?' asked the headman.

'No, no,' replied Qasim. 'We are with him because we are the greatest of friends. We are walking with him all the way to Chaghcharan.'

And I smiled and nodded, hoping our destination was also a lie; otherwise, we'd be together for the next four weeks.

Qasim took my photographs out of my diary and began to show them to everyone, saying my sister was my mother and that a photograph of me was of my (non-existent) brother. I admired a photograph of the host's sons taken in a Herat studio. They were dressed in red shirts and white cowboy hats.

*

The next day we set out into the same flat desert landscape. We were about a hundred kilometres outside Herat. The scenery would not change until we reached the hills. As before, we walked alongside the Hari Rud River. Had it been snowing or raining, the river would have been a seething mass. There had been villages built on the alluvial flood plain for thousands of years. But now it was just a thin stream, running east–west at the bottom of a flat gravel bed. The earth was parched and bare, and only the slight mounds of rectangular field boundaries were visible.

I felt quite detached from the landscape. I wondered how I might connect my Afghan walk to my walks in Iran and Pakistan. I was thinking in phrases that resembled the names of motor rallies: 'Isfahan–Herat', 'Kabul–Multan', 'Istanbul–Hanoi'. I redesigned a journey around the world, which would finish where I began in Turkey.

I thought about evolutionary historians who felt that walking was a central part of what it means to be human. Our two-legged motion was what first differentiated us from the apes. It freed our hands for tools and carried us on the long marches out of Africa. As a species, we colonized the world on foot. Most of human history was created through contacts conducted at walking pace, even when some rode horses. I thought of the pilgrimages to Compostela in Spain; to Mecca; to the source of the Ganges; and of wandering dervishes, sadhus and friars who approached God on foot. The Buddha meditated by walking and Wordsworth composed sonnets while striding beside the lakes.

Bruce Chatwin, who was very interested in these things, concluded from all of this that we would think and live better and be closer to our purposes as humans if we moved continually on foot across the surface of the earth. I was not certain that I was living or thinking any better.

Before I started, I had imagined that I could fill my days by composing an epic poem in my head or write a novel set in a Scottish village which would become more rooted in a single place as I kept moving. In Iran, I tried earnestly to think through philosophical arguments, learn Persian vocabulary and memorize poetry. Perhaps this is why I never felt quite at ease walking in Iran.

In Pakistan, having left the desert and entered the lush Doab of the Punjab, I stopped trying to think and instead looked at the movement of the canal water and peacocks in the trees. In India, when I was walking from one pilgrimage site to another across the Himalayas, I carried the Baghvad Ghita open in my left hand and read a line at a time. In the centre of Nepal, I began to count my breaths and my steps, reciting phrases to myself, pushing thoughts away. This is the way in which some people meditate. I could only feel this calm for at most an hour a day. It was, however, a serenity that I had not felt before. It was what I valued most about walking.

It was a cool, overcast day. As we entered the third hour, we were walking in a line and in step to the Hindi music from Abdul Haq's radio.

Aziz caught my eye, smiled shyly and said, 'We are brothers.'

I said, 'Yes, four brothers,' and smiled back.

We had all adjusted to each other's pace and we moved now almost in a single pack. The competitiveness between Qasim and Abdul Haq seemed to have faded. The others no longer asked me any questions about my life. I seemed almost to be accepted.

We saw a young boy drawing water below us; Abdul Haq threatened to kill him. The boy cried. Then Abdul Haq laughed and said, 'I drove over the edge of this road three years ago, in a jeep. We crashed into the ditch where that boy is whining. The other six people in the car were killed. But I was thrown over a wall and survived because God loves me.'

After about four hours we had to cross the Hari Rud. I took off my boots and overtrousers, tied them around my neck and waded in to the cold water. The river which in normal times would be impassable without a ferry boat was now barely two feet deep. Without speaking, Abdul Haq stopped on the bank, and bent slightly over, and Qasim climbed onto his back. Then Abdul Haq stepped into the stream, roaring like a bullfrog with delight at his strength and the shock of the cold. Having deposited Qasim on the further shore, he returned and Aziz clambered on. At the mid-point of the stream, Aziz dropped the sleeping bags. Abdul Haq put him down in the water and charged after the bobbing sacks. When he caught them, he spun and danced on the shore like a paper puppet caught in the wind, shouting, '*Man Ghaater Hastam*' (I am a mule.) A camel was on the flats ahead, loping easily across the sharp gravel.

I opened a packet of Iranian orange cream biscuits and offered them to Qasim. He took one biscuit, sighed heavily, said, '*Allah-u-Akbar*' (God is Great) and put it in his mouth.

Abdul Haq looked at me and winked. Qasim, the oldest and least open of my three companions, was also it seemed the most religious. Abdul Haq described himself as a Mujahid, a holy warrior, and his leader, Ismail Khan, had fought an Islamic crusade to expel the atheist Russians before implementing Sharia law in Herat. But Abdul Haq was not very religious. In Iran young city types had talked to me about Nietzsche and said they were atheists. I never met an Afghan who called himself an atheist and Abdul Haq had never heard of Nietzsche. But during the time I was with him, he never prayed, never fasted, never paid a religious tithe and had no intention of going on pilgrimage to Mecca. Generally the only time I heard him refer to God was when he was firing his Kalashnikov. Then he would sing 'Allah-u-Akbar' like a full-throated muezzin in the dawn call to prayer.

Abdul Haq took the packet of biscuits from my hands, tipped it out onto the cloth to encourage us to eat more and threw the wrapper over his shoulder. It was the only piece of rubbish on the desert plain and the silver foil glittered fiercely amongst the gentler colours of the soil.

*

We reached the village of Dideros in the early afternoon. It stood on a bank on the south side of the river, surrounded by walled orchards and divided by well-maintained canals and avenues of young poplars. We stayed with Moalem Jalil (school-teacher Jalil) in a house set in a large vineyard. He had just heard on the new Herat radio station that an Englishman called Agha Rory was walking alone on foot to Chaghcharan and would be paid two million dollars to complete the journey. He was worried this might encourage bandits to attack his friends.

'Don't worry,' said Qasim, 'we are only taking him to the edge of the plain, then he's on his own. I'm doing it to learn English. A translator can make a hundred US dollars a day.' When we were walking Abdul Haq talked as much as Qasim but inside the house Qasim still dominated the conversations. Aziz rarely said anything in either environment.

Qasim whispered something to the schoolteacher, ran his

tongue quickly over his chapped lips and then said, 'Rory. I've spent all the money you gave me. You must pay me another two hundred dollars.' The other men looked at me.

'How did you manage to spend two hundred dollars in four days?' I asked.

'For food.'

'How much is food?'

'Two dollars per meal per head.'

'We've mostly been eating bread.'

'Bread costs two dollars.'

'In Kabul it costs five cents.'

'This isn't Kabul – it is more expensive here.'

'Given that the average wage is less than a dollar a day, how can you afford to eat then?'

'I've told you we can't – we are very poor.'

A young man with a soft face and full red lips, who had been staring at me for some time, now intervened. 'You must believe us. It is two dollars per person per head, if you are travelling.'

The five people in the room nodded solemnly. I didn't believe any of them.

'Whatever the price,' I said, 'I am not giving any more money for food. If you leave me at Darai-e-Takht I might add an extra gift.'

Qasim left the room without speaking. The man with the red lips was looking at me. I smiled at him but he just continued to stare. I, therefore, took out my notebook and sketched Abdul Haq, who was lying down with his rifle on his thighs. He was asleep, with his clear, open face turned upwards to the ceiling and his large chest slowly rising and falling. He had a very honest face and I was fond of him. I found this difficult to reconcile with what I knew of his enthusiasm for killing people or making small children cry.

*

Then everyone stood up, woke Abdul Haq and left, taking him with them and leaving me alone in the room. When after an hour they had not returned, I walked out as well.

The overcast day had given way to a lemon-yellow sunset. In the distance to the north above the round tops of the shale hills, I could see a succession of tiny peaks bright with snow. Teacher Jalil appeared beside me. He seemed happy to see me. I asked him to show me his land. We walked out of the village.

The ploughing was finished. One of his uncles was standing on a split trunk, which was being pulled by the oxen to flatten the soil. He stepped off because he was tired and I asked if I could take over. He stepped back and I stood on the trunk, holding the tail of the left ox and prodding the right one forward with a stick. The ox on the left moved more quickly than the other and while I struggled to keep my balance, we went round in a circle. It took me some time to learn how to drive them straight with my voice. When I had finished the furrow Jalil called me. He was standing by a wall of open brickwork that enclosed a large tomb. Two bare wooden trees had been placed at the head and foot of the tomb.

'This is my father's grave,' said Jalil.

There are frequently tombs like this on the edges of settlements and most are revered as shrines. The most famous shrine in Herat is that of Ansari, the eleventh-century Sufi mystic and Abdul Haq's call sign. His tomb is still believed to have magical powers. The courtyard around his shrine is filled with curious marble headstones of men who wished to honour some of Ansari's holiness. In the alcoves old men sit reciting the Koran from end to end. Babur visited it and his cousins decorated its walls with rare Chinese motifs. Ansari's tomb is one of many. The rulers of Ghor built a shrine to the son of one of Ansari's friends at Chist, while recent Pakistani presidents have built gold gates and marble courtyards around the tomb of Ansari's contemporary, Datta Ganj Baksh,[12] in Lahore. The tombs are supposed to have magical powers. A medieval saint who entered Multan riding on a lion and whipping it with live snakes is still believed to put his hand out of the tomb to greet pious pilgrims.

Around these great shrines were many smaller places, still revered although the occupant's name and deeds were forgotten. More orthodox forms of Islam are very suspicious of saints' shrines, and the superstition associated with them.[13] The Wahabi movement in Saudi Arabia, perhaps the strongest theological influence on Al-Qaeda, was famous for destroying them. Babur too was sceptical about shrines. In 1504, when visiting the ruins that the Ghorid rulers left when they sacked Ghazni, he wrote:

> *I was told that in one of the villages of Ghazni there was a mausoleum, in which the tomb moved itself whenever the benediction on the Prophet was pronounced over it. I went and viewed it and there certainly seemed to be a motion of the tomb. In the end, however, I discovered that the whole thing was an imposture, practised by the attendants of the mausoleum. They had erected over the tomb a kind of scaffolding, contrived so that it could be set in motion whenever any of them stood upon it, so that a looker-on imagined that it was the tomb that had moved; just as to a person sailing in a boat, it is the bank which appears to be in motion. I ordered the scaffolding to be removed and strictly enjoined the servants of the tomb not to dare to repeat this imposture.*

Villagers were less sceptical and often assumed that each mausoleum contained a dead holy man or a descendant of the Prophet. There was a decent chance that the grave of Jalil's

---

12. Hazrat Ali Hajweri.
13. But the Taliban, who were never as close theologically to Al-Qaeda as has been suggested, left the shrine of Ansari well alone.

father, who was neither a religious teacher nor a descendant of the Prophet, would be prayed to in three generations' time. It sat oddly beside Jalil's grandfather's grave, which was merely an unmarked earth barrow.

'From this line of trees to that was my father's and is now mine,' said Jalil. He appeared to own almost a hundred acres of fertile ground.

'You are a big landlord,' I said.

'There are two bigger in this village. I have just dug this tube well with a mechanical drill. It cost five hundred dollars.' He pointed to a pit running a hundred feet into the ground, lined with concrete. Beside it was an imported Indian pump. At first, I was surprised that he had gone to this expense with the Hari Rud River so near and with the village and fields lined with flowing irrigation canals. There was surely enough water for wheat. Opium poppies, however, will die if they spend five days without water.

'Do you grow poppies?' I asked.

'I used to under the Taliban but not now because Ismail Khan has banned their cultivation.'

He may not have been lying but I assumed he was. Ismail Khan was not more strict than the Taliban on opium and heroin production. The Taliban had totally stopped production in the valley during the last two years[14] and it was their departure that had allowed it to start again. By the spring of 2002, with the foreign drug enforcement agencies focusing on the Helmand basin, the Hari Rud valley, with or without Jalil's contribution, had produced one of the largest poppy harvests in Afghanistan.

*

14. They may have been motivated as much by a desire to drive up prices as by religious considerations.

I returned to Moalem Jalil's guest room. The village men had just come back from evening prayers, flushed from the cold walk from the mosque. Three small boys were stoking the iron stove with twigs. It was a large room, laid with fine carpets, and the walls were hung with clocks and prayer rugs. Again I wondered how much Jalil made from his poppy fields. About thirty men were enjoying the warmth, seated against the walls, smoking and playing cards. It looked from the relaxed progression of the game as though many of the people were here every night: relatives, clients and allies, all dining at Jalil's expense. At the end of the room, in the senior position, was a fat old man in a faded pinstripe suit and turban. A tape was playing on the cassette recorder beside him. He was sucking on a water pipe, chuckling and singing along to a tune. I had a friend in Kabul who was from the Pushtun Ahmadzai nomadic tribe of the southeast and I thought I recognized the tune as being Ahmadzai. Jalil confirmed that it was.

I looked around the room, meeting the eyes of the men who were staring at me, following the marks on the mud walls and the borders of the bright carpets and the smoke that seeped from the stove. I could feel my calf muscles and I was grateful to be sitting down. I stretched my bare foot over the rug and dug my toes into the thick wool.

'Where are these carpets from?' I asked, half out of habit.

'That one is from the shrine of Abdullah in Mazar-e-Sharif.'

'And the silk cloth on the wall, with the picture of Medina?'

'It was bought in Saudi when my father visited the shrine of the Prophet in 1983.'

'The kilim?'

'Is from the mountains east of Chaghcharan.'

'And this?' I pointed to the bright red rug at my feet, which had a design of minarets and Soviet Attack helicopters.

'From Farah in the south.'

The Uzbek and Hazara rugs on the floor and the Pashto music suggested a sense of Afghan national identity that transcended their own Tajik province. I was about to ask Jalil what he thought of Afghanistan when the old man with the water pipe looked at me and roared, 'Hey American!'

Five or six of the men stopped playing cards and waited for my response.

'I'm not American,' I said.

Directly opposite me was the soft-featured, red-lipped man who now in his white turban and prayer robe was unmistakably a mullah. He leant slightly towards me. 'You are an American,' he said.

'No, Scottish.'

'Foreigners should stay out,' he replied.

More people were listening now, including Qasim, who was expressionless.

'I understand. What do you think of Americans?' I asked an old man by the door.

'We will accept development money from America but not soldiers.'

'Excuse me, I wish to make a statement,' said the mullah. He spoke in slow pompous phrases, as though he were in a pulpit. 'Unless I am mistaken you are a British spy.'

'No, I am not,' I said, turning away from the mullah and addressing the rest of the room. 'I am a historian, following in the footsteps of Babur, the first Mughal emperor . . .'

The mullah sat back, muttering, 'We know who Babur Shah is.'

I continued, ignoring him. 'He came down this road five hundred years ago. I am walking on foot to Kabul to write a book. I have been travelling in Iran and Pakistan, where I was treated very well because Muslims know how to treat guests.'

Various people murmured to each other, 'Of course we treat guests well . . .' 'Because we are Muslims . . .' 'We honour travellers.'

Jalil said, 'I met an Englishman twenty-five years ago in Nimruz, who was doing a journey like yours. He was crossing Afghanistan with a camel. I think he's written in one of my history books.'

'I have a history book,' said Qasim. No one paid any attention to him.

'What do you think of your new leader Karzai?' I asked the mullah.

'Good.' A pause. He smiled. 'Up till now.'

'Up till now?'

He shrugged, 'Al-Qaeda was good at the beginning.' He raised his hands to the sky. 'Al-Qaeda was very good at the beginning.'

The ewer arrived and I poured the water for my neighbour and as he washed his hands he sighed: '*Al Allah Il Allah. Muhammad rasull Allah.*' (There is no God but God and Muhammad is his prophet.) For some, it is enough to repeat this phrase to be a Muslim.

'The Englishman who travelled with his camel could say that phrase. But he was not a Muslim,' commented Jalil.

'He will go to hell,' said the mullah.

I was grateful when the arrival of the food brought the conversation to a halt.

Crown Jewels

There were three small meat dishes for dinner: mutton and potato stew, a peppery innard sausage and some lamb fat. Because there were so many of us, the meat was minutely divided, so we could have a hint of flavour with each handful of our rice.

'Is it true that Queen Elizabeth travels by carriage?' asked Jalil, when he had finished eating.

'Yes, she does.'

'Why does she not have a car?'

'England is a desert,' said the mullah.

'No, it rains a lot in England,' I replied.

'Perhaps I am thinking of Australia.'

'True, Australia is a desert.'

'What is your currency? The euro or the dollar?' asked the fat man with the water pipe.

'It's a hundred yen to the dollar in Japan,' interrupted the old man by the door.

'The pound.'

'Mr Pound,' shouted the mullah, 'do you have kerosene lamps, and rice and green tea in England? Do you grow rice? Is it green like Mazandaran in Iran?'

Everyone was talking at once. I had learnt my Persian through repetitive conversation in villages. This discussion tested my vocabulary. I must have missed a quarter of the conversation. But what I heard showed that this remote place was much more aware of foreign geography, monarchs and currencies than I had imagined.

'Where,' asked the fat old man, 'is the Koh-i-Noor diamond which the English stole from Afghanistan? When are you going to give it back?'

'When I was in the Indian Punjab people asked me to give it back to them . . . ' I said.

'But you took it from us . . .'

*

Babur's diary is the first credible report of the Koh-i-Noor because it was almost certainly the diamond that he captured himself at the siege of Agra and which he describes as worth 'half of the daily expense of the whole world'. He writes that it had been acquired first by the Delhi Sultan at Marwa in 1304.

There is no certainty about where it was before Marwa. There is little evidence for the *Indian Sunday Tribune*'s claims that the Koh-i-Noor was seized by Alexander the Great at the battle of Jhelum in the Punjab in 326 BC, and that it was then owned by the great Buddhist ruler Asoka.

Babur gave the diamond to his favourite son, Humayun, who probably carried it into exile in Persia and presented it as a gift to the Shah of Iran, who in turn sent it back to his liege-king in the Deccan. On 8 July 1656, the diamond was presented to Babur's great-great-grandson Shah Jahan at Agra, where Babur had first seized it.

In 1739 Nadir Shah, the ruler of Iran, acquired the diamond from Shah Jahan's eventual heir and carried it back to Iran across Afghanistan. He called it 'Koh-i-Noor', *Mountain of Light*. It was then about 186 carats and it was believed that whoever owned it would rule the world, provided it was worn by a woman. Nadir's son gave it subsequently to Ahmed Shah Durrani, his Afghan Chief of Horse, and the founder of modern Afghanistan.

Ahmed Shah kept the Koh-i-Noor in his capital at Kandahar as the central symbol of Afghanistan's independence from

Persia. His grandson then carried it back across Afghanistan to exile in India, where he was persuaded to give it to Maharajah Ranjit Singh, the Sikh ruler of the Punjab. In 1849 it was given to the East India Company in a tin box by Ranjit's heir as indemnity for the Sikh wars. Sir John Lawrence lost the diamond in a garden shed and when he found it, presented it to Queen Victoria, stressing that whoever owned the diamond would rule the world and that it should only be worn by a woman.

The Queen put it in the Great Exhibition of 1851. The public were not impressed by its lack of glitter. A distinguished committee decided to cut the stone and a patent steam wheel was imported from Amsterdam. The Duke of Wellington started the engine and Prince Albert laid the diamond to the drill. After a month of work by the Dutch team it was reduced into a 'brilliant' shape of 106 carats, wrecking the historical shape of the stone.

I was in India during the Queen's visit of 1997 when, on the basis of the possession by Ranjit Singh, Sikhs demonstrated for the return of the Koh-i-Noor to the Punjab. Three years later, twenty-five Indian parliamentarians demanded its return to New Delhi on the basis of Babur's ownership. When I was in Iran, the Taliban demanded its return to Afghanistan on the basis of Ahmed Shah's possession. In April 2002, a *Guardian* leader, with no reference to the claims from Pakistan, Afghanistan and Iran, supported the Indians. I last saw it lying on top of the Queen Mother's coffin in Westminster Hall.

*

By about midnight I was determined to sleep, so I lay down in the corner while the men continued smoking and playing cards. The oil lamps were extinguished an hour later. It was a difficult night. Abdul Haq had poisoned himself with the ditch water and had stomach cramps; Aziz's painful cough now sounded tuberculous. I woke at dawn and went out to the vineyards to go to the loo, and walking around a corner found Moalem Jalil squatting on the ground and wiping his bare bottom with gravel. I had been surprised that when I was shown to the fields in Afghanistan, I was never given a pitcher of water with which to clean myself. The Afghan technique was now clear and I could see why Qasim and Abdul Haq so proudly displayed their toilet paper.

At breakfast, which again was very sweet black tea and dry bread, the old fat man who had dominated proceedings the night before behaved as though he were drunk, probably because of whatever was in his water pipe. Usually Afghans sit still, revealing little with their faces or bodies. But this man, who was the headman of the neighbouring village, engaged in long heroic perorations, with melodramatic whispers, crescendos and histrionic gestures, which I found difficult to follow. Every few minutes, he would twist his head to one side like a cockatoo and stare unblinking at me for five seconds, then straighten his head again and launch back into the story. Throughout the conversation, his large body rocked back and forth, his hands waved through the air and he kept thrusting his turban back at a steep angle on his head.

His speeches concerned various groups who apparently intended to kill us on the road to Obey. Qasim, who had been quite relaxed the previous day, was frightened. When the headman had finished, Qasim told me that to walk the next ten kilometres would be suicide. 'The young Commandant of Obey, Mustafa, is planning to kill us. We must travel to Saray-Pul at least by vehicle. We cannot do it on foot.'

I refused. I was determined to walk all the way. I had been right in Nepal where people had warned me of similar things. Finally Qasim insisted that Moalem Jalil come with us to Obey. Again we waded through the cold water on an overcast day, Abdul Haq carrying Qasim and Aziz on his back in turn.

This was our fifth day of walking together. We had moved

only about one hundred and forty kilometres east of Herat, sticking to the gravel plain beside the Hari Rud. The plain of short-cropped grass and boulders, under a dark sky, reminded me of the Scottish battlefield of Culloden. On the far bank were two black wool tents of the nomadic Pashtun Kuchi people. Traditionally at this time of year the Kuchi would have moved south with their flocks. But either the politics or the climate had kept them in the Hari Rud valley for the winter.

Again, walking ahead of the others, I felt the familiar liberation of escaping the men in the claustrophobic guest room and being outside, moving in the open air, on foot.

*

Obey, which we were approaching, was in Babur's time ruled by Zulnun Arghun:

> *Zulnun Arghun . . . was madly fond of chess; if a person played at it with one hand; he played at it with two hands . . . He played without art just as his fancy suggests. He was a brave man. He distinguished himself above all the other young warriors in his use of the scimitar . . . His courage is unimpeached, but certainly he was rather deficient in understanding. The Sultan conferred on him the government of Ghor . . . With but a handful of men he bravely vanquished and reduced large and numerous bodies of Hazara . . . these tribes were never so effectively settled and kept in order by any other person. Zulnun rose to very high rank and the countries on the Damenkoh [skirts of the mountains] of Herat, such as Obeh and Chaghcharan, were given to him.*

Shortly after Babur's journey, however, Zulnun convinced himself that a warrior supported by Allah was invincible. Like others since, he was wrong:

> *Though a man of courage, he was ignorant and somewhat crazed. Had it not been for his craziness and ignorance he*

*would not have made himself the dupe of such gross flattery
and exposed himself to scorn in consequence . . . When he was
Prime Minister several sheikhs and mullahs came and told him
that they had had intercourse with the spheres and that the title
of Lion of God had been conferred on him; that he was predes-
tined to defeat the Uzbeks and make them all prisoners. He
implicitly believing all this flattery, tied a handkerchief round
his neck and returned thanks to God . . . he did not put the fort
in a defensible state; did not prepare ammunition and warlike
arms; did not appoint either an advance or pickets to get notice
of the enemy's approach, nor even exercise his army, or accus-
tom it to discipline, or battle-array, so as to be prepared and able
to fight when the enemy came . . . When the Uzbek leader fell
upon them . . . Zulnun . . . relying on this prediction . . . kept
his ground against 50,000 Uzbeks with a hundred or a hundred
and fifty men. A great body of the enemy coming up took him
in an instant and swept on. They cut off his head as soon as he
was taken.*

Bread and Water

Abdul Haq walked beside me towards Obey, talking about his life. Perhaps because he was younger and stronger than Qasim or Aziz, he did not seem tired by the walking. The others had dropped five hundred yards behind. He told me that he had become a holy warrior, a Mujahidin, ten years earlier, when he was thirteen. I enjoyed talking to him. Unlike Qasim he did not seem to be tailoring his stories in order to extort things from me.

'I was a cook in Ismail Khan's camp before I was allowed to fight that Russian agent Najibullah. When the Taliban reached Herat in 1995, I did not take to the hills with Ismail Khan. Instead I fled to Iran, leaving my wife and two daughters.'

For three years he sold spare parts in truck stops in Shiraz and Tehran, which may have been where he picked up his clean-shaven look and his baseball cap. He returned to Herat in 1998 and was imprisoned by the Taliban. He spent six months in a cell so crowded that the prisoners slept standing up. His daily ration was one piece of *nan* bread and a glass of water.

'One of the guards offered to help me escape if I could raise one thousand three hundred and fifty dollars. I told my wife to sell our clothes in the bazaar. My daughters went without meat. I sent messages to my friends and borrowed a hundred dollars from one, two hundred from another. Finally I had the money and he let me go. I went to the hills to fight for Ismail Khan against the Taliban. They were good times. We had a lot of money from Iran and other countries.

We slept in tents. Every night we bought sheep from the Kuchi nomads to feast. Four months ago I went down to Herat. There a man – not a man – a *shaitan* – a devil – reported me to the Taliban – and they put me in jail to execute me. But after ten days Ismail Khan captured Herat and I was freed.'

'Do you have any money?'

'Yes. I am a rich man. My job in the Security Service is as a driver. I am paid eighty dollars a month but I get more – much more – a great deal – for doing little contracts in the villages.'

'What contracts?'

'No one can check my truck because I am from the Security Service – so people pay a lot to use my truck. I can carry anything.'

'Aziz?'

'Aziz is very poor. He has nothing. His detachment has not been paid for months. He will be lucky to get forty dollars this month. We have taken him with us to help him.'

'And Qasim? Is he as poor as he says?'

'Qasim, no. Qasim is very rich. But his father and grandfather were nothing. Less than nothing.'

'But he is a Seyyed.'

'A descendant of the Prophet? So he says,' said Abdul Haq and laughed, 'but no one has ever heard of his family before. Now he owns two villages next to Herat. He has six thousand dollars at home in cash.'

'Because . . .'

'Because he is close to Ismail Khan. He can help himself to foreign money.'

'You are all officers in the Security Service?'

'Qasim and I are. We are Mujahidin. Most of our colleagues used to work in the KHAD.' (The body set up by the Russian KGB.)

'But I thought you used to fight the Russians?'

'What can we do? Qasim and I can't run a Security Service. We can barely read and write. We have to use the experts.

Like the man who interrogated you. The one with the goatee beard . . .' Abdul Haq blew out his cheeks and traced the shape on his chin.

'Yes?' He had not told me that he knew the man who had questioned me.

'That was Gul Agha. He has a revolver hidden here.' He patted the side of his chest. 'He is a very big man. He was not a Mujahid. He was in Iran working in the Security Service while we were fighting in the hills.'

'And Qasim? What is his job? Is he a commander?'

'Qasim? No. Qasim doesn't work in an office with paper. Qasim's job is to deal with bad men . . . question them and deal with them for men like Gul Agha.'

Abdul Haq never elaborated on this comment so I do not know precisely how Qasim dealt with people on behalf of the man who had questioned me. This, however, is an eyewitness report of an interrogation scene that took place in Qasim's headquarters building six months later in September 2002, recorded by Human Rights Watch:

> They tied his feet and hung him [upside down] from the ceiling, so that his hands touched the ground. After beat- ing him with whips, they brought two electrical wires, and they wound the wire ends, the metal part, around each of his big toes. Then they shocked him. On his big toes there were burns, like a ring about each toe. The skin there was black and bloody. A new man came in. He looked around and then said to the men who were tor- turing Arbab, 'What are you doing? You are not doing it right.' And he made the men take off the wires from [his] toes and wound it around his thumbs instead. His hands were tied together but hanging on the floor, and they stepped on his hands with their boots while they did this. Then the new man said, 'Now I will make him do the death dance.' And they shocked him again. He was mov- ing all about and shaking all about by his feet. [He was still

hanging upside down from the ceiling.] And he fainted
and lost consciousness.

We reached the graveyard on the outskirts of Obey after three
hours' walk and it began to rain. The largest tombstones
were megaliths of black granite, eleven feet tall, framed by
the obligatory piece of wrecked Russian armour and a ruined
caravanserai.

As we walked down the main bazaar street, we were
stopped by a group of armed men.

'Is this the American?'

'He is English. We have come from the Emir Ismail Khan,'
said Qasim.

'That is impossible. You would be in a car.'

Aziz and Qasim's black and white keffiyah scarves and
their military radios marked them clearly as Ismail Khan's
men, but we had reached a place where the governor's authority was diminishing. The local ruler, Mustafa, was a new commander and his loyalties were uncertain. The Obey group did
not want units coming in from other areas, but they probably
pretended Qasim was not Ismail Khan's man because they
were not prepared to challenge his leader directly.

Qasim, Aziz and Moalem Jalil were detained. Abdul Haq
and I were ordered to sit in the truck stop. We entered through
its courtyard. This was a modern version of the ruined
medieval caravanserai we had passed on the edge of town. It
was filled with truck-churned mud and the stench of human
excrement. There were rows of donkeys standing patiently in
the rain. Their nostrils had been cut open to let in more air,
which showed they were being taken to high altitudes. I had
walked some way with a mule in Iran but had left it because
the police had thought I was an Afghan using the animal to
smuggle opium or other goods on the mountain tracks. The
donkeys were being loaded with yellow waterproof bundles
by unshaven men with bloodshot eyes. They wore fake

designer hooded tops and heavy jewelled watches loose on their thin wrists. I guessed from their clothes that they lived in Tehran.

Abdul Haq and I were sitting on the floor of the restaurant eating a large meal of mutton when Qasim entered to say that we could not go any further because of the rain. Qasim would not say why, except to repeat that it was dangerous and that, if we had not had a local like Moalem Jalil with us, we would not have got this far. I wondered if the Obey men wanted to stop us seeing them loading opium onto the donkeys, but I doubted it. They didn't seem to care when we walked through the courtyard. The problem was probably simply rivalry between Ismail Khan and the Obey militia.

I told Qasim that I was leaving in an hour regardless and he went back to talk to the militia. Finally, he returned and repeated that the road ahead was far too dangerous: there were roadblocks by bandits. I wondered if the bandits were a euphemism for the Obey militia. We would be robbed and killed. We had to take a car to Saray-e-pul.

'How far is that?'

'Twenty-five kilometres.'

That was five hours' walk and there were only four hours till dark. 'I'm going to walk,' I said.

There was a pause and then Abdul Haq said, 'And I will go with him.'

Qasim hesitated. 'Well, Aziz and I will get a jeep and meet you there.'

The Fighting Man Shall

It was raining hard when we walked out onto the street.

'Five hours . . . no problem,' yelled Abdul Haq at Qasim's departing back. 'I can do it. Not Qasim. Me. Look at me . . . a gun, two magazines, three hand grenades, kung fu . . . I'll get them . . . should have seen me yesterday . . . then I had three magazines, five hand grenades.'

I walked out of Obey matching Abdul Haq's long strides and wondering whether the Obey militia would shoot us. We passed the next three kilometres in silence. We had entered camel country: there were three sheltering by a wall under their bundles, one walking beside an old man and a herd of them grazing in the desert. When we reached the next village, Abdul Haq began shouting again about how many Taliban he had killed. He had never used ear defenders when firing his automatic weapon and, although he was only twenty-three, he was half-deaf.

'Sixteen of them?' I asked.

'Sixteen? No, eighteen. I killed eighteen myself one after-noon, in an ambush, with my Kalashnikov.' He lifted up his rifle to demonstrate and shouted, 'Baah . . . Baah . . . Baah . . . I kept five of the prisoners alive and took them with me into the hills . . . walked two days and two nights, living off snow. One man died in the snow. Nineteen dead because of me.' He tilted his baseball cap further back on his head.

Further on, amongst a grove of trees, we caught up with a nine-year-old boy on a donkey. Abdul Haq gave him a cigarette and balanced his rifle on the moving animal. Then he tried to climb on. The donkey set off at a trot with Abdul Haq clinging on, one knee hooked over its bony back, and his long leg bumping along the ground. Then the boy left us. At dusk the hills closed in around us, the rain stopped and we could not see any villages. We looked up at the bare ridge line.

'If there was someone up there . . .' said Abdul Haq.

'We'd be in trouble,' I said. The path we were on was a narrow track between a steep hill on our left and the Hari Rud which was running fast below us on the right. On the far bank was a flat exposed gravel beach. There was no cover.

'Here I am,' Abdul Haq roared at the wilderness. 'No problem. I am a man. I'll get them.' He turned to me. 'Qasim is a woman, right? He can't walk. In fact he is a queer.' He turned to me to illustrate the kind of things Qasim did with other men. 'In fact,' he continued, 'when we get back I'm going to fuck him. Ahhh,' he roared, 'what a woman.'

Silence. Neither of us spoke for some time. I noticed that we were both walking and breathing more quickly than usual. A loose stone fell and we both spun around.

'You're not afraid, are you?' I asked.

'No. Are you?'

'No.' Although I was nervous, I was revelling in the beauty of the low hills and the pale dusk. Everything was very still and silent. The long line of cliffs continued above us and we could see no one on the track. Abdul Haq stopped, looked up and suddenly fired at the ridge. The muzzle flashed and the sharp explosion echoed around the valley.

'That will frighten them away . . . all of them, bandits, villagers, wolves.'

*

We continued, barely able to see the path. It began to rain again. A country without electricity is quiet and dark on an overcast night. Then, all at once, there was barking, and dogs sprinted towards us angry and invisible. Abdul Haq pulled at the cocking handle of his Kalashnikov; I shouted and threw some stones. The dogs followed us, enraged, to what must have been the edge of a hamlet. The rain increased and our boots and jackets were soaked. The four-year drought had clearly ended. After another forty-five minutes walking in darkness, Abdul Haq spun around and grabbed at something. It turned out to be a man, who had been standing behind a tree. I was impressed by the speed of Abdul Haq's reaction. I had not noticed the man.

Abdul Haq cocked his Kalashnikov, placed it against the man's head and demanded to know what he was doing. The man didn't move but replied very slowly that he was going to the loo. Abdul Haq searched him thoroughly and then released him with a warning.

A fog had closed in around us, the rain continued and we could see nothing. Five minutes later I took a step into thin air. As I fell, I managed to grab a thorn bush, which came away in my hand but slowed my drop down the cliff. I ended up spreadeagled, about fifteen feet below the road on the river bank. Abdul Haq shouted down and I shouted back, '*man khub hastam . . . man khub hastam*' (I'm fine, I'm fine) while he laughed. I found a chimney cut into the cliff wall and climbed up with difficulty to join him.

We had been walking for over five hours from Obey, it had been dark for a couple of hours, we were both now shivering and the rain was beginning to turn to snow. Our destination was on the other side of the Hari Rud River, which had swollen with the downpour. It was moving very quickly and would be difficult to cross without ropes. We had heard a truck moving behind us, the first since the morning. Abdul Haq suggested we ask it to drive us across the ford. I was reluctant because I didn't want to go a single step in a vehicle on this journey, but I knew that Aziz had probably been waiting two hours in the snow for us already and it didn't seem worth the fight.

The truck came around the corner. Abdul Haq stepped out into the road and stood in the glare of its headlights, pointing his rifle at the windscreen. The truck stopped and drove us through the ford on to the other bank. Aziz was waiting with a torch on the far bank. I stumbled beside him through the snow to the house, falling a couple of times into drifts. At the door to the house, I took off my wet boots and bashed the snow from my hair and coat. Then I entered. Our host sat me by the fire and I put my white, peeling feet as near to the flames as I could and gratefully accepted the offer of a cup of tea. It was ten o'clock at night. For once I was too tired to write in my diary, so instead I played a game of chess with our host.

Abdul Haq entered shouting at Qasim, 'You're a woman. Too scared to walk. But we made it. No one even dared to attempt to kill us. And now as I promised Rory I am going to bugger you. Didn't I, Rory? You are a woman.' Qasim did not reply.

Abdul Haq continued, 'Rory was very reluctant to get in the truck . . . and we have now to go back to walk from the same point on the beach tomorrow . . . well, I'm sleeping in . . . Aziz, you can do it . . . Best of all just before that we were tiptoeing along in the dark and the snow and suddenly there's a sound of something tearing and then rocks clattering down into the river. Then there's a thump and from as deep as a well below this small voice saying in an English accent: "Man Hoob hass-tam. Man Hoob Hass-tam."'

A Nothing Man

Aziz and I went the next morning to retrace our steps on the right bank and he told me he was leaving me now and that Qasim was leaving the next day and Abdul Haq the day after that. I was going to be walking the next six hundred kilometres alone. This news was a relief but not a surprise. Qasim's blister had swelled, burst and swelled again inside his red leather boots. He felt exhausted and humiliated because of the walking. He was happy, therefore, for me to continue alone, as I had suggested earlier, from Darai-e-Takht, the frontier of Ghor. He was no longer going to come to Chaghcharan.

It had continued to snow during the night, covering the tracks of my stumbling walk to the house. The air was cold and dry; the sky was a dark blue and the snow crust glittered. Sheets of ice spun across the surface of the swollen current.

'I am poor,' said Aziz.

'I know,' I said.

'I need some money.'

'I was going to give you some – here is a hundred dollars. Thank you for your help.'

Aziz took it, smiled briefly and put it in his pocket. 'I am very ill,' he said. 'I am going to stay in bed for a month after this journey.'

'Thank you for coming with me. I hope you get better soon.'

'I have a difficult journey to get back to Herat.'

'Good luck,' I said.

Aziz did not reply.

We returned inside for some walnuts with our bread and sweet tea. After breakfast, Abdul Haq and Qasim said good-bye to Aziz and we walked on, through the hills on the south bank of the Hari Rud. Half an hour later, I heard a cry. It rose quickly in an ascending ululation, 'lalalalalala . . .' It was made by more than one voice. The sound ceased and returned ten minutes later punctuated by howls and whistles, from a hidden valley to our left. Then a dog pack streamed past, baying over the crest, followed by a hundred villagers stumbling through the snow.

'A wolf hunt,' said Qasim, 'they are crying the "Aaabag" to drive their hounds onto the wolves.' More figures appeared on the ridge-line on the other side of the river. One of them shouted and the pack wheeled east and dropped from sight.

Qasim explained that we had left the stretch around Obey that had worried him most.

'God loves you, Rory. That is why you have made it this far alive.'

'Thank you for bringing me here safely.'

'No. Thank God, not me. From here to Chist you will be fine – they are good men.'

'And the men beyond Chist?'

'Men? Beyond Chist they are donkeys.'

*

We stopped for lunch in a village ten kilometres before Chist. Water was dripping through the mud roof into a bucket that stood on a dark rug in the middle of our host's guest-room floor. He had bought a poster in Herat, which showed a yellow convertible sports car parked outside a Swiss chalet with flower-decked balconies. Written below in capital letters in English was: 'ANYONE WHO HAS EVER STRUGGLED WITH POVERTY KNOWS HOW EXTREMELY EXCITING IT IS TO BE POOR.' He asked me to translate it. I told him I could not understand the inscription.

*

Qasim said that he was leaving. I asked him not to tell the Security Service that he had left me, but instead to take ten days going back to Herat and tell them that he had taken me to Chaghcharan.

'That is fine,' said Qasim. 'We will take it slowly, staying a long time with all our friends and eating well on the way back. They will never know. Please give us some money now. We are very poor.'

'Of course,' I said. 'Thank you for everything.'

'You don't have to if you don't want to – you are my brother,' said Qasim. 'Even if you give us nothing, of course we will be pleased.'

I gave each of them one hundred and fifty dollars.

Qasim seemed particularly disappointed. There was a pause.

'Please could you give us some money for Aziz as well? He is very poor and very sick.'

'I have already given him some.'

'How much?'

'A hundred dollars.'

Abdul Haq interrupted, angrier than I had ever heard him, 'That is completely wrong. He is nothing. A nothing man. He stopped two days ago. He only came with us because we invited him.'

'If you gave him one hundred dollars you should give us three hundred,' snapped Abdul Haq. 'Why did you give him that money?'

'Because he is very poor and very sick.'

'He told me you had given him nothing,' said Abdul Haq.

'I gave him a hundred dollars.'

'Then I will kill him,' said Abdul Haq.

I said nothing.

'You do not believe me, do you?' he continued. He unclipped his magazine and pushed five rounds onto the carpet. 'These are for Aziz. He told me you had given him nothing. I was going to give him some of my money. He tried to steal from me. From a friend. He will die when I meet him next.'

'Please don't,' I said.

'It is too late – you should not have told me.'

'Don't – I gave him that money and then told you – I will be responsible for his death.'

'There is nothing you can say. He lied. He betrayed a brother. He is dead.'

We continued to discuss this throughout the night but Abdul Haq would not change his mind. Qasim, who was Aziz's brother-in-law, said nothing.

The next morning, Qasim embraced me and his face broke into his warm, paternal grin, which I had never learnt to interpret. I wished him luck. He nodded but like Aziz he did not wish me luck in return. In Pakistan and Nepal, men who met me for ten minutes wanted to add my address to scraps of paper, which recorded in biro the best wishes of couples from industrial towns outside Stockholm. Qasim, however, did not ask for my address. He said goodbye and then went inside for some tea.

Part Three

The country of the Eimauks is reckoned less mountainous than that of the Hazaurehs; but even in it, the
hills present a steep and lofty face to Heraut. Their
tents are almost universally of the kind called
Kirgah . . . all the Eimauks keep many sheep . . .

– Mountstuart Elphinstone,
The Kingdom of Kaubul and its Dependencies, 1815

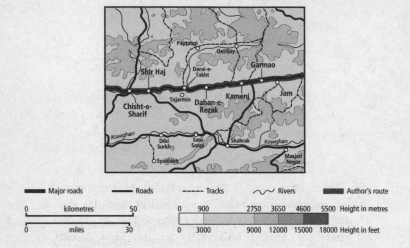

Highland Buildings

After six and a half farsang [days' walk] from Herat
you reach the boundary of the hill-country of Ghor,
at a place named Chist.

– Ibn Haukal of Arabia, 976

At sunset on the seventh day, Abdul Haq and I climbed the
first hill across our path. Until this point whenever we had
looked back we had seen the gravel stretching flat to the
horizon. Now we had reached the mountains. Caught by the
north wind, scraps of snow danced and glittered like white
fireflies in the setting sun. From the crest we looked down on
a neat plateau set between symmetrical rows of snow peaks.
There was no electricity in the village below, only the small
lights of fires and candles. The roads had been closed by snow
for two days now and there were no vehicles. The only sound
was our boots on the thin mud and the creak of my pack.
Then two shattered domes rose above the skyline of the
plateau in front of us, framed by the twilight. This was Chist,
at the frontier of the province of Ghor, the ancient site of a
dervish order and an empire that had conquered India.

Ahead lay the greatest mountain massif in the world
which brooded, in the shape of a mythical bird, over four
thousand five hundred kilometres of Asia. Chist was the bird's
head; the Hindu Kush was its neck; its chest the Himalayas;
its body the Tibetan plateau and its plumage spread over
the coast of China. Ghor was one of the poorest and most

obscure provinces in Afghanistan. It was not on the way to anywhere. There were no lapis mines and no great cities. It was one of the only places in the classical world not to be named or recognized by either the Persians or the Greeks. Aristotle believed that from these mountains, which we had reached, the Paropamisus, one could see the eastern edge of the earth.[15]

I climbed up to see the domes on the plateau of Chist-e-Sharif the next morning. Powder snow had covered all the ground and lay in wedges on the crumbling shoulders of the buildings and the external silhouettes of the squinches. But the vertical faces of pale yellow brick were warm in the morning sun.

The western dome was decaying with age but seemed largely unharmed by the war. The eastern dome had been struck by a tank shell since it had been last described by an archaeologist. Its rear wall had disappeared and the facings

---

15. Elsewhere in Asia, ancient rulers could travel at an astonishing speed. Alexander sent his assassins one thousand two hundred kilometres from Herat to kill his friend in Hamadan and they covered the distance in eleven days. In seven days Alexander's enemies, the Persians, could cover two thousand two hundred kilometres on the Royal Road from Sardis to Susa, and Genghis Khan's 'arrow messengers'could travel four hundred and fifty kilometres a day. This speed was the key to conquering or governing a large ancient empire.

Everything changed at Chist. In the mountains, travellers were reduced to the speed of men on foot. Here, the ancient English sense of journey, 'a day's travel' (French *journée*), meant the same as the Old Persian word '*farsang*', 'the distance a man could travel on foot in a day', and the territory was in effect ungovernable. In the month which it would take me or Babur to journey from Herat to Kabul through these mountains, Alexander could get from Herat to Athens. He could reach Jerusalem from here before he could have reached Yakawlang, Cairo before Bamiyan. A Mongol arrow messenger would have been in Baghdad in the time it had taken Abdul Haq and me to walk from Herat to here. Little wonder that, with one exception, the ancient world left Ghor well alone.

had fallen from the front. What remained was an isolated arch, set like a high triumphal portal leading to the mountains beyond, and a fragment of the roof set with splinters of dark blue sky.

The locals called them the '*madressah*', or school buildings, but their shapes implied that they were tombs. They followed a model for tombs whose prototype is in Bokhara in central Asia and whose culmination is the immense mausoleum of Genghis Khan's grandson in Iran. I could see no trace of a tomb under the domes, but beneath the covering of snow the plateau was scattered with graves.

*

Two people I met over the next two days claimed family connections with the buildings. One was a fat, middle-aged man with a broad beard, bright red with henna, and a little puppy. When we arrived at his house, at Shir Haj, one day's walk beyond Chist, the puppy tried to bite Abdul Haq. Abdul Haq took off around the building, with puppy in pursuit and our host, who had been badly wounded during the wars, limping heavily after it, entreating it to stop.

'Such a good dog,' he said, when we had slammed the guest-room door behind us. 'Always tells me when someone is coming.'

Then, having never met us before and without any introduction, he sat us by his warm stove and fed us eight boiled eggs.

His name was '*Agha Ghori*' (His Excellency man of Ghor). Everyone from Chist to Chaghcharan called him 'His Excellency' so automatically that it had become part of his name. But it was not because he had any power or wealth. He lived in a small mud hut by the side of the Hari Rud River and he had no job any more.

Agha Ghori had lost both his sons. One had been killed fighting the Russians; the other had been killed fighting

Najibullah. Whenever anyone mentioned it Agha Ghori smiled, a broad smile that emerged from his hennaed beard.

During the war he had commanded the eastern Chist forces. Before that, he had been the manager of a hydro-electric project on the Hari Rud River. People still talked of it with awe.

'It cost a billion dollars to build,' Abdul Haq told me.

'It would have given money and electricity to everyone in Herat,' said Qasim.

But the war had come before it could be completed. Earlier that day we had passed what remained of it. There was a tunnel, thirty feet high, cut two hundred feet through the rock and flooded with water. There were girders thrusting out over the gorge. Twenty-five rusty yellow JCBs stood in a line next to a group of collapsing concrete buildings. Around these ruins still hung tales that might be told of the capital of a lost civilization. They spoke of the fabulous wealth of the Japanese engineers. They talked of a three-thousand-strong workforce and machines that could cut through walls of rock. They said that the plain we had walked across would have become a lake, ten kilometres long, heavy behind the dam walls.

Agha Ghori did not call himself a Tajik or an Aimaq. He was, he said, a Ghorid, a descendant of the rulers of the province of Ghor who had built the Chist domes in the twelfth century to honour a local sect of dervishes. He had grown up beneath their great fort at Taiwara. But he said he knew little about his ancestors.

These Ghorid rulers were the one exception to the other-wise obscure history of Ghor. They had begun as chieftains of the inhospitable terrain of central Afghanistan. They were surrounded on every side by dynasties of nomadic horsemen. Because horses were the foundation of military success and Ghor was too mountainous to support many horses or move at speed, the Ghorids seemed unlikely ever to defeat their neighbours.[16]

In 1141, however, the Ghaznavid Turks, one of the neighbouring nomadic dynasties, killed a Ghorid chief. In revenge the chief's brother attacked Ghazni. According to Babur, who visited Ghazni four hundred years later:

> *Alauddin the 'World-incendiary' Ghorid [brother of the murdered chieftain] burned and destroyed the royal tombs, ruined and burned the city of Ghazni and plundered and massacred the inhabitants . . . there was no act of desolation and destruction from which he refrained. Ever since that time the mound of Ghazni has remained in a state of ruin.*

*

The Ghorid chieftain then forced the inhabitants of Ghazni to carry every mud brick of their city on their backs up to the mountains of Ghor. There they executed the captives and mixed their blood with the mud to make more bricks for their highland capital, the Turquoise Mountain. The Ghorids went on to conquer much of Asia from Baghdad to the east of India, and took control of the Silk Road to China. For the next half century this obscure mountain province of Ghor became the seat of one of the most powerful dynasties in the world, and apart from the last flowering which Babur witnessed in Herat, Afghanistan was never to experience such a civilization again. As Muslim ruler of India, Babur saw himself as the Ghorids' successor.[17]

The domes of Chist were one legacy of the Ghorids' improbable success, so too was the Friday Mosque in Herat

---

16. Like the seventy small kingdoms of mountainous Nepal.

17. *'Three foreign kings have subdued India . . .'* wrote Babur, *'one of these was Sultan Mahmud of Ghazni . . . the second was Sultan Muizuddin the Ghorid . . . and for many years his slaves and descendants swayed the spectre of these realms. I am the third.'*

and the minaret of Jam further up the Hari Rud River. Their capital, the Turquoise Mountain, was described by Juzjani as consisting of an enormous Friday Mosque, filled with the wealth of India and dominated by two giant golden birds on the castle battlements. This capital city was not on a flat plain near their great conquests, nor on a trade route or fertile farmland. It was in the centre of the mountains, in such an inaccessible place that no other dynasty ever attempted to occupy it and in such an unlikely location that archaeologists have since been unable to find it. The Ghorids continued to rule from this mountain city in defiance of all the economic and administrative conventions of their time. In 1216, however, Genghis Khan invaded and the already declining Ghorid Empire was destroyed. The city was lost and with it all details of this strange mountain civilization.

In Chist that morning, looking at the Ghorid domes, I realized that they were unlike any Islamic mausoleum that I had seen. The nomadic Turks and Mongols often built their domes as though they were pitching yurt tents. Their buildings in Tabriz, Sultanijeh, Marageh and Samarkand seem to have been simply dropped at random on the plain, as though all that mattered for a site was that it should be level and cool and have pasture and water for the animals.

But the mausoleum at Chist had apparently been placed more carefully. The domes were positioned in the centre of a symmetrical plateau, which was lower than the western approach ridge. From above, they had no silhouette and from the bottom of the slope they were invisible. Only for a moment, halfway down the slope, did they rise above the skyline. They were then lost again until the summit of the final climb when the curved roof slowly reappeared framed by the mountain range beyond, with the shape of the arches mimicking the shape of the peaks.

They were decorated with pale mud bricks, the colour of the earth, cut to imitate a pattern of brambles or thorns, which spelled out a Koranic text.[18] The Seljuks at the same period covered their domes with blue tiles but the Ghorids had not used coloured tiles here.[19] The shape of the dome, the colour of the pale brick and the script had all apparently been chosen to echo and enhance the surrounding landscape.[20]

Perhaps it was their attachment to their mountains and pride in being the only indigenous highland people to found a medieval Asian empire,[21] that led the Ghorids to mark the gateway to Ghor with these domes and to position them in a way that emphasized their mountain setting. But why did they choose to dedicate them to the Chistiyah dervishes?

---

18. This Kufic script was unique to the Ghorids. I had seen it also in the alcove of the Herat mosque, where the Al-Qaeda men use to chat in Urdu.

19. See the Kabud dome in Marageh.

20. The ancient peoples of highland Asia were very sensitive to the landscape. During the earlier stages of my walk, in Turkey and Iran, I was often struck by the symmetry and isolation of a rock in the desert, only to find on approaching it that the Phrygians had carved a lion into its surface; or that forty feet up a sheer cliff, the Medians had placed the facade of a shrine; or that beside a volcano cone and beyond livid copper walls, the Persians had built water temples.

The Ghorids seem to have shared this delight in the shape and colour of rock. Unlike the Seljuks or the Mongols, they were not nomads from the steppes but instead, like the Phrygians, Medians and Persians, people who had lived for centuries among their mountains.

21. A pride reflected in the Ghorids' use of the epithet Malik-I-Jabal, or King of the Mountains, as their royal title.

The Missionary Dance

As I turned away from the domes an old man rode up on a white horse decorated with a finely woven saddle cloth coloured with soft vegetable dyes. The horse was bony and lame and he rode it timidly. He looked as though he was wearing not a turban but a barber's basin on his head.

'I,' he said, 'am Khalife Seyyed Agha, son of Haji Khalife Seyyed Ahmed, direct heir and descendant of Hazrat Maulana Sultan Maududi, the saint of Chist who died in 1132. My ancestor is buried beneath that dome. I am the lord of all the land that you can see.'

'So you are the head of the Chistiyah dervishes?'

'I am but there are no dervishes living here any more. Can you draw a picture of my horse?'

'I'll try.' It was cold in the snow and my hands were stiff but my drawing looked like a horse. We were joined by a younger man who stood silently, watching us.

'Can I keep your drawing?' asked the old man.

'OK.' I ripped it out of my notebook and handed it to him.

'I like your sunglasses. Can I try them on?'

I handed them to him and he hung them on his long nose. 'Excellent. Can I keep them?'

'No, I'm sorry I need them – I am walking through the snows of Bamiyan – I need them for the glare.'

'Please.'

'I am sorry.'

'Just the sunglasses . . .'

'I'm sorry.'

'A pity; I might have offered you hospitality.' The patriarch turned and rode off. The Chistiyah dervishes were once famous for refusing gifts.

The young man who had witnessed this laughed. 'He is nothing now. His ancestors were great Chistiyah teachers, men of mystical power and great lords. There are no Chistiyah here today. He was too scared to fight the Russians, too scared to fight the Northern Alliance, too scared to fight the Taliban. He has done nothing in twenty-four years; I had almost forgotten that he existed. He is lucky that we haven't taken all his land.'

Only hints remained of why this local Sufi sect whose tombs these were (they were called Chistiyah because they came from Chist) had become one of the four most powerful dervish orders in the world. Surviving descriptions suggest that they had a great deal in common with other mystics, even non-Muslim mystics. They repeated sacred phrases and used rosaries like Hindus, Buddhists and Christians who may have encountered Sufis during the Crusades. They seemed intoxicated with an almost erotic love of God, drowning details of religious doctrine in a transcendental fervour, and their saints talked of being able to see the ultimate oneness of God.

They also differed from other mystics in very particular ways. It was not just that one of their saints, Baba Farid, prayed suspended by his feet for forty days, or that, with the distinguished exception of Amir Khosrow, the Chistiyah wrote little poetry. Nor was it their theological views on *walaya* (the spiritual authority of a Prophet) and *welaya* (divine love). Nor was it that they carried a toothbrush attached to their turban and wore four-cornered conical hats. What made the Chistiyah most famous was their music. Whereas some dervishes achieved mystical union by praying and others by walking or whirling, the Chistiyah did so by playing instruments and dancing.

The Ghorids brought their local sect with them when they

invaded India, and the Chistiyah must have given some religious legitimacy to an invasion that was presented as a jihad. They may have built the domes to honour this association. But Juzjani, who chronicled the Ghorid dynasty, suggests that they were not acceptable to all Muslims. He presided as a judge over a complaint made about a ceremony called Sama, in which the Chistiyah experienced religious ecstasy by dancing and playing music. Juzjani found in favour of the Chistiyah saint,[22] who died in ecstasy during one of these performances a little later. A later Chistiyah saint,[23] who was born in the thirteenth century, records that these Sama sessions lasted throughout the night. They were led by male singers reciting Persian poetry and accompanied by drums, timbales and tambourines, but not string or wooden instruments because they 'blocked the taste and pain of the mystic'. Hindus were allowed to attend and everyone was encouraged to dance and sing. Later descriptions showed how disturbing these practices must have seemed to the orthodox.

The disciple of this saint[24] stressed that the visitation of the unseen in the Sama dance ceremony should be seen as a form of love-making: Sama must happen at night, not in a mosque, but in a closed hall, perfumed with sandalwood. Garments may be torn or thrown off in ecstasy. The dancing could overcome you as a feeling of uncontrollable agitation, it could develop into a feeling of total harmony or it could be assimilated by conforming to the other dancers:

> *The Sufi may go round in circles in ecstasy, leap about, beat the ground in his place with his feet or lift his hands over his head, twisting them together and rotating them before bringing them down again.*

22. Qutb-al-Din Baktiar Kaki.
23. Nezam Al-Din Aulia.
24. Gisuderaz.

It is clear from the lavish domes that the Ghorids had a particular affection for this dancing sect.[25] It was also a relationship, which they advertised by placing the domes so visibly at the entrance to their lands and engraving them with long passages from the Koran. Was this their answer to the Arabs and Seljuks who had mocked the obscure province of Ghor as one of the last pagan enclaves in the Persian world? Again, I was looking at evidence of a very different society and a very different Islam from what existed on the same site today.

*

The police chief at Chist had a generator, which powered a video and his black and white television. Twenty of us gathered to watch a film of dancing. He handed me the cassette sleeve. It showed a girl in a red sequinned mini dress with thigh-length boots. But when he switched on the video, the star was an overweight middle-aged lady in a puffy ballgown. She was dancing in a tent in Peshawar. To the delight of rows of Afghan men, who were seated on the floor, she had released her hair and bared her forearms. The film was shot in the dark by a man with unsteady hands, but he had captured

---

25. Not much, however, is known about their relationship. I found a myth in India of how a great Chistiyah saint walked through Multan and Lahore in the late twelfth century and, reaching Ajmer, appeared to the Ghorid prince in a dream saying, 'Arise, the land of India is yearning to kiss your feet and the crown and throne await you there', encouraging the Ghorid to conquer all of India. Muinuddin Chisti Sanjari went from Multan (which they conquered in 1175) to Lahore (1186) and then to Ajmer (where they held their decisive battle in 1193). The saint's march into India seemed to pass through the cities which the Ghorids conquered and in the order in which they conquered them. It suggested at least that the military conquerors supported the work of missionaries and then were in turn encouraged by the missionaries. The conquest was a jihad, a holy war, and both warriors and saints were required.

most of her scowls. She danced by hopping stiffly up and
down with her hands on her hips. Disappointed with her
sloppy footwork, the cameraman zoomed in on her enormous breasts, which lurched from side to side and filled the
frame for a minute.

'Was there dancing here before?'

'Not in Chist, but we used to have it in Herat and Kabul
when the King was in power,' replied the police chief. 'There
was less with Najib because of the war. The Mujahidin stopped
it completely.'

'The Taliban?'

'No, Ismail Khan and the Northern Alliance stopped it as
well. It is forbidden in Islam.'

'Do you like dancing?'

'Me?' said the police chief. 'I like it very much.' Everyone
laughed.

*

Then I sat down and wrote a long letter to my parents, in case
I was killed. In the past sixteen months, I had bribed, flattered,
pried, bullied, begged and wheedled to keep going on my
walk. I was more of a tramp than a mystic, but as I wrote I felt
at peace. I wrote to my parents about the moments on the
way which seemed to have a deep, unified relation to my past.
I wondered if walking was not a form of dancing.

I was happy then and I slept well.

Mirrored Cat's-eye Shades

Abdul Haq behaved in his last hours with me much as he had during the previous week. In a three-hour period he got lost, said we were almost there, changed his mind and decided we were still a night away, laughed, said he was a mule and shot some bullets at a mud house. Then he turned towards me and asked, 'How much does it cost to buy a wife in England?'

'But you are already married.'

'I want a second wife.'

'Nothing. You don't have to pay in England.'

'Then why don't I just go to England and get one for free – instead of paying five thousand dollars here?'

'No reason,' I said.

Abdul Haq looked at me suspiciously.

If you couldn't get around the system by marrying your sister to your wife's brother, you had to pay far more for a wife than most could earn in a decade of work inside Afghanistan. In some villages you had to give your father-in-law two horses and fifty sheep in addition to cash. Everyone seemed to think that the sums were ridiculously high but no one seemed to be able to get around the custom. Abdul Haq said that most of his friends had had to leave Afghanistan and work for three years in Iran just to earn the money to pay the bride-price.

Then someone fired three shots behind us. We ran a little and then stopped. They fired again. We ran on. Abdul Haq had no idea who was shooting but he thought they were aiming at us. The shooting stopped.

At about midday we came down into Darai-e-Takht, a

large village nestled in a gorge of the Hari Rud River. Darai-e-Takht formed the modern frontier of Ghor province and of the formal territory of Ismail Khan. From now on Ismail Khan's authority was more indirect, although he had appointed the governor of Ghor. Abdul Haq said this was where he was stopping. We sat in the inn. I was used to the ritual of greetings that took place in private houses. Here everyone ignored us entirely. I was conscious of not having washed for eight days, the stink of my socks and walking boots and the dust on my pack.

A slender thirty-year-old entered and everyone suddenly stood up. He was wearing gold-rimmed, mirrored cat's-eye shades and a silver turban over his gold cap. Followed by a group of armed men, he moved up the line, shaking hands in a steady, smooth glide to the most senior position in the room. He did not urge anyone to sit down or try to put someone else in the senior position. It would have been difficult for him to stop because of the thirty men pressing behind him who, all older than him, held bandoliers and heavy machine guns designed to be mounted on vehicles, which must have been almost too heavy to lift. One of his retainers wore a soft Russian tank commander's cap with ear flaps beneath his turban; another wore a blue naval jacket with brass buttons.

This was Mustafa, the commandant of Obey, who had apparently tried to kill me on the road near Obey and who, it transpired, had just been shooting at us again. I never found out why: perhaps it was for fun or perhaps he was asserting his anti-American credentials. When he was seated he began to speak in a soft, high-pitched voice. His conversation had none of the solemn grandiloquence of Persian oratory.

'At last the walking foreigner, I see. Welcome. And where are you wandering – you must be cold . . . have you eaten?' He spoke quickly and did not give me time to answer; he seemed to be very amused by something – perhaps by having just shot at us.

As he spoke a grey-bearded secretary wrote down every word. The commander took off his turban and cap and ruffled his gleaming, newly washed, black hair. His followers gazed at him.

'You are lucky to have me,' he continued. 'I will provide you with an honour guard of five men.'

I smiled. 'Please excuse us for a moment,' I said and took Abdul Haq outside. I did not want to lose one group of armed men only to be given another. I told him to tell the commandant that I needed to travel alone.

When we re-entered, Abdul Haq sat down and talked to the young commander. 'His Excellency Rory is travelling alone for his book. He should remain alone.' He talked about the Emperor Babur, about anthropology, about my close friendship with Ismail Khan, about my travels in other countries. I had assumed that Abdul Haq had little knowledge and less interest in what I was doing. But he had apparently remembered almost everything I had said along the way. He spoke convincingly and fluently and the audience listened attentively.

When he had finished Mustafa laughed out loud at me and Abdul Haq. 'Then you will walk on Englishman and I will give you a letter of introduction, which my secretary will write, and you,' he said to Abdul Haq, 'can travel with me to Herat. I am sorry I don't have more time.' He stood and walked down the line, shaking hands, and left followed by his men. Abdul Haq embraced me, kissed me three times and hurried after them. I walked outside to watch him go. He was the only bare-headed and clean-shaven man. Everyone else wore a beard and turban. He had his shoes only half on and he was stumbling through the mud with his rifle on his shoulder. He didn't look back. I stood ready to wave a final time but he still didn't look back. I was a quarter of the way through my journey.

Marrying a Muslim

A man called Gul Agha Karimi had written some letters to introduce me to people in Ghor. Gul Agha was a wealthy businessman, originally from this district, who owned a pizza restaurant and shop in Kabul. I was very grateful for the letters, but I did not know how he was perceived in Ghor or how his introductions would be received.

He had told me that people from one village would accompany me to the next village. The custom of escorting visitors was once common throughout Asia. In Iran, Pakistan and India, city dwellers often said to me, 'Don't worry . . . someone from one village will always walk with you and hand you to someone in the next . . . they won't let you walk alone.' But such traditions and social structures had, in reality, vanished, and in eighteen months of walking, no one had ever offered to accompany me to a neighbouring village.

Gul Agha's first letter was addressed to Dr Habibullah Sherwal, who owned the inn in Darai-e-Takht where I had just met the young commandant. I found Dr Habibullah; he glanced at the letter and simply said, 'Give me a minute to change my shoes.'

He reappeared a minute later in sunglasses with a Kalashnikov on his shoulder, locked the door and we set off. He had not been warned that I was coming, and yet without hesitating or asking any questions he set out with a stranger on a two-night journey.

Dr Habibullah was a portly man of thirty-six. He had to keep hitching his rifle up on his round shoulders, and he took small, quick steps in his tasselled brown loafers. He did not speak to me at all in the first twenty minutes walking together.

I liked Abdul Haq but I preferred travelling without him. He had dominated my view of the landscape. The dangers and the geography of the country and the villages had been filtered through the mind of a man who was a Mujahid of Ismail Khan, based in Herat. Habibullah was a local. The fields through which we were walking belonged to him. The people on the road recognized him. I was pleased at last to have reached the hills and be moving further away from the vehicles and deeper into Ghor. The valleys were narrow and the Hari Rud River ran through gorges. It had not snowed for two days, but there was still a dusting of white in the hollows and on the upper slopes. Above our path were pillars of sand, and high in the cliff walls were caves used as sheep pens in the winter.

We passed a large, round fort by the river. Habibullah waited patiently outside while I wandered among the crumbling walls, half buried in snow, and climbed into a round tower to look across the valley. The castle seemed to dominate the path from every direction. I had no way of finding out how old it was: mud bricks could be almost any age. Then, having checked I couldn't be seen from the path, I squatted down in the snow.

I had had diarrhoea for a day. I had tried to avoid it by drinking only tea or purifying my water with chlorine tablets. The breads and soups, which were the staple diet, were relatively safe, but no one washed their hands and we all shared the same bowls. I was surprised that I had not caught it three days earlier when Aziz and Abdul Haq complained of stomach cramps. But I had it now and I knew that it was dehydrating me and would weaken me for walking. I still felt quite strong but, if it persisted, I would have to try some antibiotics.

When I reappeared, Habibullah was squatting on his heels in the afternoon sun. I apologized for taking so much time but he just shrugged. We started walking again, with me trying to adjust to his short steps after a week of Abdul Haq's stretched and rapid pacing. We crossed the ford below Darai-e-Takht on a small bridge marked 'ECHO – built with funds from the European Community'. It had been built five years earlier and was already crumbling, but it was an important contribution, since this ford had been frequently impassable.[26]

When we reached the far end of the bridge, Dr Habibullah pointed at a large black rock, high on the slope behind us and said, 'Commandant Mustafa – the young man whom you just met and who shot at you – shot two Taliban from there. They died here on this ground, which is my wheat field. Before that he was nothing – a small-time mullah – but because he was the only man in this village to fight the Taliban he is now a commander.'

'And you?'

'I didn't fight the Taliban. I fought the Russians from when I was fourteen for ten years with Rabbani's Jamiat, but when the Taliban came I went to work in Iran and Herat.'

We walked that afternoon for four hours along the Hari Rud River without a break. Everyone we met greeted Habibullah with respect, not wariness. Dr Habibullah embraced some of the men; others bowed over his hand and kissed it, while he looked fastidious and uninterested.

*

'How much do you pay for a wife in Scotland?' asked Dr Habibullah.

I told him.

'What is your religion?'

'*Jesewi* – Christian,' I said.

'You believe in God?'

'Yes.'

'One God?'

'Yes.'

'Would you marry your mother's sister's daughter?'

'I don't think so.'

'How about your mother's brother's daughter?'

'No.'

'Your father's brother's or your sister's daughter?'

'No, not them either.'

'Then who would you marry?'

'Probably someone not related to me.'

Silence. Habibullah's questions suggested he was interrogating a Stone-Age tribesman about kinship structures. But these were not anthropological questions at all. They were religious questions. Islam, much more than Christianity, is a political and social religion. Clear rules govern who and how you can marry. In this area most people married their first cousins.

A tall bearded man came running after us. He ignored my greeting entirely, and asked Dr Habibullah, 'What religion is he?'

'He's a Jahdui – a Jew,' said Dr Habibullah.

'No, no – I'm an *Esawi* – a Christian.'

Dr Habibullah turned around, looked at me and then said to his friend, 'I can't work this out – is there a difference?'

Many people who fought in the holy war against the Russians must have known less about other religions than Dr Habibullah.

The man led him aside, whispered to him and then we were on our way.

'That man was a mullah,' said Dr Habibullah. 'He said that you can marry our daughters – you are a type of Muslim.'

This idea seemed to relax Habibullah. I wasn't going to point out that Muslim women were not usually encouraged to marry Christian men.

Habibullah explained that he was called Doctor because he had done a part-time veterinary course in Herat.

'Why are you carrying a weapon?' I asked.

'For the wolves.'

'Are they dangerous?'

'Six months ago on that slope on my way to vaccinate some of the sheep on that hill, I came across the clothes and then the leg of a friend who had just been eaten by a wolf in the middle of the day. Two years ago five wolves killed my neighbour at eleven in the morning. Your stick wouldn't keep them away.'

Habibullah told me about long walks which he had done when he was young. He had led fifty men across the hills to Quetta from Darai-e-Takht to collect weapons. It had taken them two months to walk there and two months to return. They slept mostly in caves. Now, however, his brown tasselled loafers were cutting up his feet, and towards the end of the day he was hobbling.

'I can speak English,' Habibullah said in Farsi, and then added in English, 'My father name Aziz.' He counted to twenty in English, only missing out number eight.

'Well done,' I said.

'That is nothing – I can count to one thousand – perhaps later . . .'

*

That night we stopped in Dahan-e-Rezak, which was Habibullah's mother's village. This was my first night in an Aimaq tribal hill village. The valley was narrow and there was no room for large fields and the houses were built in terraces into the hillside. Two large sheepdogs were asleep on the roofs.

The villagers referred to themselves as Tajik, which seemed to mean that they were Persian speakers who were not Uzbek, Hazara or Pushtun.[27] But other people called

---

27. They sometimes refer to themselves also by tribal names such as Taimani, Firuzkuhi, Jamshidi and Hazara-e-Qala-e Nau.

them the Aimaq of Ghor. Although they were famous for
their colourful tents, there was no sign of the tents on my
visit; they only lived in them during the summer on the high
pasture. In the winter they lived in villages of flat-roofed
mud-houses, not domed like many of the villages of the Herat
plain. More recently the Aimaq, who numbered over half a
million people, had settled into four major tribal groups.[28]
Dr Habibullah said that this tribe was known as Firuzkuhi,
which is to say, Aimaq of the Turquoise Mountain. They lived
in the heart of the old Ghorid Empire.

There were six houses and seventy people in the village.
They claimed there were thirty houses because that meant
they got more food aid from international agencies. Everyone
in Rezak was descended from a single grandfather. Their
wealth was traditionally linked to their sheep flocks, but many
had died in the war and the villagers now lived off UN grain
and by selling a few sheep. The men had supplemented this
by working as builders in Iran. The women wove carpets in
styles that could be sold in the markets of Iran and Pakistan.[29] The development agencies called this area 'the hunger
belt'. They had predicted that a hundred thousand people
would die from starvation that winter. No one seemed to
be starving, but the diet was limited to plain *nan* bread for

---

28. Some of the Aimaq have Mongol features. They are supposed also to
use many more Turkic words in their dialect than other Persian speakers.
Perhaps because my Persian was not good enough or because they were
avoiding dialect in talking to me, I never noticed this. Even the Aimaq
disagree about which are the four main tribes. Among the groups, however, are the Firokuhi, Taimani, Taiwara, Hazara, Jamshidi and Timuri.
Elphinstone in 1815 added the Zooree and has the Firuzkuhi and Jamshidi
as sub-tribes of the Hazara.

29. Their carpets would often be sold as Bokharan or 'Khoja Rushnai' –
areas hundreds of miles away. The main cost of the carpet lay in the wool.
The women and girls who wove were often paid less than ten dollars for
work that took them a month.

breakfast and lunch and occasional beans for dinner. One household, however, had so little food that its members had left for the large refugee camp near Herat. As in the case of many villages, however, their main source of cash was money that they had been given by the West, Iran and Pakistan to encourage them to fight against the Russians and then against other Afghan groups.

The headman of Rezak, Seyyed Agha, had been a military commander for twenty-four years. First, he had fought the Russians, with a group funded by Pakistani intelligence, then, 'because they weren't killing enough people', he had fought for a group partially funded by the British. Then the Russians withdrew and he fought the pro-Russian Najib government and the rival Northern Alliance groups. When the Taliban took over the province, five years ago, he decided, he said, to 'retire from fighting'. This probably meant that he had been the Taliban commander in the area, but he would have denied it if I had asked. Perhaps to compensate for this lapse the headman had presented Ismail Khan with his personal horse when the Emir had come through here on his triumphal ride back into Herat two months before.

The headman asked me if I knew where mullah Mohammed Omar was. I replied that I imagined he was in the south. 'No, he's not,' said the headman, 'he's sitting there . . .' and pointed to a one-eyed man. Everyone roared with laughter, except the one-eyed man, who seemed to have heard the joke before.

As we went to sleep someone put the BBC Dari service on the radio. Bill Gates was making a speech on American policy towards technology monopolies, which was being translated into Dari. The men listened intently. I wondered what these illiterate men without electricity thought of bundling Internet Explorer with Windows.

War Dog

I woke the next morning to find Habibullah trying to wind another empty clarified butter packet around the butt of his Kalashnikov. The barrel was swaddled in biscuit packets. Beneath the yellowing transparent tape, used to bind the wrappers, were fragments of Hindi, English and Persian script, advertising food factories in Tabriz and Bangalore. The dawn light was weak through the small window and he was struggling to find the end of the sticky tape. He saw me looking at him and asked, 'Would you like a dog?'

'What dog?' I replied.

'There is one outside, which they'd give you . . . he's a good dog.'

I didn't know how I could keep a dog. On the other hand I like dogs.

'Show him the dog, Sheikh,' said Habibullah, addressing the twelve-year-old trainee mullah.

Sheikh led me out of the mosque. In the dim dawn light members of the family were beginning to emerge from their mud houses, stepping carefully over the patches of ice, pulling their blankets closer around them. Three old men were already squatting with their trousers down. They coughed noisily and spat into the damp air. Women were dipping tin jars in the cold river water at the bottom of the hill. The sun would not enter the narrow valley for another hour.

On a mud roof, a large dog was asleep on a blanket. There was a dusting of the previous night's snowfall on his coat. While I looked at the dog, a small group of boys looked at me. It was two hours' walk from here to their nearest neighbour, so the children spent all their time with their cousins. When they were fifteen or so they married their cousins.

A young man called Hussein emerged from a doorway with a hastily tied turban. 'This is the dog,' he said, 'do you want it?'

Hussein walked over to the sleeping animal and kicked it. The dog opened one eye and looked up at the man and the dim morning light. He closed his eye again, shook his bear-like head and, still lying on his side, pushed out his front legs, arched his long back and stretched his hind legs. Then he sighed, rolled laboriously onto his front and stood up. The village boys backed away so quickly that they fell over each other. He was about the size of a small pony.

'He is very strong, very dangerous,' said Hussein. The dog, oblivious to the boys, looked around and then took a couple of steps, stiffly on three legs, holding his left paw in the air. Then he lay down again. His back was shaped like an Alsatian's or a wolf's, but he was much taller and quite thin. His coat was a deep gold except for the brindle of black hairs, which stood up in the cold air. Hussein put his foot on the dog's neck, rolling him on his side. 'OK, come over.'

The dog peered at me, craning his neck under the man's boot. His eyes were bloodshot and he was missing his ears and his tail.

'Do you want him?' asked Hussein.

'I don't know. What is his name?'

Hussein shouted over his shoulder, 'Does he have a name?'

'No,' they replied.

'What sort of dog is he?'

'*Sag-Jangi*,' Hussein replied, which means 'a dog of war', a fighting dog.

'What does he do in the village?'

'He is here to kill wolves.'

'Please take your foot from his neck,' I said.

The man released his foot. I squatted down and called the dog. He rolled onto his front and lay there with his huge paws in front of him. I whistled and snapped my fingers. He lay there, immobile as a Trafalgar Square lion. Then one of the boys made a tutting sound and the dog stood up heavily.

'Look how fit and strong he is,' said Hussein.

The dog limped slowly over and looked up at me. His eyes were still and yellow like a wolf's. I gave him my hand to sniff and then cautiously touched his head. I heard an old man mutter, 'That infidel is going to get bitten.'

He would not have called me an infidel if he had known I could hear him but that was how villagers perceived me. This was a pious Muslim community. They had built a mosque for a hamlet of five homes, and every man prayed there five times a day and listened to long Koranic readings in the evening.

I backed to the edge of the roof and called the dog again – this time by tutting. After a long pause and some consideration, he followed me. His left foreleg was undeniably stiff. He rubbed his earless head against my leg.

'What happened to his ears?'

'We chopped them off.'

'Why?'

'So he could fight better. He's very ferocious.'

The dog yawned, revealing that he was missing most of his teeth.

'What happened to his teeth?'

'Hussein knocked them out with a stone.'

Hussein grinned. He still had his teeth.

'Why?'

'Because he bit me.'

'And why has he got white hair on his muzzle?'

'People get white hair very quickly around here.'

'How old is this dog?' I asked

'Five,' said Dr Habibullah, who had emerged on the terrace and was acting in his capacity as a vet.

'He's not. He's ancient. He's got a white beard,' I replied.

'He says the dog's got a white beard,' repeated Dr Habibullah, and everyone laughed.

'And he's missing his teeth.' I added.

'That's not from age – that's because Hussein knocked them out with a stone.'

'Look,' I said, 'he's a lovely dog, but I don't think he's going to be able to walk with me to Kabul. It's seven hundred kilometres from here and there's a lot of snow and we have to do thirty-five kilometres a day. Look at how stiff he is.'

'Nonsense,' said Dr Habibullah, 'We know these dogs – he's not old, it's just a cold morning. He comes from a very famous line of dogs . . . all raised here. He's one of the biggest dogs in the province. You're very lucky they're offering him. He's killed many wolves.' I didn't ask whether that was before or after he lost his teeth. 'This is a very poor village. They can only afford to give him one piece of *nan* bread a day. If you took him you could get him meat. He'd be much stronger. He's a great dog for you. In any case you're going to walk alone through the mountains; you'll need him to protect you against wolves and the Hazara.' He was Aimaq and he believed the Hazara were untrustworthy and violent and certain to kill me.

'Why did you touch the dog?' asked Sheikh, the twelve-year-old trainee mullah.

'I like dogs. Does no one ever touch him?'

'Of course not. He's an unclean animal – our Prophet tells us not to touch dogs – particularly when we pray. We must do special ablutions if we have touched a dog.'

'Where is that in the Koran?'

'I can't remember exactly,' said Sheikh, 'but it's there.'

'I thought you were a "Hafiz" – that you had memorized the entire Koran . . .' Sheikh had come here from an even more remote village to study with their mullah. He recited passages for the village in the evening. In honour of this, he had been allowed to join me and the adult guests at dinner.

'I have memorized it,' Sheikh replied. 'I can recite it in Arabic from end to end – more than one hundred thousand words. But I don't speak Arabic, so I don't understand precisely where the individual pieces are.'

I walked outside again. A small group of bored, dirty children were shouting at the dog. One of them threw a stone at him, which hit his flank, but he didn't react. I wondered how it felt to have lived here and never to have been stroked. There was something ponderous about his movements; there was no eagerness, no playfulness and no curiosity. I couldn't decide whether he was very depressed or very old or both. He looked over his shoulder and saw me. The stump of his tail moved slightly and he took a slow step towards me. I decided to take him back with me to Scotland.

When Dr Habibullah said goodbye, he added, 'Do you know about Dr Brydon? He was English. We killed you all but we left him alive to ride into Peshawar . . . I think Afghans shall send you alive like Dr Brydon.'[30] Half an hour later, having given some money to the villagers, I left with the dog.

I called him Babur, which means tiger, because of his brindled back and because we were taking Babur's route. Babur the dog followed me up the shoulder of the first hill,

---

30. The British retreat from Kabul took place in January 1842, almost exactly a hundred and sixty years before my conversation with Dr Habibullah. The Afghans killed at least twelve thousand of the British troops and their followers in six days in the snow-filled gorges below Kabul. Only Dr Brydon, a medic, managed to ride into the fort of Jalalabad. Apart from a few prisoners released later, he was the sole survivor of the army of the Indus. Lady Butler's painting of him shows him half-dead on his pony at the gates, looking, in his long-tailed tunic like a pre-Raphaelite knight ending a Grail quest. He took the pony, which he had taken from an Afghan village and which had carried him to safety, back with him to Scotland.

which was deep purple and sat like the plateau of Chist neatly framed by the surrounding hills. It was called 'the Hindu's mountain' and the headman told me there had once been a Hindu village on the top. He had no idea when. Historians were not sure what Ghor's religion had been before its conversion to Islam. This name suggested it had been Hindu.[31]

We turned a corner and Babur's village was hidden from sight. For as long as Babur had been alive, he had seen nothing but those six mud houses and the high pastures where they moved into their tents for the summer grazing. He spent his days beside the sheep in the same pastures every year with his giant paws in front of him, waiting for the wolves. He had never been more than a day's walk from the place and he had never seen a motorized vehicle, electricity or a village of more than six houses, still less a school or a clinic. The same was true of the women of Rezak who, I was told by their proud husbands, had not even visited the village three hours' walk away. Only the men had had some exposure to other places. Babur would never see his home again. After ten minutes walk Babur met the cold wind on the crest, lay down and wouldn't move. Only a piece of stale *nan* bread, which I'd been given by Sheikh, convinced him to descend the slope.

After another half an hour of sniffing and trotting further away from his village, he lay down again and looked at me steadily, narrowing his yellow eyes. He would take no interest in the bread. When coaxing failed I grabbed on to the orange nylon string which they had tied around his neck and hauled, dragging his ten-stone frame along the gravel. To my relief, after a couple of feet, he stood up heavily and, shaking his head roughly, walked behind me, more slowly now. But by forcing

---

31. Arab historians also refer to it as a Hindu area, but they had a tendency to call all pagan kingdoms Hindu. Bosworth, who is the great authority on the Ghorids, suggests they may have had their own individual local religion, which simply vanished with the Islamic invasion.

him on, I had finally confirmed that he was coming all the way to Scotland. As if in acknowledgement of our new relationship, he no longer took any interest in the smells around him and we walked for an hour without a pause until we met a man on a white horse, accompanied by a herd of goats.

'Hey, boy,' shouted the man on the horse, 'come here.' No one had talked to me like that before. He apparently assumed that I was a very low-grade Afghan villager because I was walking with something as unclean as a dog. 'When's the dog fight? What does the dog do? Where are you taking it?'

I replied politely that there would be no dog fight, that Babur didn't do anything and that I was taking him to Kabul.

'What are you talking about?' he said. The man thought I was talking nonsense. Afghan dogs are not pets. They are for hunting, for protecting sheep from wolves or for dog fights. Babur, who was unusually large, was obviously a promising gladiator, and the man on the horse wanted to match him against his own dog and start some betting.

It was not as if this man didn't like animals. Over his horse, he had thrown a large kilim saddle blanket with thirty bands of colour that would have taken six weeks to weave. But a dog was religiously polluting, dirty and dangerous. Later, Afghans were variously to describe Babur as big, strong, ferocious, useless, tired or decrepit. I called him beautiful, wise and friendly. Afghans would generally only use such adjectives for a man, a horse or a falcon.

Commandant Haji (Moalem) Mohsin Khan of Kamenj

We walked on through the hills, whose brilliant colours showed the presence of metal ores in the soil: a rock face striped like seaside candy, a crest of snow-softened russet, then slopes of green and orange sandstone and finally a cliff streaked with bands of bull's blood red. After four hours we reached the compound of Commandant Haji Mohsin Khan at Kamenj.

It snowed throughout the afternoon and I spent much of my time on the veranda of Haji Mohsin's house looking at the dog. I gave him some *nan* bread and he held it between his large paws like a bear as he tore strips off with his teeth. When he had finished he sniffed earnestly around the pillars to see if he could find any last crumbs and then lay heavily down with his head between his two paws and closed his eyes. The wrinkles of loose skin on his forehead made it look as though he was always anxious when he was sleeping. I returned to the guest room.

In the middle of the afternoon, Wazir, Commandant Haji Mohsin Khan's servant, entered, kicked the snow from his boots and laid a new water pipe by the stove. It was warm inside the room and Commandant Haji Mohsin Khan leaned back against the cushions, letting his camelhair gown fall open from his thin chest and fingering his grey beard, as though congratulating himself on its length and unusually neat shape. A young man and his father were in the room, having walked a full day from their village to see Haji Mohsin, but he had barely spoken to them. The young man mixed the cannabis and tobacco for Haji Mohsin's water pipe.

When the pipe was placed in front of him, Haji Mohsin sat up, swung the tail of his silk turban over his shoulder, put the stem between his lips and inhaled. After a few sharp breaths he passed it to the old man and asked me if I had had enough to eat. Although Haji Mohsin was a grand feudal commander he had only fed us dry bread. I thanked him.

'Green tea or black tea?'

'Green please.'

Wazir walked back into the snow to fetch the tea and the commandant leaned forward to pick up my rosary beads and put his own plastic beads in his pocket. For a few minutes he ran my beads through his hands, watching the light on the opaque Tibetan amber.

Silence.

There was a small window in the side of the room and through it I could see the snow falling on his orchard and on the water pump and lavatories marked with the acronym of an international aid agency. The compound was some way from the village and on the other side of the fast Hari Rud River, so that no one except Haji Mohsin's immediate family was able to use this sanitary gift from the people of Scandinavia.

'Commandanthajimohsinkhan,' said the boy, passing the water pipe back. The boy pronounced the commandant's name as though it were a single word. Commandant indicated that Mohsin was a military commander, 'Haji' meant he was wealthy enough to have performed the obligatory pilgrimage to Mecca, 'Khan' that his family had been one of the two largest landowners in this district for a couple of hundred years. Such titles didn't always go together, but it was not uncommon. It was also normal that such a man should be in charge of a visiting guest, just as he was in charge of deciding where the development agency put their lavatory and water pump. I had read an account of his family from British officers in 1885. They were described as hereditary rulers of one of the Aimaq confederacies.

'Show me your letters of introduction,' said Commandant Haji Mohsin.

I gave him the letter from Gul Agha Karimi. He scowled and laid it aside, muttering that Gul Agha had collaborated with the Russians. Then I handed him the letter from Agha Ghori and the one which Abdul Haq had persuaded the young Commandant Mustafa to write. They were supposed to introduce me to everyone along the way, but Haji Mohsin simply put them into his pocket. He wanted to keep the letters because they would allow him to ask favours from these men in the future.

'Can I have them back?' I asked.

'No. They're for me.'

'But I need them for others along the way.'

'Then they should have given you more than one copy. I will give you letters of introduction to the others.'

I went outside. Babur was asleep on the edge of the veranda. There was a thick crust of snow on his left flank. I led him down to the Hari Rud. He looked gloomily at the water and then at me, but he wouldn't drink. I led him a little further upstream, stepped onto a rock in the stream and waited. He scooped up the water with his tongue so it spattered his chops and dribbled from his large lips. He drank for a full minute and then raised his head. I waited. He drank again.

When I returned to the house, the others stood to greet me, but Haji Mohsin merely raised an eyebrow and continued smoking on his cushion. His air of superiority apparently reflected his social position. Unlike many feudal lords, Haji Mohsin had retained his land and power throughout the war.

'Agha Commandant Haji Mohsin Khan, what have you been doing for the last twenty-five years?' I asked.

'Well, originally I was a malem – a teacher.' Others fixed the title 'Moalem' to their name, in the fashion of doctors in the West. But Commandant Haji Mohsin Khan had enough titles already. 'Then I fought the Russians as a Mujahidin and they dropped sixteen bombs on Kamenj, killing forty-five of my villagers. When the Northern Alliance took Kabul, I was made Head of Security in Chaghcharan. Then, when the Taliban came into power, I retired to my estate and played no further part. I am still retired.'

Haji Mohsin's guests, however, had come to discuss politics, and from the tone of the discussion I couldn't believe that he had been retired for five years. His family had attended the Loya Jirga assemblies of the previous kings and they expected to attend the new assembly.

'Will you join Karzai's party?' asked the young man's father.

Haji Mohsin Khan said nothing, focusing on his water pipe.

Five minutes later, he was asked again.

'I am old and tired, this is nothing to do with me,' said Haji Mohsin Khan.

Ten minutes later the old man asked for a third time and this time got the answer that perhaps he always expected,

'With all respect to this British boy,' drawled Haji Mohsin Khan, indicating me, 'Karzai is a tool of the British and the Americans and I will not be supporting him.'

Later I learned that Haji Mohsin Khan had not been in retirement during the Taliban era. He had defected to the Taliban and become their district commander; he and his brother-in-law, Rais Salam Khan, had opened fire on Ismail Khan's party as Ismail Khan made his final march on Herat and killed two of his senior lieutenants. He was therefore under threat from Herat. If I had still been with Qasim or

Abdul Haq, who were Ismail Khan's men, it would have been impossible for us to enter this house.

*

Much of the afternoon and evening was defined by the rhythm of Haji Mohsin's mosque. Three times between lunch and evening, Haji Mohsin's private mullah walked out into the garden and, with the snow falling gently around him, sang the call to prayer for Haji Mohsin's private mosque. Three times the commander and his guests disappeared and returned again to their water pipes and cups of tea.

For dinner, Haji Mohsin gave us only a small piece of salted meat each and a plateful of rice. Perhaps without my armed escort I no longer had enough status to deserve a serious meal, or perhaps he enjoyed providing frugal food to a foreigner.

After supper, which was eaten as usual in silence, he leaned very close to me so that I could smell the tobacco on his breath and said; 'Rome – Riga – Madrid – Kiev – names correct?'

'Correct.'

'Do you build ships in Britain?'

'Not any longer.'

'You see,' he said to the group, 'in Britain they are so rich from stealing when they ruled the world that they pay their workers a fortune. They do not need to manufacture – they import everything from America and Japan, where labour is cheaper.'

'Is England very rich?' asked the old man.

'Of course,' said Haji Mohsin. 'It all looks like Dubai.'

Wazir stuck his head through the door, 'At least a metre of snow has fallen now. The foreigner will be here for two months.'

The old man whispered something and they all laughed.

'Twenty-five years getting rid of the foreigners,' said Haji Mohsin's younger brother, 'and here they are again.'

Everyone laughed.

'He better be careful,' said the old man, 'or we'll do to him what we did to the CIA officer in Kunduz.' The CIA officer in Kunduz had been killed.

'He can't really think that dog can defend himself against wolves?' asked the young man.

'Don't forget his metal-tipped staff,' said Haji Mohsin, for once forgetting his dignity and rolling onto his back on the cushion laughing.

*

The next morning it was still snowing and they tried to persuade me not to go. They said that if there was a metre of snow in Kamenj – there must be at least two metres in Chaghcharan. But I didn't want to be trapped in Kamenj for the next two months.

Wazir, Haji Mohsin's servant, muffled up with three jackets, led Babur and me out through Haji Mohsin's orchards. He walked with a rolling seaman's stride and kicked the snow high into the air with his tall leather boots. The snow lay heavy on the thin black branches of apple and mulberry trees and formed a thick crust on the drystone walls. Babur padded happily alongside us, making his own tracks in the fresh powder. But it needed both of us to drag him across the ice on the river.

As we entered a broad valley, the snow stopped falling, the sun broke out of the clouds and we saw other footprints.

'Where are you from, Wazir?' I asked.

'I am the man of Commandant Haji Mohsin Khan. I fought for him during the jihad, went into hiding from the Russians with him in these mountains and work for him now for my bread. He is a good man.'

After another mile, the valley narrowed and the mountains were suddenly alive with figures, following the ridges, tumbling down the slopes and beating the hills for wolves.

Men waited with large dogs at the bottleneck on the valley floor.

It looked like a dangerous point for either a wolf or an army. I said so to Wazir.

'We were encircled here by Najib's troops,' he replied, 'and forty men were executed there.' He pointed to a slender stream running gently between the snowfields and the orchards.

I presumed then that it was Haji Mohsin Khan's troops who had been executed. But that evening I was told the story again and it appeared that the victims were on the other side. President Najib had ordered a helicopter-borne Special Forces operation to disarm Haji Mohsin. Ten of Haji Mohsin's men were killed but many of Najib's men were captured. Three of them were locals whose names people still remember: Maulani Jalami, Hazrat Gul and Akbar Mohammed. Haji Mohsin had executed them in front of the villagers beside this river.

Outside Guk three dogs came snarling at us with their teeth bared: one a sort of husky. I raised a stone to warn it to keep back. Babur padded along solemnly as though they were not there. Wazir told me to put my stone down. When I did so, the lead husky sprinted forward and sprang on Babur's back, sinking his teeth in. Babur turned, enraged, and flung the husky on the ground; the other two dogs charged in and I ran at them, swinging my staff. I hit one hard and it retreated whimpering. I didn't like hitting dogs but I was not prepared to let some mongrel savage Babur and I was furious with Wazir for letting it get to the stage where I had to lash out. For the rest of our morning together Wazir flung a stone whenever a dog looked at us.

As we turned up the side valley to Garmao, we saw a column of men approaching. Seven of them were walking through the snow and the last one rode a white horse. They were all wearing webbing as well as carrying their rifles. They passed without greeting us.

'Who are they?' I asked Wazir.

'I don't know. They're not from around here.'

Cousins

Three kilometres further up the valley, we reached Seyyed Umar's village of Garmao, where I was to stay. We entered the guest room and found a very tall man surrounded by his bodyguards. He was sitting by the door. Judging by his manner and his escort, he should have been in the senior position at the other end of the room. Something was wrong. He was not talking to his host, he refused to acknowledge Wazir and after asking me sharply if I had a satellite phone, he left. Our host, Seyyed Umar, watched him leave and then said, 'Once I would have killed a sheep for that man – now he is lucky I gave him tea.' Then he ordered someone to bring me an omelette. I was hungry and grateful.

Seyyed Umar's treatment of the tall man was a symptom of the rapid shifts in power that had followed the coalition bombardment. The flat plains were half controlled by militias such as Qasim's operating from Herat. But in the hills of Ghor I was moving between Aimaq leaders who were barely speaking to each other and stumbling over distinctions that were only half visible to me.

Islam does not encourage strong social distinctions and the war and social revolutions in villages had destroyed many of the old feudal structures in Afghanistan. Nevertheless, villagers were very aware of each other's backgrounds. A multitude of points of etiquette, tradition and tribal identities differentiated a servant such as Wazir from a feudal lord like Haji Mohsin and Haj Mohsin from a middle-class vet like Dr Habibullah Sherwal or an upwardly mobile mullah like the young commander of Obey. Class did not necessarily reflect education and experience. My current host, Seyyed Umar, was a wealthy man from a respected family of landowning clergy, but he could not read or write and had never been abroad. Abdul Haq, who was from a much humbler background, was literate and had travelled. What mattered was power and that in turn depended on your allies.

Many of my hosts had been war leaders. Most of them had fought against the Russians but not all for the same groups. The red-bearded Agha Ghori and Haji Mohsin had been two of the leading Jamiat commanders in the province, but the headman of the dog's village was a commander for the Pakistani-funded warlord Gulbuddin Hekmatayar.

A few, such as Gul Agha Karimi, who wrote my letters of introduction, had worked with the Russians. He and some others seemed to have been largely forgiven for collaborating. But the man who had been the Russian chief of the KGB-Khad and who ordered the planes to bomb Haji Mohsin's village would be killed if he stepped into this area.[32]

Things had become even more complicated under the Taliban era because anti-Russians now found themselves on opposite sides. Some men, such as Agha Ghori, genuinely retired. Haji Mohsin Khan had been pro-Taliban and attacked Ismail Khan. He had therefore been allowed to run the valleys for five years during the Taliban period.

The defeat of the Taliban meant that everything had changed again in less then two months. The anti-Taliban

---

32. Among those who had been forgiven was the Russian-era governor of Ghor, Fazal Ahmed Khan, who was now the Christian Aid representative in the province, living in Shahrak. He came from a feudal family even grander than Haji Mohsin's. Haji Mohsin's family were *khan zada*, important district figures, but Fazal Ahmed's family had been Taimans, effectively controlling the province under the royal court. His Khad Security chief, Moheddin, and he had been forced into hiding.

commander[33] had now taken back control of the whole
area from Haji Mohsin and was policing Haji Mohsin's
territory with his own men from Shahrak. That was why
Wazir had not recognized the gunmen who passed us on the
snowfields. Meanwhile, Haji Mohsin was refusing to hand
over his Taliban deputy.[34]

My host, Seyyed Umar, was the man of Haji Mohsin Khan,
while the tall guest who had just left was the man of Haji
Mohsin's enemy. But ten years before they had stood beside
each other to shoot Najibullah's men by the river.

'Why did you become a Mujahid?' I asked Seyyed Umar.

'Because the Russian government stopped my women
from wearing head-scarves and confiscated my donkeys.'

'And why did you fight the Taliban?'

'Because they forced my women to wear *burqas* not head-
scarves and stole my donkeys.'

It seemed that if you did not interfere with his women's
headdress and his donkeys he would not oppose the government. But Seyyed Umar had not fought the Taliban. As
Haji Mohsin Khan's man, he had been one of their represen-
tatives.

*

There were five of us in the guest room and for two hours we
sat in silence. It was an overcast afternoon. Seyyed Umar sat
by the large window, clicking his rosary. He shifted his head
to look down at the black ridge, the mud below the river
and the tracks in the snow. Occasionally he sighed or cleared
his throat. Outside a door creaked, a horse whinnied. Half an
hour later, two ragged men came up the hill with donkeys and

33. Haji Gul. He and Dr Ibrahim, who had suddenly become governor of
Ghor, were among the very few who actively fought the Taliban in this
area.

34. Mullah Hussein of Guk.

the children of the village threw snowballs at them. The men who were exhausted and at the end of their day's journey smiled.

Seyyed Umar and the others could not work in the fields because of the snow; they had lived here together since they were children; nothing had happened recently that was worth talking about and they were illiterate so they could not read. They waited in silence throughout the long afternoon for the call to prayer, dinner and bed.

A hundred years ago this valley had been uninhabited. Seyyed Umar's great-grandfather was a mullah who had come here from the mountains in the south. Four local landlords each gave him a plot of land – and on each plot he placed one of his sons and built a village. One of those villages was this one, Garmao, which was given by Haji Mohsin's ancestor and passed eventually to three of the mullah's grandsons – one of whom was sitting in the room with me. There were eighty-two male descendants of the mullah's son in Garmao (Seyyed Umar could not be bothered to count the women) and the plot of land, which had been generous for one man, was now overcrowded. Everyone had either married a cousin from the village or one of their second cousins from one of the other three original villages.

Dramatic differentials of wealth and power had emerged amongst the descendants in forty years. Seyyed Umar was a wealthy man and a much more generous host than his chief, Haji Mohsin. Following the omelette for lunch, he served me a whole chicken (a much more expensive delicacy here than lamb) with rice, a clear beef broth, a bowl of fried lentils and soaked breadcrumbs in rehydrated goat's curd. I had had difficulty getting Haji Mohsin to let me have even a little bread for the dog. Seyyed Umar gave me four loaves for Babur, to which I added a little meat when the others weren't looking. But Seyyed Umar's older first cousin was in rags. He was older than Seyyed Umar and paralysed down his right side. He sat in the corner, muttering to himself over a cleft tongue. He begged money off me and I gave him some.

It was my eleventh day of walking without a day off and despite the generous meal I was beginning to feel rundown. I had had diarrhoea for four days, which seemed to be as a result of giardiasis, and that evening I decided to start a course of antibiotics to try to clear it. My knees were also feeling the strain of the hills and I was preparing to strap them. I had run through all my letters of introduction for this district. The one I had been given by Haji Mohsin had been pocketed by Seyyed Umar. His illiteracy added a double complication: he could not read the letter and he could not write another one for me.

Part Four

The Eimauks are rigid Soonees. In their wars . . . they show a degree of ferocity never heard of among Afghauns. I have authentic accounts of them throwing their prisoners from precipices and shooting them to death with arrows; and on an occasion at which a Zooree with whom I had conversed assisted, they actually drank the warm blood of their victims and rubbed it over their faces and beards.

– Mountstuart Elphinstone,
The Kingdom of Kaubul and its Dependencies, 1815

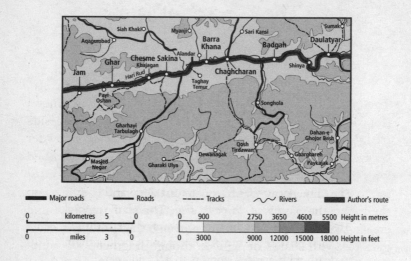

The Minaret of Jam

The next morning the sun had just hit the valley floor when I
stepped out onto the snow with Babur stepping high beside
us. It had been snowing all night and there was virgin powder
on every side. Seyyed Umar rode behind me, heavily swathed
with blankets, on his horse. He was puzzled that I was refusing to ride. The snow was barely a foot deep and the climb up
the hill to the pass was an easy one. The staff trembled and
creaked in my hand as it moved through the snow. The crust
glittered with shards of light as though fragments of windscreen glass had been scattered over the powder.

Halfway up the slope, Babur paused to sniff a jet-black
boulder. His long nose thrust gluttonously through our footprints towards the desert floor, seeking the frozen smells of
vanished animals. Having completed his survey, he raised
his head, stared solemnly into the distance and lifted his leg.
Then, scuttling soil with his front paws to cover his marks,
he walked quickly on, head averted, distancing himself from
the act. A minute later another boulder caught his attention.
We stopped six times in ten minutes.

Babur seemed prepared to examine, mark with urine and
take possession of every metre of the next six hundred kilometres walk. Only once or twice in my eighteen-month walk
across Asia had I felt as though I had some magical claim to
the territory I had touched with my feet. But Babur apparently felt it all the time. The warm stream of urine was set
like a flag to mark his new empire. All his movement was
conquest and occupation. He seemed ready to ponder and

possess every place in the world. He was like a canine Alexander. He had never encountered a space so large or a time so small that it was not possible to sniff and ponder every rock. In this mood, his coat bristling with cold and energy, he strode up to the crest.

At the pass the snow was thicker and Seyyed Umar was forced to dismount before we descended. At the bottom, in a narrow press of orchards, with smaller tighter hills along a winding river, the scale of the peaks and snowfields was suddenly lost. Here, Seyyed Umar spurred ahead. He was very keen for me to get rid of Babur, who he thought was likely to get us killed by packs of village dogs. He said that if I disposed of the dog he'd accompany me all the way to Chaghcharan, but since I insisted on keeping Babur, he regretfully took his leave.

As Seyyed Umar had predicted, dogs swarmed over every orchard wall, teeth bared, and I turned again and again to drive them back. Swinging at another dog, I clipped Babur by mistake and he cowered whimpering at my feet. The day before he'd helped me by barking at the other dogs and trotting along beside me. But from now on whenever I raised the stick to try to protect him, he would lie down terrified, thinking he'd done something wrong and waiting for me to hit him again. This left him very vulnerable to the angry packs and I had now to drag his ten-stone frame with me as I backed up the street throwing stones and lashing out.

*

We left the village, the dogs fell back and beside the road the cliffs closed in and the river twisted more aggressively. For twenty minutes we were walking alone in a deserted maze of narrow gorges, following a small path. Pale yellow cliffs rose on either side. Apart from the brisk clatter of the river, it was silent. There was no human in sight and no sign of the last twenty-four years of Afghan war.

We came around the edge of a scree slope. Then we saw the tower. It rose two hundred feet, sixty-one metres, in a slim column of intricately carved terracotta set with a line of turquoise tiles. There was nothing else. The mountain walls formed a tight circle around it and at its base two rivers, descending from snowy passes, ran through the ravines into wilderness. A dense chain of pentagons, hexagons and diamonds, formed from pale slender bricks, wound around the column. On the neck of the tower, in Persian blue tiles the colour of an Afghan winter sky, were the words: 'Ghiyassudin Muhammad Ibn Sam, King of Kings . . .'

Ghiyassudin was the Sultan of the Ghorid Empire who had built the mosque in Herat, the dervish domes in Chist-e-Sharif and the lost city of the Turquoise Mountain.

I walked around the base of the tower following the tall exuberant chain of polygons, which spelled out (though I couldn't follow the geometrical script) the Arabic text of one of the longest chapters of the Koran.[35] It was as finely worked as an ivory chess piece. The octagonal base, the three storeys, the remains of the balconies and the ornate complexity of the geometrical surface were all subdued by the clean, tapering lines and the beige fired brick. The snow on the ground was in shadow. Only the narrow blue line of mosaic, lit by the bright sun, stood out from the pale coffee-coloured hills. The shape of the circular tower was reflected in the curve of the surrounding cliffs. Just as in Chist-e-Sharif, the Ghorids had used the natural landscape to emphasize the colour and shape of the building.

Although the people that lived in the area had never talked of the tower and none of the nineteenth-century travellers had known of its existence, a foreigner did reach it in 1957. André Maricq's careful study confirmed that this had been the tallest minaret in the world at the time of its construction.

---

35. The Mariam Sura on Mary the mother of Jesus.

Thereafter a number of archaeologists had made the difficult journey, but they were unable to decide how it related to the mysterious Ghorid Empire. The Russian invasion of 1979 stopped further visits.

Some archaeologists concluded that it had been part of a mosque, called it 'the Minaret of Jam' and looked for the Turquoise Mountain in the valley. They discovered very little except, to add to the mystery, a small, twelfth-century Jewish cemetery two kilometres from its base. Others, according to Nancy Dupree in 1978, citing the 'smallness of the valley, its inaccessibility and its absence of significant architectural remains [argued convincingly] that the Turquoise Mountain had been at Taiwara, more than two hundred kilometres south'. Still others asserted that this had been a pre-Muslim holy site and that this was a single victory tower, built by the Ghorids to mark the conversion of a lonely and sacred pagan spot to Islam. The archaeologists did, however, agree on two things: that the tower was a uniquely important piece of early Islamic architecture and that it was in imminent danger of falling down.

By the time of my visit, officers of the Society for the Preservation of Afghan Cultural Heritage had had no reliable reports on the tower of Jam for eight months. In the last decade, much of Afghanistan's cultural heritage had been removed or destroyed; the Kabul museum had been looted and the Taliban had dynamited the Bamiyan Buddhas. No one in Kabul was sure whether the tower was still standing.

*

Leaving Babur to sniff around the base, I clambered up into a hole four feet from the ground and dropped down into a circular staircase. Narrow skylights had been worked into the design above, but here it was dark and the steps were steep, worn and narrow. I had not climbed far when I slipped and came accelerating down in the darkness, cracking my head against the staircase, grabbing at bricks to try to stop myself. I tore the skin from my palm, the bricks came away in my hands and the tower seemed to shake as I hit the outer wall. For a moment I wondered if I would be remembered as the man who died while knocking down the last remaining masterpiece of Ghorid art, then I came to a halt and the tower was still. It was quiet at the bottom of the stairwell and cold. When I started to climb again, I did so slowly, pressing off both brick walls with my arms. My right leg was shaking.

After perhaps a hundred and twenty feet, I came out into a circular chamber from which a second spiral staircase ascended. Here, the smaller brick steps had fallen away from the wall and I had to pull myself up by my arms to get onto a ceiling. I continued, climbing between portions of an old staircase, up over another three chambers, till I emerged just below the lantern. Above me were smoke-blackened wooden beams, which must once have supported an external balcony. I looked out from the skylight and saw on the facing ridge two small ruined towers and, to my surprise, a line of trenches cut into the gravel slope.

*

When I descended and emerged, I found Babur lifting his leg against the base and a man, squatting on the ground, looking warily at him, cradling his Kalashnikov and stroking his long white beard. Standing to greet me, he put his hand to his chest and said, *'Salaam aleikum. Chetor hastid? Be khair hastid?'* very quickly, while I spoke over the top of him saying, *'Jur hastid? Sahat-e-shoma khub ast? Khane khairiat ast? Zinde bashi . . .'* and other politenesses at a rapid pace with no pause for an answer. I gathered that this man was Bushire, the commandant of the area. I had heard of him before. He had led eighty men against the Russians and then during the last five years he had fought the Taliban, while his old commander supplied the Taliban. He had been fighting Seyyed Umar, my host from the previous night. Bushire was not at war at that moment but he was still called 'commandant' and was a power in the valley of Jam.

Bushire invited me to stay and led us across the ice on the Hari Rud River and up the western gorge. We passed one of Bushire's cows, which was carrying a live goat in a saddle-bag. 'We don't have enough grazing land in this valley,' said Bushire, 'so the goat is too hungry and weak to walk.'

Near Bushire's mud house, Babur sniffed around a curious boulder in the snow. I picked it up and found that it was a piece of grey marble carved with a floral frieze. Inside the guest room, we sat on the carpets while his son fed the fierce fire in the stove with dry twigs.

'What are you doing at the moment?' I asked.

'I am a director of a society which has been set up to protect the tower,' Bushire replied. 'We get money from foreigners abroad to preserve its history.'

'And have you found out anything about the history of the tower?'

'Well, we've dug up quite a lot of stuff from the ground.'

'What kind of things?'

'Oh, we've sold most of them to traders from Herat, but I'm sure there are a few pieces left. Son, go and see what there is next door.'

His son, Abdullah, returned with a tray of green tea and some objects wrapped in a cloth. There was a marble slab with a floral pattern (part of the same section as the piece that Babur had found outside); a terracotta ewer, covered with a bold black design of waves and fish eyes; a bronze six-sided dice with five spots on each side; a hemispherical bead carved from bone and a large clay disc, with a peacock in the centre.

'And where are these from?'

'From all over the mountainside.'

After tea, I climbed up the hill beside the tower. The gravel was loose and the slopes steep and I needed to use my hands.

I soon found myself clambering over rough trenches, some almost ten feet deep. Along the rim of the pits were piles of sand and broken fragments of pottery. I passed shards of brilliant yellow porcelain, half a terracotta bowl, a section of ancient guttering and some new spades and pickaxes. Clearly the antique robbers did not steal each other's tools. Those digging had made no attempt to preserve the shape of the buildings they had found; only in a tiny section on the ridge could you even trace the walls of the rooms. The villagers were tunnelling as deep and as quickly as possible to reach whatever lay beneath and destroying a great deal in the process. The trenches, which had been invisible from the base of the tower, now stretched across every slope in sight. The villagers had clearly succeeded where the archaeologists had failed and had uncovered an ancient city.

I was looking down at the pits beneath the tower on the ridge when there was a shout from Abdullah, Bushire's son, as he pushed up the steep slope to join me. 'This was the palace of the princess,' he said as he reached me.

'How do you know?'

'We found an inscription on an old stone here, which a trader deciphered for us. It said that this palace had been built by the daughter of Ghiyassudin the Ghorid.'

'Where is this inscription now?'

'Sold. We have found houses on slopes three kilometres up this valley.'

I followed him along the narrow walls of the trenches, sliding down the steep face towards Bushire's house. 'Do you want this?' asked Abdullah, pausing to pick up a complete terracotta pot.

'No, thank you. Actually I think these things should be in a museum.'

'Indeed,' said Abdullah, 'Do you think you could bring us a metal detector next time you visit?'

That evening, there was a large group in Bushire's house.

Someone had told them I was interested in history and they were hoping for advice on where to dig.

'When did you move here?' I asked.

'A year ago. Before that there were no houses in this place, the slopes are so steep that building is difficult, and so narrow that there is very little sun. We cannot grow crops here and the animals are weak from lack of food. We only moved here to dig.'

'How many of you are digging here?'

'A few hundred. People are now coming down from all the surrounding villages, two hours in each direction.'

'Do you control this?'

'No, no, anyone is free to dig,' said Bushire, who as the commandant had some authority in the area. 'You can have a go yourself.'

'When did you find this city?' I asked.

'Really only in the last two months. We tried to do some digging during the five years when the Taliban were here, but it was difficult. Some of the Taliban mullahs had good links to the antique smugglers but they also killed people for illegal excavations. Now it's fine. There is no government any more and in any case the snow has closed the passes so no outsiders can interfere.'

I was clearly wrong in assuming that the American operations had had little effect on this valley – they had freed up the antique smuggling market.

'And what have you found out about the life of this ruined city?'

'I don't understand. What do you mean?'

I tried again. 'Have you found out roughly what the plan of the city was . . . where the bazaar was, the religious schools?'

'No.'

'The smaller mosques, the gardens, the military barracks?'

'No. You are asking difficult questions. We just dig downwards and we find a jumble of things. It can be very frustrating – yesterday, we dug a pit ten metres wide and didn't find anything worth anything.'

'What did the ordinary houses look like?'

'Like this house – built from mud, but the rooms were very small and crowded, and many of them were multistoried, perhaps because they were built on such a steep cliff. We can sometimes guess which the better houses were from the state of their foundations. But it doesn't help us find the treasure – many of the houses have nothing in them. Nothing at all.'

Abdullah interrupted, 'I think I've found a bathhouse, there were a lot of pumice stones in it and guttering which brought the water up to the ridge from a spring three kilometres away.'

'That is very interesting. Anything else?'

'No.'

'What do you think about the people who lived here?'

'Gamesters,' said Bushire, and everyone laughed in agreement. 'We find so, so many playing pieces like this bronze dice. This old man,' Bushire said pointing to a toothless villager, 'found a whole set of beautifully carved ivory chessmen a month ago, in one of the smallest houses on the hill. Our ancestors weren't Taliban.' The Taliban banned chess. 'And he's just sold a wonderful carved wooden door, one and a half metres high, with tigers and hunting scenes, to a merchant from Herat for a lot of money.'

'How much do you sell these objects for?'

'This,' replied Bushire, holding up the twelfth-century ewer with its bold wave pattern, 'is worth one or two American dollars – good money. That's why we are here. The door or chess pieces can go for more. But it isn't as much as we would like. The people must have taken a lot with them before the city was burned.'

'Burned?'

'Yes. There are charred roof beams in most of the houses.'

'There was once a famous city in Ghor called the Turquoise Mountain, which Genghis burnt and which has been
lost ever since,' I said, not sure whether these people, all of
whom were illiterate, would have heard of it.

'This is the Turquoise Mountain,' said a man from Beidon,
a village eight kilometres away. 'We found it here two months
ago.'

'But the foreign experts in the seventies?'

'We remember them,' replied the old man who had found
the chess pieces. 'There was even a hotel by the minaret
where they used to stay, which we blew up during the war.
I always used to tell the professors that my grandfathers
believed the Turquoise Mountain was here. And they never
listened – why do you think our tribe has always been called
Firokuhi Aimaq (the Aimaq of the Turquoise Mountain)? The
foreigners didn't know how to dig; they worked so slowly,
a few centimetres at a time. All they found were the Jewish
headstones, which were lying above the ground. They should
have worked like us.'

*

'We all heard stories about the Turquoise Mountain, the
Ghorid capital, when we were children,' said another man,
the next morning. 'There were legends of a causeway built of
wooden beams, covering the river for kilometres because the
gorges were too narrow and the passes too steep to get the
camel caravans in any other way. There was a tunnel, which
ran under the minaret, beneath the river and up the hill to the
princess's palace . . .'

'And' the old man interrupted, 'there were two giant
golden birds on the battlements, except one was melted down
to make that cauldron in the mosque in Herat.'

'In my village,' said the man from Beidon, 'we have found
weapons where my father said Genghis's first attack was
defeated. He made his second attack at this very time of year,

while the snow still lay on the ground, sending one army up the old wooden causeway from Kamenj.'

'It was destroyed twice,' Bushire added, 'once by hail-stones and once by Genghis.'

'Three times,' I said. 'You're destroying what remained.'

They all laughed.

Traces in the Ground

If this was the Turquoise Mountain, then the bricks of the minaret were made from the blood of the citizens of Ghazni and the village was digging through the traces of more than just a single Afghan culture. As the capital of a Silk Road empire, the Turquoise Mountain would have contained art imported from all over twelfth-century Asia. The new colours and motifs of Iranian porcelain and the new forms in Seljuk metal would have lain alongside Ghorid innovations in architecture. We know very little about this period because, just as Genghis buried the Turquoise Mountain, he also obliterated the other great cities of the eastern Islamic world, massacring their scholars and artisans, turning the irrigated lands of central Asia into a waterless wilderness and dealing a blow to the Muslim world from which it barely recovered. The Turquoise Mountain could have told us much, not only about Afghanistan but also about the lost glory of the whole of pre-Mongol Asia.

The chronicler Juzjani, who was alive when the city was at its height, wrote that the Friday Mosque was filled with Indian treasure looted from Delhi and that on 'the palace-fortress are placed five pinnacles inlaid with gold and also two gold humae[36] each about the size of a camel'. Juzjani has often

---

36. If the villagers were right these were gilt bronze not gold and were melted to form the famous cauldron in the mosque in Herat. The man credited with commissioning the cauldron was one of the last direct descendants of the Ghorid dynasty and may, therefore, have been reusing a family heirloom two hundred years after the fall of the city.

been accused of making up his description of the city, but the villagers' discoveries suggest he may have been accurate. The huge Friday Mosque beneath the two giant minarets must have filled the entire base of the gorge, straddling the Hari Rud River. Above it, a wall of tightly packed houses must have risen almost vertically to the castles on the ridge line. The city would have reflected the Ghorid sense of architecture in the landscape and their pioneering use of terracotta decoration, calligraphy and tile work. The magnificence of the city can now, however, only be sensed from the grandeur of the lone surviving minaret.

The villagers have already done so much damage with their excavations that the site may never reveal much about the mysterious culture of the Ghorid period. Most of its artistic treasures are on their way through Pakistan and Iran to European markets. But even the scattered debris around their trenches hints at how unusual this culture was.

*

I had thought at Chist that the Ghorids were defying the economic and administrative logic of their time by building in the mountains. But I had not expected them to go to this extreme. The valley floor was barren and hardly a hundred metres wide and provided so little fodder that even Bushire's goat was too weak to walk and had to be carried by the cow. There was barely enough in the valley to support Bushire's family alone. The food and all the goods for the city must have been carried in, either over the snow passes which we had just crossed or, if the villagers were right, on a causeway of planks laid for five kilometres up the Hari Rud River.

The valley walls were steep, prone to landslides and difficult to build on. The lower houses must have received at most an hour's sunlight a day. No easy roads connected the city to the Ghorids' kingdoms in Herat, Bamiyan or Ghazni, still less Delhi. Nevertheless, the villagers' excavations suggested that more people had lived in this remote, unpleasant, impractical gorge eight hundred years ago, than lived in any town in Ghor today. This suggested a great deal about the power of the Ghorids and their desire to emphasize their mountain roots in opposition to their rivals, the nomads of the plains.

The Turquoise Mountain is only the most dramatic victim of a general destruction of Afghanistan's cultural heritage. But the pillaging of Jam (unlike the destruction of the Buddhist sites) was a recent post-Taliban phenomenon. As an Islamic site, Jam had been relatively well protected during the Taliban period. It is the lack of central control following the coalition's operations that has allowed the looting of the Turquoise Mountain to take place. The demand for these objects and the money for the excavations comes from dealers and collectors predominantly in Japan, Britain and the United States. A month after I left the village, items from Jam were being offered on the art market in London, described as Seljuk or Persian to conceal their Afghan origin.

Antiquity looting is an ancient and highly controversial problem and because of the money involved, it is almost impossible to stop.[37] But the situation in Jam is comparatively simple. There is a single, small site of immense historical importance in a remote location that can be manageably enclosed, policed and monitored. Any items reaching the international market from Jam are not chance finds, but deliberately stolen. The local villagers are only earning a dollar or two a day digging and could be employed by an archaeological team to work with an official excavation, rather than against it. Ismail Khan, the most powerful man in the province, does not earn much from the illegal antiquities trade in comparison with the cross-border trade in other

---

37. Ancient because it seems to have been taking place even in 2000 BC Egypt – hence the elaborate security precautions around the pyramids or, later, around King Midas's tomb in Turkey.

items from Herat. He would see providing security at the site as an inexpensive and uncontroversial opportunity to cooperate with the international community. One reasonably energetic and committed foreign archaeologist with decent funds could have stepped in to protect the site any time. I guessed, however, at the time, that the international community would not act before it was too late. I was right.[38]

*

Just before I left the site of the Turquoise Mountain, Abdullah, Bushire's son, showed me three pieces he'd found that morning, which suggested that the Ghorid Dynasty was in some ways more open to the world in the twelfth century than the government in Herat is today. One was a fragment of porcelain, which appeared from the delicate design in underglaze red to have been imported eight hundred years ago from China on a trading route four thousand kilometres long. The other was a coin depicting Zoroastrian fire worshippers, one element in the complex religious patchwork from which the minaret emerged: the Hebrew tombstones showed there had been Jews; the indigenous people had perhaps been Hindus, while the Ghorids' second capital of Bamiyan was dominated

---

38. In 2002 UNESCO, the UN body responsible for cultural heritage, visited Jam, more seminars were held and a 'world heritage site' was announced. But nothing was done to stop the pillage. In mid-August 2002, UNESCO was still refusing to acknowledge the scale of the looting or the quality of the objects removed. As a result, they continue to refer to the minaret as 'possibly a victory tower' and would not concede that the Ghorid capital had been found and was being destroyed. Professor Andrea Bruno, who led the excavations of the seventies and the recent UNESCO visits, still maintained that '"Firozkuh" is only a legend for the moment'. When I confronted him and others at a British Museum seminar in November 2002, I was told that an archaeologist would begin work on the site in April 2003, sixteen months after my visit and long after the villagers had removed everything they could.

by two giant Buddhas.[39] The third piece was a fragment from the rim of a plate. On the surface, cross-legged, in a brightly coloured robe, a man with a halo was preaching in a flower garden. Mani, the founder of the now dead Manichean religion, was associated with bright robes and flower gardens. It has always been assumed that the Manicheans left this area centuries before the Turquoise Mountain, but the shard made me wonder whether they had not survived under the protection of the Ghorids until Genghis's invasion.

'These pieces suggest very interesting things about the culture of the Turquoise Mountain and about Afghanistan,' I said, handing them back to Abdullah.

'I don't know about that,' he replied, 'and I won't be able to sell them. But,' he said smiling, 'I like the man on this plate and I think I'll preserve him.'

---

39. There were a very large number of faiths in medieval Muslim Asia. In the mountains of western Iran and Iraq there are still Yezidis, whose syncretic faith combines Islam, Zoroastrianism and Christianity and centres around the worship of a fallen angel in the form of a peacock. Their idols traditionally included vast bronze birds – reminiscent of the Huma birds on the city walls. The peacock, which they worship, is depicted like the peacock on the Ghorid clay disc that I was shown by Bushire.

Between Jam and Chaghcharan

Babur and I had eaten well at Seyyed Umar's but we were living mostly on dry bread, which did not provide much protein. I had not had a day off to rest in fourteen days and despite the antibiotics my stomach was still very weak. I was looking forward to reaching Chaghcharan, which was the district capital as it had been in Babur the Emperor's day. Although all the roads had been closed by snow, there was an airstrip there and, I had been told, British soldiers and a small mission from the Red Cross. I imagined resting for a day in a private room, talking English and getting Babur some meat, before I continued into the mountains of Hazarajat.

For the next four days we walked on the narrow path to Chaghcharan, which led through the village of Beidon. Judging by the Mongol arrowheads which I was shown in Beidon this was also the route that the Mongol armies took for one of their attacks on the Turquoise Mountain. They, according to Juzjani, surprised the Ghorids by doing the journey, like me, 'when the snow still lay on the ground'. I stayed the first night in Ghar, the second in Chesme Sakina, the third in Barra Khana and reached Chaghcharan on the fourth. It had snowed more heavily in this region and it was higher and we were walking through snow most of the time.

In the Indian Himalayas, villagers had described their landscape in terms of religious myth. 'This hill is where Shiva danced', they said or 'This lake was made by Arjuna's arrow.' But like Abdul Haq in Herat, these Aimaq villagers defined their landscape by acts of violence or death. I was shown the hundred yards which the young Commander Mullah Rahim Dad galloped when mortally wounded, after an ambush by men from Majerkanda, then the grave of a young man who had died of starvation on his way to the refugee camp.

Places in the Scottish Highlands are also remembered by acts of violence: the spot where Stewart of Ardvorlich shot a MacDonald raider or where the MacGregors decapitated Ardvorlich's brother-in-law. Around my house in Scotland the Gaelic place-names record death: 'Place of Mourning' or 'Field of Weeping'. But here the events recorded were only months old.

They were inflicted not by Russians but by one community on another. The settlement of Tangia was now only a line of red mud pillars like giant rotting teeth. The school in Ghar had been destroyed. Everyone knew the men who did these things. They had watched them at it.

*

On the second afternoon after leaving Jam, Babur and I turned from the broad snow-fields of Chesme Sakina into a small side valley, invisible from the main path. When we reached a line of leafless silver poplars along a stream and a small group of mud houses, a man ran towards me crying, 'Welcome, Welcome.' Seizing me by the hand he told one man to feed Babur and led me straight into his guest room, without asking who I was.

This was Dr Paende, a veterinary doctor like Habibullah Sherwal. His room was decorated with Hikmatyar posters attacking Russia and America: 'Let us combine to fling out the Red and Black imperialism'. He lived with two servants and his wounded brother. Dr Paende asked his servants to get some food. They smiled and did not move, and then he smiled and got it himself. While he was out of the room, his servants picked up my jacket and inspected all the pockets minutely.

When they heard him return they sat back in their positions beside the door.

Dr Paende's brother was walking on one leg. He was working for Afghan Aid and had been driving to the road-head in one of their jeeps three months earlier, before the road was closed by snow. He ran into an ambush and took three bullets in the leg. His driver was shot in the head beside him and died 'quite quickly'. Paende had been wealthy enough to send his brother to Pakistan for an operation. He had just emerged from hospital with six pins in his thigh. The attack had been a mistake, he told me. The ambush party thought the jeep belonged to Commander Abdul Salam, who had killed four men from Barra Khana. They were apologetic. Because they were illiterate they had not been able to read the Afghan Aid sign. There was no sense taking this to court.[40]

Dr Paende persuaded his younger servant to guide me. Shortly after dawn we set off across a plateau of fresh snow. It seemed endless and we did not see a track for hours. The snow was deep and came over the tops of my boots. After some time my feet were wet. To our left, a range of mountains ran in a silhouette of waves, endlessly repeated, trough and crest, trough and crest. It stretched for sixty kilometres. I took out my sunglasses, but the guide had none so I lent him mine. The glare from the flat, shadowless snow-plain stopped

---

40. Abdul Salam apparently took his revenge six months after my visit. Residents of Ghor told Human Rights Watch that during late August 2002 a commander under Ismail Khan, whom they called Abdul Salam, attacked a rival commander in a village near Chaghcharan called Barra Khana. He killed the commander, arrested several of his troops, tortured, and then killed them. 'The corpses were returned to the families,' said one of the residents. The troops mutilated some of the detainees while torturing them: 'When the families were given the corpses, they saw that the hands were cut off, eyes were pulled out, ears were cut, and then people understood that they had been tortured terribly in the prison.' Human Rights Watch Report, October 2002.

my seeing more than a few yards ahead. I had no idea whether
we were climbing or descending. After half an hour without
glasses I could hardly see at all. When I closed my eyes lights
danced behind my lids and my head ached. The young man
got lost and it took us two hours more than it should have
done.

Dawn Prayers

After the snow-plain, Dr Paende's guide left me. I pressed on and reached Barra Khana when the sun was still just above the horizon. The snow had melted off the south-facing slopes, revealing a mustard-yellow soil. The snow-peaks were a gentle mauve and the distant mud houses glistened like oil. In the village I was interrogated for half an hour in the street by the headman, Bismillah. When he invited me in, his dogs attacked Babur. I slammed my staff on the ground to scare them away. My staff snapped in the middle and everyone laughed except me. For dinner I was given dry bread and a bowl of water with sugar dissolved in it. Nine people shared the floor with me that night.

My host, Bismillah, woke at half past four and, having gone outside, returned, washed his hands and feet and began praying. The stars were fading slightly and the sky was paler over the snow-peaks but it was not yet morning. I was still exhausted from walking eleven hours the previous day and could have slept more. When he had finished his prayers he put brushwood in the stove and the others, who were sharing the floor with me, hurried to roll their blankets away and then knelt in a line facing west towards Mecca. It was cold and they shivered as they prayed, each speaking and bowing out of sequence.

The mullah chanted a long sura of the Koran, revelling in the guttural sounds of the Arabic. The villagers did not speak Arabic and I suspect that they understood little more than the set phrases: 'In the name of God'; 'the only God' and 'God be praised'. Finally everyone bowed, announced in clear voices 'God is Great', then stood and knelt again and turning to their right and left said, 'Peace be with you' twice.

Then they leaned against the walls, with their blankets draped over their knees against the cold, looking at me with solemn, half-awake eyes and, like Habibullah, they asked me questions, which sounded anthropological but were based on Islamic practice: 'In Scotland, can a widow remarry? How much of her husband's wealth can she keep? Can she marry her husband's brother?'

The mullah told me that he had recited the *mariam sura* about Mary, the mother of Jesus, to show how much Jesus was loved by Muslims. It was the sura which was inscribed on the minaret of Jam.

I went outside. A thin band of yellow light had just appeared on the eastern ridge and the snow glowed under a dark sky. I gave Babur a scratch and he stretched elaborately, groaned, rolled and stood, greeting the morning, facing south, with four gruff barks. This was the village where the brother of Dr Paende had been shot. There were signs that the graveyard on the hill had been recently excavated. Almost every village I passed was digging for antiques, often in old graves. They showed me corroded spearheads, incised terra-cotta pots and bronze bangles that they had removed from the wrists of skeletons.

Dr Amruddin, my host in Ghar three days earlier, was the first man to take me to the private quarters of an Afghan house. As we entered the dark room, with its single oil lamp, the women scattered into the shadows. But I saw that they wore pillbox caps and bright scarves, and had painted their eyebrows with thick bands of black dye. Later Amruddin brought out some highly stylized female heads, which he had excavated on the hill. The heads formed the tops of clay beakers. They were decorated either with white slip on a dark brown background or with bright yellow on a red background. Their eyebrows were defined with exaggerated bands of black glaze. I was shown the same beaker-heads, with the same eyebrows and the same sharp chins, in many villages along the route.

West of Dr Paende's house we passed the 'snake stone' at Dahan-e-Choqur, a four-metre-high pillar of coarse mud and gravel with a head that arched forward, flat like a python's head. They had found a pre-Islamic burial site beside it. Snake cults are the earliest surviving religions in the Indian Himalayas.[41] I wondered if there had been one here too.

But again the villagers were not interested in recording or preserving historical evidence. They were digging up things from very different periods. They had found people buried eight or nine to a grave with wooden bowls and they had found tiny mud houses with pottery, but were these sites related? Who made the bowls that depicted men on horseback with lances? Were they the same men whose lances and helmets and shields they had found?

I spent half an hour handling a fragment from a vase, which must once have been two feet in diameter. It was decorated in black, cream, red and brown. In the centre of a circle neatly drawn in black on white were two isosceles triangles, one equilateral triangle with a ribbed edge, a spiral, an oblong and a human eye. The geometric forms were elegantly balanced by the surreal eye. It was presumably pre-Islamic, but again there was no clue as to which Afghan culture had been responsible for this strange and confident symbolic composition.

---

41. And are important for the peacock-worshipping Yezidis.

Little Lord

The only feudal lord whom I spoke to at length between Jam and Chaghcharan was a twelve-year-old.[42] He had been summoned from Pakistan to meet his father, Rais Salam Khan, and he had been riding for a month with a small group of retainers. I met him in the village of Beidon, where they had found the Mongol arrowheads. His father, a brother-in-law of Commandant Haji Mohsin Khan of Kamenj, was not a popular man. A number of the villagers had told me that he had stolen land, had collaborated with the Taliban and was now in hiding because he had killed some of Ismail Khan's men. But his twelve-year-old boy was riding towards Chaghcharan like a young prince.

The boy entered the room in which I was sitting, followed by six bodyguards. His long fawn coat was identical to the one worn by his uncle, Haji Mohsin, but in this case, it emphasized how small he was. I stood to greet him and he acknowledged this by putting his small hand in mine before taking the senior position in the room. I felt very large and unwashed

---

42. I had barely met the great commanders and chiefs of the area. My hosts were all minor Aimaq headmen who owned small holdings like Bismillah in Barra Khana who ran a mechanics shop, and Dr Amruddin and Dr Paende who were vets like Dr Habibullah Sherwal. On the first day, I saw a chief's son cantering his white horse slowly across the snow but he did not approach me. On the second day, an old chief rode past me across the snow with a column of armed men running behind him. He told me that he and the others were on their way to Herat, where they had been summoned to meet the new president.

beside him. He introduced himself in a sing-song unbroken voice then added in English, 'It is rather dirty here. Are you not displeased?'

'I like it very much. Do you not?'

'I am not really familiar with this. I study at a boarding school in Pakistan. A madressah for Koran and English.' He stroked the black down of hair on his cheeks. I had not heard anyone speak English for a fortnight. 'A most excellent school. I like Pakistan very much. We have a big house in Peshawar. But I fear these people are only village people. They are not educated or civilized people. Yes,' he concluded, 'I prefer Pakistan.'

'Well you mustn't say so. They would be disappointed.'

'I'm afraid they would,' he said, frowning, 'but then they cannot speak English and you would not tell them what I said? Please.'

'Of course not.'

'Good. I like you.'

'Why are you here?'

'Because my father summoned me. I have not been in Afghanistan for four years. This is all quite unfamiliar to me. I have had to come in from Quetta to Herat. I think my father is in trouble. He wanted me to return to help. I would rather remain in school. But I am already twelve and I am the eldest son. What can I do?'

'Where are your brothers?'

'In Pakistan. Tell me please where are you going?'

'To Chaghcharan.'

'Then you should travel with me. I am going to Chaghcharan. You can keep me company.'

'When are you going?'

'I will arrive there in about a fortnight. It is not safe at the moment. We are going to visit some of my father's estates before I join him there. You will come with me. I can practise my English and you will stay with my father and me in Chaghcharan.'

'I am afraid I would like to be in Chaghcharan sooner than that.'

'How soon?'

'Three days.'

'But how can you go so fast? You don't have a horse. I will give you my horse.'

'Thank you but really I must walk.'

'I had hoped you would be my friend. I have no friends here. They are all very old.'

An old man appeared at the door and whispered 'Your Excellency' to the young boy.

'This is my retainer,' said the boy. 'He is a fine man who knows many things. You must meet him. Abdul this is Rory, a Scotsman, who is walking across Asia.'

'Peace be with you,' said Abdul. 'But your Excellency, it is time for us to go. It is getting dark and the path will be dangerous for us.'

'Yes. Yes. Well then I hope to see you in Chaghcharan.'

I never saw him again and when I last heard his father was still on the run from the coalition and from Ismail Khan.

*

Perhaps because I was sick, I was often irritated by villagers and village hospitality. On the fourteenth day, when I came off the snow-plains after five hours walking and turned into a village hoping to get some lunch, I was left standing in the snow with my pack on my back for half an hour while the headman decided whether to speak to me and another villager told me I would never make it to Barra Khana by dark. Finally I shouted, 'Right that's it. If there's no welcome here, I'm off to Barra Khana now,' and began to walk away. Only then did he invite me in and give me some dry bread. After the meal I walked off to a gully, a necessity with diarrhoea, and half the village followed to watch me defecate. Back in the village, the headman's son asked if he could try my camera and proceeded to finish the roll of film by pointing the camera at the ground and clicking again and again. I now had only one roll to see me to Kabul. I was angry for the rest of the day. That night I dreamed that I was buying a plane ticket to Venice.

*

On the last day before Chaghcharan, Babur and I were alone again, following a track into a snow-plain and squinting into the morning sun. Babur paused frequently to chase smells in the cold wind or to relieve himself. I turned around a number of times to take in the rich light on the low hills, to look at our footsteps in the snow or to readjust my pack. It was twenty minutes before we found our stride and settled into the silence and the space. There was no birdsong and the high, dark blue sky was empty. The only sound was the regular groan of my pack and the creak of firm snow beneath our feet.

We reached a village. It was fifteen kilometres to the next village and I wanted to let Babur drink. Off the path, the snow was knee-deep and, perhaps because he was wary of mines, Babur walked carefully behind me in my footprints. The Hari Rud was frozen and it took a number of blows to break the ice with the stump of my staff. Babur simply stood, head up, staring at the mountains. I tried to pull him down and he pulled back. We had found no water the afternoon before and I knew that we had a whole day without water ahead. I squatted by the new icehole. Hoping the sound would interest him, I splashed the water and dripped some on his nose. Eventually, he spreadeagled his front legs in the snow, cautiously stretched his neck forward and began to drink. He drank for three minutes.

As we re-emerged from the snow-fields onto the track, we were stopped by a man with a Kalashnikov, leading a group of young men. 'Hey, boy! Where are you taking that dog?'

'To Kabul,' I said.

He came closer and stared at me. Not too close, because he was wary of Babur.

'You're a foreigner, aren't you?' the man said.

'Yes, I'm from Inglistan (Britain).'

'From Hindustan (India)...' he said thoughtfully.

'No, Inglistan.'

'Yes.' Most people in this area had not heard of Britain, though they had heard of America. Some had even heard of the World Trade Center, but they had no real concept of what it had been or why the coalition had bombed Afghanistan. The man paused for a moment and then suddenly shouted, 'Give me your dog.'

'No, this is my dog, he goes with me. I'm taking him to Inglistan.'

'Give me your dog, and you can go free,' he said again. Babur and the crowd watched us, impassively.

'What is this?' I shouted back. 'Who do you think you are? This dog was given to me by Bismillah of Barra Khana. I was a guest in his house last night. He is my close friend. If you have any questions you talk to Bismillah.' I barely knew Bismillah and Babur was not Bismillah's dog, but the man seemed suddenly uncertain, perhaps because a man with a demeaning animal was speaking with the confidence of a village headman.

'What is this? Who is this?' he said to the young men.

'We heard a foreigner was in Barra Khana at Bismillah's last night.'

'And this is Bismillah's dog.'

'Perhaps . . .'

'It is, indeed.' I said coldly. 'Now if you'll excuse me . . .' and I stepped past him. Babur was lying down but I was in too much of a hurry to plead with the dog. I yanked at his collar, dragging him through the snow, until he found his feet and we strode off. Shouting at people could be dangerous. For ten minutes, I was waiting to hear a voice or a shot from behind me, but they never came.

Frogs

I reached Chaghcharan, the capital of Ghor, after a lonely walk down a series of gorges just before dusk. The town consisted of a scattering of mud and brick compounds alongside the river. I walked towards the airfield to the east of the town. Fair-haired men in jeans carrying large automatic weapons were feeding an Afghan dog with cornbeef hash from a British army ration pack.

They looked at me walking in with Babur, stinking in Afghan clothes, and one of them said: 'Who the fuck is this?' in a cockney accent.

I replied in English and, when they had stopped laughing, one of them asked if I was working for the British government. I said I wasn't. I was on holiday.

'Like fuck you're on holiday,' he said, and they laughed some more.

I had heard about these men at the Chaghcharan airfield in many of the villages along the way. The villagers liked them. The headman of Barra Khana, Bismillah, had said: 'British soldiers have chests as broad as horses. We wish there were more of them to keep the peace. Every morning they hook their feet over the bumper of their jeep, put their hands on the ground and push themselves up and down on their hands two hundred times without stopping. I don't know why.'

These men were not in a position to discuss what they were doing, so I didn't ask them any questions and didn't hang around. They were in a difficult situation, dropped by helicopter and left for months in the middle of Afghanistan with the nearest back-up two hundred kilometres away, but they didn't show it. They brewed me a cup of Tetley's tea with milk and gave me a giant bar of Cadbury's Dairy Milk, and I told them a little about my journey. They seemed to enjoy the story. They were funny and relaxed. I liked them and it was refreshing to be able to talk English. When I left, they gave me an airport thriller, some rations, some Wagon Wheels in a Marks and Spencer bag and some meat for Babur. It was a fine welcome to Chaghcharan.

*

The Taliban captured Chaghcharan in 1995 and immediately executed sixty-four members of the Northern Alliance who had surrendered their weapons. On 20 October 2001, three months before my arrival, the Taliban retreated. Some of the people of Chaghcharan came out to celebrate prematurely. A returning Taliban column saw them in the main bazaar and killed forty-four of them between midday and two in the afternoon.

As I walked through the bazaar, I saw a number of fair-haired children. Afghans are often fair-haired. They sometimes say it is because they are descended from Alexander's troops, but there were probably blonde inhabitants here before Alexander's arrival.[43] The marines at the airfield, however, thought they were descended from the Russians who had been based in Chaghcharan when it was one of the few permanent Russian bases in the interior of Afghanistan. Some of the Afghans in the bazaar told me that a Russian had deserted, converted to Islam, and was still in Chaghcharan

43. The Chinese chroniclers long before the birth of Christ describe the barbarians in Mongolia as red-headed and archaeologists have excavated 4,000-year-old bodies with red hair preserved by the dry air in northwest China.

twelve years after the Russian withdrawal. They wouldn't tell me where he lived.

That night I found the other foreigners in town. The office of the International Committee of the Red Cross consisted of a Swiss manager, a Dutchman and Colin, who was from somewhere near London. They all seemed to have worked in Rwanda. Now they were coordinating food aid and running flights in and out of Chaghcharan, which was the centre of the 'hunger belt' where the relief agencies had predicted so many famine-related deaths. The snow had blocked the roads and you could only get to the town by plane or on foot. These men had one hundred and seventy-five trucks, loaded with grain, stuck in the snow on the road from Herat. The next day the bazaar heard that I knew the Red Cross and I was besieged with requests for extra ration tickets.

The ICRC men did not seem interested in making their own lives more comfortable. They wouldn't buy local meat or fruit in the bazaar because they said it was too expensive. They were opposed to importing foreign food on their airlifts. For a month they had been living mostly on rice and *nan* bread, supplemented with brown sachets of strawberry jam. They did not seem to be very interested in the history or culture of the area. They did not socialize with the soldiers, because they wanted to remain neutral. It must have been quite depressing. But they were very kind to me. They shared their rice dinner with me and, against regulations, let me sleep on their office floor, and gave me some food to take away.

*

The following afternoon the third pillar of the international involvement in Afghanistan arrived in two giant Chinooks. The choppers swept in low over the hills from the east, with machine-gunners seated on the open rear ramps. Two foreign civilians in their thirties emerged flanked by soldiers. One was a German in a Chitrali cap. The other was a large Irishman, bare-headed in *shalwar kemis*. These were the political officers of the United Nations.

The agreement setting up the future shape of Afghanistan had been signed in Bonn a month earlier. In five months there was to be a 'Loya Jirga' assembly to choose a new government. Lakhdar Brahimi, the UN Special Representative who was running this process, had staffed his Political Affairs office with some of the most experienced expatriates in Afghanistan: people who spoke Dari or Pashto well, had worked there for years and had experience of village culture. But there were few of them and they had to manage the conflicting interests of foreign governments, other UN agencies, warlords, international organizations and Afghan technocrats. They knew too much of the reality on the ground to be popular either with the new Afghan government or the international bureaucracy. By the end of the year they had been moved sideways into almost meaningless jobs.

At this point, however, they were still in charge. They were driven down in jeeps to the only concrete building in town. Its flat roof was packed to the edges with spectators, and there were heads crammed into every window and a crowd of a thousand in the forecourt. They stepped out of the jeeps and moved down the crowd, shaking hands. They sat in the front row. It was a sunny day and everyone was enjoying the warmth.

The Irishman stood at the microphone to explain the Loya Jirga process in Dari and, as he did so, caught the eyes of the three foreigners in the crowd: Colin from ICRC, me and one of the military team from the airfield. He smiled. We smiled back, each I suppose surprised at being in the middle of Afghanistan.

The Irishman explained to the audience that they could select a new kind of representative for the Loya Jirga. Traditionally this assembly has been dominated by feudal landlords and district chiefs like Commandant Haji Mohsin

Khan of Kamenj. The plan was for more ordinary people to be nominated, including women. Everyone applauded. I wondered, however, whether anyone thought it was possible. Haji Mohsin certainly intended to go to the Loya Jirga and it would be a brave villager who stood against him. Three months later, three of the new Loya Jirga delegates from Ghor were killed by local militia before they could reach the assembly in Kabul.

Dr Ibrahim, the new governor of Ghor, who wore a turban and a pair of large aviator sunglasses, stood to talk about democracy.

'Don't use the word "democracy". It is un-Islamic,' shouted a mullah beside him.

'Democracy is not an Arabic word; it is English,' replied Dr Ibrahim.

'Well in that case it's all right,' said the Mullah. I don't suppose this exchange meant anything to anyone but everyone seemed satisfied.

Half an hour later the helicopters took off again.

*

I left Chaghcharan the following morning. I had had two days off, but had not experienced the rest I had hoped for. I had spent a night on the floor of the night watchman's room in the ICRC compound, a cold night in a swept-out donkey stable in the centre of town and one night in the office of Afghan Aid. But my hosts were busy and wanted me to clear out early in the morning. During the days I had nothing to do but limp between the two teahouses in the bazaar with my pack on my back and Babur behind me. I had kept the metal top and bottom of my walking stick when I broke it and I persuaded the ironmongers to fix them to a new pole. I wrote nothing in my diary. I had a bad migraine; everything I tried to eat made me sick, so for a day and a half I ate nothing.

The Windy Place

Any regrets I had about leaving Chaghcharan faded after half an hour on the road. My pack was still heavy, the hills tall and Babur reluctant, but I felt with the familiar motion of my muscles confidence and ease returning. The road ran gently up from the Hari Rud onto a flat plateau and then into rolling hills. Among the pug marks, footprints and hoof blows on the pale track, melting snow had left patches of dark, glutinous mud. To my right the same line of mountain peaks was curling, falling and rising again, in a silhouette, as regular as waves or ocean liners, heading east.

I pressed through a group of teenage donkey drivers in shabby turbans with dust-caked faces. They were fighting about who would ride the donkeys. When they saw me they poked Babur with their sticks, whistled, shouted questions, beat their donkeys so they careered into the side of my pack nearly toppling me over and told me I would never make it to Badgah by dark.

We soon left them behind. After another hour I sat down beside a mud wall and opened a green packet of army biscuits marked 'Biscuits Fruit S'. I didn't feel up to eating more than one so I offered the rest to Babur. He wouldn't touch them. Finally, in the late afternoon, we came down into a valley, with an old mud caravanserai at the base and two mud towers on the slopes above. The Hari Rud was mostly frozen and there was a line of bare silver poplars along the bank. A shepherd sat by the ice, playing a flute.

This was Badgah, 'the windy place', the home of

Commandant Haji Maududi, who had once been with the Pakistani-supported warlord Gulbuddin Hikmatyar, and was now the owner of the only Stinger missiles in Ghor. I had a letter to him but he was away. We found his sixteen-year-old son in their mill. His hair and clothes were covered in a thick dusting of flour and he was very uncertain what to do with me, but after a long delay he led me to a guest room and then left me for the rest of the evening. He did not come to say goodbye the next day. I was grateful to be left alone.

The next morning it began to snow again. I turned off after ten minutes of walking to let Babur drink. Just above us the river was frozen. We watched four men from a neighbouring village stamp across the thirty-foot width of ice without pause. Then we turned away from the Hari Rud, following a gorge through low hills. A gentle snow-hail started. Black hairs rose on Babur's golden coat and each one had a small ball of ice at its tip. But for some time the weather was still warm enough for me to walk without a coat. Then the hail strengthened and I pulled a coat out of my pack. We continued for about three hours through winding, brown, snow-stained hills, with the sun hidden in thick cloud. We had been luckier so far with the snow than the Emperor Babur:

> *The farther we advanced, the deeper was the snow. At Chaghcharan the snow reached above the horses' knees. Two or three days after Chaghcharan the snow became excessively deep; it reached up above the stirrups. In many places, the horses' feet did not reach the ground and the snow continued to fall.*
>
> *One Sultan Pashai was our guide. I do not know whether it was from old age, or from his heart failing, or from the unusual depth of snow, but having once lost the road he never could find it again, so as to point out the way. We had taken this road on the recommendation of Qasim Beg [Babur's ancient chancellor]. So, anxious to preserve their reputation, he and his sons dismounted, and after beating down the snow, discovered a road, by which we advanced. Next day, as there was much snow, and*

the road was not to be found with all our exertions, we were
brought to a complete stand.

Babur the dog, in the heart of the blizzard, stopped to savour
the bouquet of a wet grass hummock. The weather shifted
and as we moved on, so did the sharp angles of the slopes,
revealing new valleys on each side. My mind flitted from half-
remembered poetry to memories of things I had done of
which I was ashamed. I stumbled on the uneven path. I lifted
my eyes to the sky behind the peaks and felt the silence. This
is what I had imagined a wilderness to be.

At midday I reached the village of Gandab and from
there left the road and took the narrow footpath up into the
mountains. 'Stay high and right,' said the villagers. 'Don't be
tempted by the path to your left.'

Halfway up the mountain the snow fell faster, obliterating
the line of footprints that I had been following. Babur and I
stumbled again and again into drifts, which were three or four
feet deep, so we were both drenched. Visibility was down to
fifty yards. Eventually we reached a ridge and a sudden clearing in the clouds revealed some peaks. But there was no sign
of any path or village. Nine hundred feet above to my right
was what appeared to be the shoulder of the mountain and a
potential pass. I started up the hill through deep snow, sinking
on every step and making slow progress. The powder slopes
below seemed very long.

On this slope Babur lay down and wouldn't move. The
weather was closing in again and it was snowing harder. I
leaned over him. He was shivering and sucking air into his
lungs and panting in an asthmatic wheeze. The fit continued
for two minutes, while I held him and he trembled and fought
for breath, and then it passed and he was able to stand again.
I thought we should turn down the hill. But I could see no
promising path.

We were both tired and cold and we would be pressed to

reach Daulatyar by dusk. We were supposed to be travelling east so I set off on a traverse across a slope, dragging Babur behind me, hoping there were no crevasses. After half an hour of stumbling through more deep powder, we came over a lip. The fog lifted again and we could see on the next ridge a line of footprints heading downhill. We began to follow the prints and a little later, to my delight, saw an arrow of dark purple rock pointing into a village and tiny figures moving among the stands of poplars on the bank of the Hari Rud. We ran and slid down the snow-slopes into the broad valley of Shinia.

From the village, I kept moving east, walking across two half-frozen streams, jumping the cracks in the ice. Babur was reluctant and I struggled to drag him across the ice. We were now walking through hard sleet. Fog descended and the low hills on either side were hidden.

We came onto a vehicle track. Tyre-tracks had gouged the earth, leaving a glutinous dark-brown strip perhaps twenty feet wide. Because my boots stuck to the mud, I walked on the ice that had formed on the roadside ditches. This was better, except when the ice broke and soaked my feet in cold water. Babur was now coated in black mud. We had been walking for nine hours.

There were only another fifteen kilometres to Daulatyar and probably two hours of daylight left but I had forgotten how much deep mud and wet snow could slow my pace. I felt muffled in the snow-fog and imprisoned by the rain hood that I was wearing. I threw back the hood. I could hear and see again. The day was very silent and the plain seemed very large. The snow driving into my eyes at a forty-five-degree angle made me feel much freer, but my left foot seemed to be frozen to a cold, rigid iron plate.

Exhaustion and repetition created within the pain a space of calm exhilaration and control. And at this point, I saw two jeeps, weaving slowly towards us through the fog, over the rough track with their headlights on. They were the first vehicles I'd seen since Chaghcharan and the first people I'd seen for hours. When they reached me, an electric window went down. It was the Special Forces team from the airstrip.

'You,' said the driver, 'are a fucking nutter.' Then he smiled and drove on, leaving me in the snow. I had seen these men at work when I was in the army and in the Foreign Office and I couldn't imagine a better compliment. I walked on in a good mood.

*

We reached Daulatyar just after dark. This was the last Aimaq village before the Hazara areas. Its headman was Rauf Abdul Ghafuri. Everyone had spoken about him in Chaghcharan, emphasizing his feudal background,[44] his position on the frontier and his connections with the Hazara. 'He knows the Hazara Begs [their chiefs],' they said. They implied that dealing with the Hazara was a strange and dangerous thing. They made him sound like a Yankee colonel on the edge of Sioux territory.

Rauf Abdul Ghafuri did not enter the guest room immediately and when he did it was with an air of condescension that I had not seen since I left Haji Mohsin Khan. There were a number of other men in the guest room, all of whom leaped quickly to their feet. He shook my hand with the others but he did not attempt to speak to me. I went outside to check on Babur.

My relationship with Babur was developing. He was never a playful dog and he growled if I ever came near his food, but he was beginning to trust me. If anyone else approached he would back away. That night I was able to lift him into a

---

44. He is a wealthy military commander from a feudal family. His uncle, who had held the village before him, was imprisoned by the Russians in Chaghcharan and executed.

manger and tuck a blanket around him, and in return he rubbed his great head against mine.

I was very proud of him. Although he had drunk some of the bad water that had given me dysentery, he had just walked a twelve-hour day without a break, crossing a ten-thousand-foot pass through snow four feet deep. But I was still not certain that he would be strong enough to complete the journey.

He was a type of mastiff, bred to fight and guard against wolves, dogs and other humans. I did not think he was designed to walk thirty to forty kilometres every day. His was a very ancient breed. In build he resembled the Tibetan mastiffs, which the Romans had imported along the Silk Road, and in temperament the English mastiffs which the Celts had used to fight the Romans. The mastiff is perhaps the oldest breed of dog in the world. There are mastiffs on early Egyptian wall paintings and on the friezes of the Assyrians. His closest living relative is the Anatolian mastiff shepherd, a breed that has spread right across the kingdom of Alexander from Turkey, where they are called Kangal or Karabash (meaning black-faced), to Uzbekistan. There is a copy of a Greek statue of a mastiff of the period of Alexander in the British Museum. It is two and a half feet high at the shoulder. It is sitting with its great paws in front of it and its hindquarters folded sideways. It has cocked its head. Its ears and tail, like Babur's, have been cut off.

From now on people would refer to him as a Sag-e-Aimaq – an Aimaq dog – with some awe – recognizing from his size that he came from Ghor. The dogs of Ghor are mentioned in the earliest descriptions of the province and were always regarded as particularly special mastiffs. According to the Seljuk chroniclers of the eleventh century, there was: 'A *remarkably fine breed of dogs in Ghor so powerful that in frame and strength every one of them is a match for a lion.*'

The king of the Turquoise Mountain had two Ghor dogs, one named after him and one after the ruler of Ghazni. He would make them fight. It was dangerous to be around him on days when his namesake lost. These dogs formed part of the tribute from the Ghorids to the Seljuk and became such proverbial parts of Islamic culture that a medieval scholar is recorded as saying that 'Avicenna could not fight with a dog from Ghor'.

The next morning, having pulled on my two pairs of wet socks and my wet boots, I walked outside to the manger and called. Babur didn't come out. He was lying in his own vomit, with pus filling his bloodshot eyes and thick saliva flapping from his muzzle.

I couldn't bear to leave Babur so I delayed a few hours hoping he would recover and drew a picture of Abdul Rauf Ghafuri. Unlike my other sitters, he insisted on keeping it. I gave the commander a cigar. He hadn't seen one before, but put it hastily in his pocket without thanking me, which was a kind of compliment.

Part Five

The country of the Hazaurehs . . . violent Sheeahs
. . . is still more rugged than that of the Eimauks. The
sterility of the soil and the severity of the climate are
equally unfavourable to husbandry. Their women . . .
have an ascendancy unexampled in the neighbouring
countries . . . there prevails a custom called Kooroo
Bistaun by which the husband lends his wife to the
embraces of his guest. The Hazara are very passionate, and exceedingly fickle and capricious.

– Mountstuart Elphinstone,
The Kingdom of Kaubul and its Dependencies, 1815

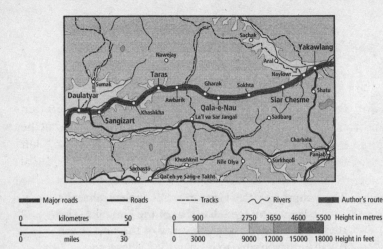

Days 20 & 21 – Sangizart

Day 22 – Taras

Day 23 – Qala-e-Nau

Day 24 – Siar Chesme

Day 25 – Yakawlang

Name-Navigation

Four hours later, having slept, Babur looked much better, and the various villagers who inspected him agreed that he could manage a short day. At about eleven, Babur and I left the vehicle track behind and turned into the long Sar Jangal valley.[45] Babur was walking well. In the early afternoon we entered a settlement where, for the first time, I saw women in the streets. They wore bright pillbox hats and clothes decked with silver. Rather than covering their faces, they stood still and watched me. I noticed how pale their skin was and how, unusually for Afghans, they had slender Mongolian eyes. One of the girls smiled. In the central square were stocky men with broad ruddy faces and high cheekbones. They immediately invited me into the mosque. It was the first mosque that I had been invited to in Afghanistan. These people were the Hazara.

Their ancestors were probably colonists from Mongolia, who arrived in central Afghanistan with the armies of Genghis Khan, displacing the previous occupants.[46] When Babur, the Emperor, encountered the Hazara they dominated a large area

---

45. We had left the central route here to take a short cut. The normal vehicle central route runs from Daulatyar to Lal. We only rejoined a branch of this road a week later at Yakawlang.

46. The 1911 Britannica states, 'The Hazara are of Mongolian origin . . . descendants of military colonists introduced by Jenghiz Khan . . . they have absolutely displaced the former inhabitants of Hazarajat and Ghor.' I had initially assumed this was just another racial myth. The nineteenth century was particularly keen on the idea of whole races migrating homogenously. Hence the attempt to argue that the Neolithic people

between Ghor, Kabul and Ghazni. Some still spoke Mongol but they were mostly Persian-speaking. Their heartland was ruled by the chess-mad Zulnun Arghun.

Babur had probably been in a village close to this one, about fifty kilometres beyond Chaghcharan, when he sent a party of sixty or seventy men to try to find some Hazara who might be prepared to guide him. They returned alone. This was probably because the Hazara feared and hated him.[47] With reason. This is Babur's diary from the previous winter:

> *The Turkoman Hazara had erected their winter habitations in the valley of Kesh and we now pushed forward to fall on them.*
>
> *A fat hairless camel belonging to the Hazara was found, brought in and killed. We ate part of it roast, part of it sun-dried. I never ate such fine-flavoured camel's flesh: many could not distinguish it from mutton . . .*
>
> *In a narrow defile, the Hazara fortified and strengthened a ford with branches of trees . . . But Qasim Beg [Babur's old chancellor] discovered a ford and having gained a footing on the opposite side, no sooner charged with his horse than the Hazara, unable to keep their ground, took flight. The party that had got in among them, followed in close pursuit, dismounted and cut down large numbers of them . . . we fell in with the sheep and herds of horses of the Hazara near their winter habitations, I collected for my own share to the number of four or*

---

whose beaker-style pottery has been excavated in Europe were ethnically distinct from their predecessors. I assumed that much more intermarriage with the previous inhabitants took place in all these encounters. But the facial features of the Hazara are so distinctive that it does indeed appear that they drove out their predecessors. Babur, who knew them well, writes that 'among the Hazara are some who speak Mongol' – implying that they had a strong Mongol ingredient, but that by 1507 they were mostly speaking Persian.

47. This is also suggested by the fact that he thought it necessary to send sixty or seventy armed men just to find a Hazara guide.

five hundred sheep and twenty or twenty-five horses ... The
wives and the little children of the Hazara escaped on foot to
the snow-covered hillocks and there remained. We were rather
remiss in following them.[48]

Although there are three and a half million Hazara, they are
the least-known people of Afghanistan. This is in part because
they are concentrated in the high, isolated central mountains.
Until the late nineteenth century, despite the efforts of rulers
such as Babur, Hazarajat was in practice an independent
country. An intensive military campaign by the Afghan king,
Abdul Rahman, in the 1880s finally conquered them and
incorporated them into Afghanistan. He gave much of their
land to the Pashtun, made many of them slaves and left them
as the poorest of the four ethnic groups in Afghanistan.[49]

For the next hundred years, it was fashionable to describe
the Hazara as ineffectual, cowardly and irrelevant. During
the Russian war, foreign journalists, who tended to enter
Afghanistan from Pakistan in the east, could only usually
reach the Tajik or Pashtun communities and, therefore, hardly
acknowledged the existence of the Hazara in their report-
ing. Then, in the mid-1990s, the Hazara seized parts of Kabul,
and other Afghan ethnic groups began to describe them as
vicious and inhumane. 'They are Mongols,' one said to me,

---

48. He continues:

A few Hazara lay in ambush in a cave near the valley. Sheikh Dervish my foster-
brother who had been in many an action with me, had gone up close to the mouth
of the den, without suspecting anything, when a Hazara from within shot him
with an arrow under the nipple, and he died the same day ... [Later] I directed
[some soldiers] to proceed and take the Hazara who had shot Sheikh Dervish.
These wretches, whose blood had curdled through fear, still remained in the cave.
Our people on coming up, filled the cave with smoke, took seventy or eighty
Hazara, and passed the greater number under the edge of the sword.

49. In the nineteenth century, the Pashtun dominated the court and were
exempt from taxes, while the Hazara in the capital were largely slaves or
manual labourers.

'and therefore they are as cruel as their ancestor Genghis Khan.'

The Taliban evicted the Hazara from Kabul in 1996, and in 1998 seized the Hazara capital at Bamiyan, forcing the Hazara resistance into the hills or into Iran. The Hazara were once again the victims and the Taliban treated them with particular brutality. This was in part because the Hazara were mostly Shia, unlike the majority of Afghans who are Sunni Muslims. The Hazara Shia saw themselves as more civilized, more mystical, more tolerant towards women and other faiths than the Sunni Taliban. The Taliban saw the Shia as heretics or even infidel.[50] They thought their Shia reverence for saints' shrines and pictures of the Prophet's family, and their respect for the twelve Imams, or leaders, was idol worship. They believed that the wailing and self-flagellation in their processions, and the small clay discs which they placed beneath their foreheads when they prayed, were signs of superstition.

Hatred between Shia and Sunni is not uniquely Afghan. I had watched the Pakistani military manning truck-mounted machine guns to stop Sunni radicals from attacking Shia Moharram processions in Sahiwal in the Punjab. In Hazarajat, the religious violence had a strong ethnic and cultural component. The Taliban, who were mostly Pashtun, despised the Hazara for their Mongol features, their traditions and their behaviour in Kabul.[51]

No Sunni ever invited me into a mosque on my walk, but in Hazarajat I was usually asked into a mosque long before I was invited into a home. This had been true in Shia areas in Iran. In this case, an old Hazara man sat me on the prayer

---

50. The Taliban leader in Mazar made an explicit statement about this and encouraged 'good Muslims' to exterminate or convert them.

51. It is difficult to generalize about either Shia or Sunni Islam. The dispute was originally over who had been the legitimate successor of the Prophet

floor and went to get some tea. As we sipped and chatted, three men were praying in the corner and another three were asleep. I asked the old man about the route ahead and he listed the villages and the distances between them.

'How far have you come from and where are you going?'

'I am walking from Herat to Kabul.'

'By foot? You are at the very mid-point. I was told by my grandfather that it is fifteen *farsang* from here to Herat and fifteen days on foot from here to Kabul. My grandfather could recite every night's halt of the month's journey. I'm sorry he is no longer alive to speak to you.'

*

I was not carrying a detailed map because I did not want to be thought a spy, and I was concerned that Babur the Emperor had lost his way on the stretch between Chaghcharan and Yakawlang. I had, therefore, been discussing routes and

---

Muhammad in the seventh century. But each sect had gathered its own collection of traditions and practices over fourteen centuries. Some Christian observers saw the Sunnis as the Protestant and the Shia as the Catholic sections of Islam. They pointed to the authority of the ayatollah priests in the Shia tradition and their emotional and colourful penances, their incorporation of local traditions and their concern with saints and miracles. But others saw the Shia as Protestants: reformers who had returned to the original religion of the Prophet when the earlier Sunni tradition had been corrupted by power.

This conflict between the two sects, whatever its theological basis, is an old theme in Afghan history. The Ghorids of the Turquoise Mountain were Sunni and had aggressively persecuted Shia in their region. A Shia movement, called the Assassins after its enthusiasm for hashish, then claimed credit for murdering Muizuddin, the Ghorid prince and conqueror of India. (Ironically, this was a rare case of one mountain power destroying another. The Assassins were based in the remote country of the Elburz and led by the 'old man of the mountain'. The Ghorids were governed by the malik-e-jabal, 'the king of the mountains'. The Mongols destroyed both.)

distances in the teahouses in Chaghcharan with Aimaq men, who knew all the villages on the main road from Yakawlang through Lal.

Three days earlier, in Chaghcharan, an old man, overhearing us, said, 'Are you really walking?'

'Yes.'

'Then forget the road,' he said, 'because you don't want to go to Lal at all . . . it will add two days to your journey at least. You should turn off the vehicle track at my home at Daulatyar, which is only two days walk from here, and walk on the ancient path straight up the Sar Jangal valley and then cross the high pass into Yakawlang. You could do it in a week.'

'Have you done this route?' I asked.

'Not all of it but I was told about it by my father.'

'It would not be safe for us. We have been fighting the Hazara,' added a young Aimaq man.

I turned back to the old man. 'Can you give me the names of the big men in that valley?'

'Mir Ali Hussein Beg is the greatest man in the Sar Jangal valley.'

'Can I reach him in a day's walk from Daulatyar?'

'No,' he laughed, 'he is three days beyond Daulatyar. In a day you could get to Mukhtar, the place of Mirza Beg, and then to Charasiab, home of Abdul Rezak Khan.'

'No, no, Hamid Khan at Dahan Gulamak,' shouted another old man from the other end of the room.

'Then Mir Ali Hussein Beg at Katlish,' continued the first man.

Everyone nodded in agreement and repeated, 'Yes, Mir Ali Hussein Beg.'

'Then Ghulam Haider Khan at Shahi Murri,' continued the old man.

'No,' interrupted another, 'Wakil Hadim Beg at Espiab first.'

I looked at the old man. He shrugged.

'Wakil Hadim?' I asked writing it down.

'Perhaps I have that wrong . . . not Wakil Hadim . . . Wazir Beg.'

'Then Shahi Murri,' repeated the old man, 'one day and then you are in Yakawlang.'

They were describing more than a hundred kilometres through villages that they had been unable to visit in twenty-five years, and which belonged to the Hazara whom they mistrusted. Much of the route they knew only from tales told in their fathers' guest rooms, but everyone had memorized a chant of names and villages along footpaths in every direction. This was a very useful map. It specified everything in terms of a man on foot: the best tracks, the distances you could walk in a day, whom you should speak to in each village. It was less accurate the further you were from the speaker's home (in this case they said it was only one day from the castle of Mir Ali Hussein Beg to Yakawlang, when it was four, because they didn't know the names of the villages in between). But I was able to add details from villages along the way, till I could chant the stages from memory:

> *Day one: Commandant Maududi in Badgah. Day two: Abdul Rauf Ghafuri in Daulatyar. Day three: Bushire Khan in Sang-izard. Day four: Mir Ali Hussein Beg of Katlish. Day five: Haji Nasir-i-Yazduni Beg of Qala-e-Nau. Day six: Seyyed Kerbalahi of Siar Chisme . . .*

I recited and followed this song-of-the-places-in-between as a map. I chanted it even after I had left the villages, using the list as credentials. Almost everyone recognized the names, even from a hundred kilometres away. Being able to chant it made me half belong: it reassured hosts who were not sure whether to take me in and it suggested to anyone who thought of attacking me that I was linked to powerful names. But they were the names of living men and different names provoked different reactions. 'How do you know Mir Ali Hussein Beg? Who told you to call Haji Nasir "Beg"?'

All the men on the list lived in mud forts, mostly on the valley floor by the Hari Rud River but occasionally high on the slope above their villages. They were the old tribal chieftains of the Hazara people and the most senior of them were called 'Begs' like Babur's ancient chancellor Qasim Beg, a Turkic word for a leader.

The Greeting of Strangers

The Aimaq had frequently complained about the Hazara hospitality, but I had been very impressed by the welcome in the mosque. That afternoon I met a group of ten-year-old boys on the outskirts of a village and asked one where Sangizart was. He said he didn't know, which surprised me. It was supposed to be close. As soon as I turned he flung a stone which hit me on the back of the head.

I shouted, 'How dare you? Where is your father?'

'I don't have one.'

I tried to catch him and he ran up the hill followed by his friends. When I turned again, they all threw stones at me and howled the Aabag wolf cry to make their dogs attack Babur, sending a pack in full tongue streaming down the slope towards us. And while Babur raged and I lashed out with my stick, an old man from the village sat calmly watching.

This was the first time in eighteen months of walking that anyone had ever thrown a stone at me and it was only my second Hazara village. I ran up the hill towards the grandfather, with the children sprinting away in front of me. 'Why don't you stop your children,' I shouted. 'Is this how Hazara treat a traveller?'

The old man shrugged. Various adults emerged from their houses to watch. Another village dog leapt on to Babur's back and I hit him hard with my stick so that he limped away. The men said, 'Kids will be kids. Why did you bring a dog? It's your fault. That's what encouraged them.' I wondered if they would have reacted any differently if one of the stones had cut open my head.

★

Half an hour further along the road, I reached another small bazaar where three young Hazara men were standing. One of them came straight up to me and smiled a little too easily and asked me whether I was tired and where I was going. Usually people were wary of me and the dog, but he was very confident. I answered and walked on.

After a few minutes, the path turned into a narrow gorge beside the Hari Rud. The sun was about to set. There were no houses, just a scree slope and the cliff falling on my left towards the water. I looked back and I noticed that the three men were following me. I continued. There was a sudden crash behind me. I started, turned and saw that they had dropped a boulder into the river. I stopped and waited for them.

'What is your name?' I asked the one who had spoken to me.

'My name?' said the man smiling more broadly.

'Yes. What is your name?'

'My name is . . . Muhammad.'

'And yours?' I asked the second.

'Aziz,' he said and simultaneously the first man said, 'No, his name is Hussein.'

'What village are you from?'

'One of the villages ahead.'

'What is its name?'

'Its name?'

'Yes. What is the name of your village?'

'Emir Beg.'

'Where is Sangizart?'

'Two days' walk away.'

I slowed my pace and so did they and when I stopped to tie

my shoe lace they gathered around. One of them was whispering to the others. I turned around and saw a man coming along the path, three hundred yards behind us. I didn't like these three men so I turned around and started walking back towards the other man.

They sauntered on a little way and then stopped, waiting to see what I would do. The man coming towards me was an old Hazara, with a wispy white beard.

'Peace be with you,' I said to the man. He was quite old.

'And with you,' he muttered, and tried to step past me as though he did not like being stopped, on this path at dusk.

'I am from Scotland,' I said, 'I am a traveller, a guest in your country, can I walk with you?'

He took a couple of steps as though he was going to ignore me and then stopped and looked at me and Babur. 'Yes. Walk with me.'

I walked on beside the old man and the three men began walking again ahead of us.

'Those three,' I said, 'are they from one of the villages ahead?'

'No they are from the village behind us. They are bad men.'

'And what is its name?'

'Mukhtar.'

It began snowing. We walked on together in silence. After a few minutes we reached a group of houses. The three men turned around and saw that I was still talking and walking alongside the old man. They were only wearing shirts and could not have been comfortable standing in the snowstorm.

After a moment, they shuffled towards a house, went inside and closed the door.

'Where is Sang-i-zard?' I asked.

'About half an hour's walk away. Would you like to stay with me in this village?' asked the old man, 'This snowstorm will not stop for a couple of days.'

'Thank you, but I should keep going.'

'God be with you.'

The snow kept falling and the three men did not follow
me.

*

It was twilight when I saw a village on a slope on the far bank
of the Hari Rud River. The valley was narrow and its sides
were steep. Where the ice had broken were dark, troubled
patches of quickly moving water. The river was thirty feet
across and there was no bridge. Babur and I crossed on a
narrow, snow-dusted causeway of ice, then climbed up
through the snow to the edge of the village. The houses were
low mud huts, cut into the hill. Snow lay in drifts up the walls
and over the flat roofs, covering the twigs and the dried dung,
which had been stored for fuel. The snow on the path had
melted, revealing a mixture of mud and human excrement.
Perhaps because it was so cold, there was no smell.

This was Sang-i-zard. There were no canals, gardens or
avenues of trees, such as those near Obey. The fields were
narrow. Qasim had called the irrigated flatlands 'poor'. This
was a much poorer place. We walked up the steep path to the
castle gate, followed by a large crowd of children.

The castle walls were about forty feet high. At each corner
was a round tower topped with battlements. Through the
gate, which was twice the height of a man, came a group of
women with pale Chinese faces. They ran at the children
and hit them with thorn switches. The children scattered. I
stepped into the courtyard, which seemed very small for such
a large castle.

I showed the eldest woman my introduction letters from
Abdul Rauf Gafuri, the wealthy commander of Daulatyar.
'You can leave your dog here but you cannot stay here,'
she said, 'my husband is away. You will have to sleep in the
mosque.'

I settled Babur in a stable and then returned to the mosque at the bottom of the hill, where I took off my wet socks and sat on the prayer rugs. I was drenched and the mosque was cold. As soon as I sat down I began to feel ill. I wondered when I could change out of my wet clothes. For an hour I watched the prayers and answered questions about my journey and then I was asked by a man called Akbar to stay in his house.

He lived at the edge of the village. The house was built on two storeys with a pair of living rooms above and a large sheep pen below. There was only one sheep in the pen.

I took off my *shalwar kemis*, put on my extra clothes and hung the wet set near the stove. Then Akbar fed me a rich bean soup. As I ate, his women gathered along the walls to watch me. One of them was breastfeeding her baby. Akbar's grandmother asked me where I came from. The Aimaq had told me that, 'the Hazara have a quite uncivilized attitude to women'. Perhaps they were referring to the old myth that the Hazara lent their wives to their guests. Perhaps they merely meant that Hazara women talk to guests.

This was the first time I had been allowed in the same room as a woman in an Afghan village. I wondered if this was not one of the few legacies of Mongol customs among the Hazara. In a Mongol tent, women play a prominent, respected and noisy part in conversation.

On his guest-room wall, Akbar had a photograph of himself taken five years before. It had been hand-tinted in the studio so that his pink cheeks and lime green jacket were highlighted by the backdrop of a vivid tropical sunset sky.

Leaves on the Ceiling

Nine times during the night, I had to clamber over Akbar, who was sleeping by the door, to go to the loo. I groped my way down the unlit stairs, past the sheep pen, opened the heavy wooden doors and stumbled into the continuing snowstorm. The candles in the village had been extinguished shortly after dusk and there was no light anywhere. My dysentery was so bad that I twice soiled my trousers before I could get to the door. I was losing a lot of fluid and none of the antibiotics or antispasmodics that I was taking seemed to be curing me. The nearest primary medical care was three days' walk in the wrong direction and they would not have the appropriate drugs. I had to hope I could recover by myself. I wondered whether this was going to be the way that I would die.

It had now been snowing for most of the previous three days and it was still snowing hard the next morning. The villagers insisted that I should not try to walk through the storm and, for once, I was pleased to take their advice. I was invited to rest in the castle guest room and spent most of the day on my back on the floor. The castle could not afford much fuel and therefore did not light the stove although I was allowed to light a small fire. It was as cold as any Scottish castle. I wore my coat indoors but I kept shivering.

The ceiling of the castle, which I stared at for hours, was made from a frame of poplar branches, which still had the brown, curled leaves attached. The bare mud floor was partly covered by a shabby striped blanket, two pieces of dark felt and a small cheap rug in the Bokhara style. In the corner, under a grimy white sheet, was a stack of mattresses. The walls were undecorated, except for a photograph of my absent host, the feudal lord, Bushire Khan, with a pencil-thin moustache and trilby hat. He looked like a 1930s Shanghai gangster.

My fever made everything slow and indistinct. I could not follow a train of thought for more than a moment without it collapsing into surreal and disconnected events. I kept seeing myself stumbling for hours through snow with occasional interruptions by angry dogs. I wondered if it was going to be the same all the way to Kabul.

That afternoon a young man entered and shook me awake. 'I am sick, what can you give me?' he asked.

'I am not a doctor,' I said.

'You have medicines. We have seen you take them.'

'What is wrong with you?' I asked.

'My whole body is aching,' he replied.

I gave him two of my eight Ibuprofen tablets and closed my eyes. I was woken again by an ancient lady dressed in what seemed to be seven layers of cotton printed cloth. She was seated on the ground with her thin legs stuck in front of her. 'I am sick,' she said.

'What is wrong with you?'

'My whole body is aching.'

I took out my six remaining Ibuprofen and gave her two of them. She snatched the other four as well. I took them back from her.

She moaned at me about the unkindness of the world and about her pain: so I found a Panadol at the bottom of my bag and gave her that.

A man with a scarred face entered, stooping under the low lintel. He was called Mohammed Amir and he was wearing faded camouflage trousers and a black bomber jacket. He lectured me on the drought, the wrecked fields and the empty wells, and made me write down statistics about the harvest:

'eight thousand tokm-roi-Zamin' I wrote in my diary. I didn't understand what the words meant except they had something to do with land yields. Then he asked me to get help from international organizations in Kabul and requested some pills for the wife of a friend. He said she had very bad diarrhoea and I handed over my last course of antibiotics, gloomily because I felt I needed them myself. He asked me to draw him, which I did although I found it difficult to concentrate on the page.

*

I woke later feeling a little better to find a girl by the fire. She looked about seventeen. Her beautiful pale face was scrunched in concentration as she crumbled the dry animal dung into the hearth. Both her hair and eyebrows were very black, as though she had dyed them. On her head was a gold cap wrapped in a blue embroidered turban. Over her dress of blue chintz she wore a purple waistcoat and a green embroidered wool cardigan. I could see that beneath the skirt she was wearing a pair of blue corduroy trousers. She raised her head and met my eyes. I smiled. She looked at me expressionlessly and then turned and left the room.

The next day, a different young girl with dark eyes watched me talking to her father. She wore a long necklace of artificial pearls over a purple waistcoat, embroidered with gold and silver thread. She held the pearls in her hand and swung them slowly from side to side, staring at me all the time. I looked back as I left the room and said goodbye to her but she turned away, smiling, and did not reply.

Flames

That night Bushire's old uncle slept in the room with me and snored throughout the night. I woke feeling rested and more cheerful. I walked outside into bright sunshine to find that the children had let Babur out of the stable and that he was prancing on the roof of the castle. He did not usually respond when I called but this time he came running down when he saw me.

Inside, the flames were bright beneath the blackened kettle in the dusty room. The old uncle was warming his socks by the fire and stroking the few wispy tufts of hair that grew on his jaw and upper lip. Other Afghans mock the Hazara for being unable to grow proper beards. When we sat down to our bread and tea, I asked him about the chiefs of the area.

'I am sorry,' he said, 'do not judge this castle and this family by its current position. The owners are Begs, chiefs of the Blackfoot tribe of Hazara, descended from Muhammad Ali Beg Tehsildar of Sang-i-zard, Tehsildar for King Abdul Rahman and hereditary chiefs of two thousand households. One of four great families in this valley with Daulatyar, Mir Ali Hussein Beg at Taras and my own family at Mukhtar.'

'And now?'

'They cannot afford the firewood for one stove to heat the castle guest room.'

'Why?'

'Because they did not fight well in the wars.'

'Were the Russians here?'

'No. The fighting was between and within villages. The Iranians gave arms to mullahs and paid them to take land away from the feudal Begs and give it to the people. This family has lost everything in the last ten years, all their flocks and all their land. This castle is all that remains.'

'And who has their land now?'

'Our new commander. He lives in a house down in the bottom of the village and no one can touch him.'

My host asked a man called Nadir to guide me from Sangizart. It was very cold. When we set out from the castle, Babur blinked and turned away from the wind and I pulled my blanket up around my face. It was difficult to judge the temperature but I guessed it was about minus twenty.

Perhaps because I was rested, I was unusually aware of the landscape that day. A dark blue sky stretched over snow, and where the sun fell the furrows in the earth showed like shadows on white velvet. We walked on the ice in the very centre of the Hari Rud for about an hour, the snow being so thick that you could only guess where the banks lay. Babur described such conditions in his first attack on the Hazara:

> That winter the snow lay very deep, which rendered it danger-
> ous to leave the common road. The banks of the stream about
> the ford were all covered with ice and it was impossible to pass
> the river at any place off the road, on account of the ice and the
> snow . . .

By the Hari Rud were tall stands of bushes that resembled dogwood. Their branches were orange and yellow and they rose like stands of flame out of the river ice. There were silver-trunked willows, too, with dark brown buds and a few pale gold leaves that clattered like cicada wings in the freezing wind. As the snow melted in the sun, the Hari Rud became at first a clean turquoise ice sheet and then a torrent of black-blue water. We climbed onto the bank.

For our first couple of hours on land, the snow crust held us but after a while we were plunging up to our knees, so we began to step in the compacted footprints of other people who had used the path that morning. Sometimes we passed a pair of bright nylon flags on the hill, which marked the site of a martyr's grave.

Despite my protests, Nadir carried my pack for the first three hours. Until that time I had always carried my own pack in Afghanistan, but I was grateful for the rest. I took it back off him for the next five hours until we saw the coffee-coloured walls of Taras castle, dwarfed by mountain slopes which were piled with smooth scoops of snow like ice cream.

The castle guards were keen for me to stay with them but when I found that none of the Beg's family were at Taras, I decided to press on to Mir Ali Hussein's other castle at Katlish. I thought that there would be better food and conversation there than in the guard room and I wanted to try to get a letter of recommendation from the Begs since they were the most important rulers in the valley. Nadir and the villagers tried to dissuade me, saying it was an hour till dark and four hours' walk to Katlish. But something about their tone suggested this was not true.

Babur, however, was less keen on continuing. He lay down in the snow and refused to move. I tried to pull his lead but he remained immobile. I half lifted him and finally in an effort to get some movement into his exhausted limbs, dragged him stumbling down a snow slope to what I thought was a snow field where, to the delighted screams of the village, he and I fell through the ice into the Hari Rud.

We pressed on for the next hour, very wet. The sun had left our bank of the Hari Rud and the wind was strong. There was a strong mauve light on the peaks above us. We reached Katlish just after dark. People were reluctant to find shelter for Babur but I insisted. He must have been very cold by the time the argument was resolved because it went on for some time. I was relieved when I could dry him, get him some food, put him to bed and go inside myself.

Zia of Katlish

That night I was again asked to sleep in the mosque beside the castle. Zia, the twenty-year-old nephew of the feudal lord Mir Ali Hussein Beg, apologized and said it was only because his castle was unheated, but it seemed to me that visitors usually slept in the mosque. The mosque functioned not only as a chapel and a guesthouse but also as a dining hall, a conference room and a school. There was a blackboard on the wall and a small embroidery of the Kabaa at Mecca. The walls were of scratched mud, stained with grease and dimpled with marks, which resembled worm casts and moth holes. In Iran there would have been posters of Ayatollah Khomeini, but here there was no government figure to idolize, no father of the nation, no king. Nevertheless, the Beg had clearly spent money on the mosque: it had a felt carpet, three full-length windows and plaster flowers on the ceiling.

As if to confirm its secular aspect, three ibex heads with curling three-foot horns hung in the atrium. The ibex, a very large mountain goat, is with the snow leopard the most revered of the Asian mountain animals. It once lived right along Asia's bird-shaped mountain massif from Afghanistan to the Hazara's original homeland in Mongolia. Like snow leopards, however, they are now almost extinct: there were certainly none left in this area.[52]

---

52. The ibex is a very common motif in Mongol art and pickled ibex blood, thick, half-congealed red liquor, which I find difficult to swallow, is considered by the Mongols to be a very powerful tonic.

About forty men gathered in the mosque that evening. Zia sat at the head of the room with me on his right and the mullah on his left. The villagers were well wrapped for the winter. The older men wore hemp trousers on their legs and thick socks knitted by their own wives, which they tied with wool at the calf. Camouflage trousers were worn by many of the younger men. All had put on vests, shirts, cardigans, waist-coats and jackets, one on top of the other, and they may have had some more layers underneath. They had wrapped their black turbans under their chins and over their ears, framing faces that were lined, tanned and bearded. Villagers don't wash in the winter. There was a strong smell.

Zia wore a neat, embroidered prayer hat and a fancy acrylic cardigan, which looked as if it had come from a Tehran shopping arcade. His face was pale and he was the first clean-shaven Afghan I had seen since Abdul Haq. He opened the conversation. I had listened again and again to ponderous old men delivering speeches about the goodness of Islam; the glory of the jihad; the need for medicines and development aid and the fact that Afghanistan was destroyed, while their listeners chimed in, in chorus, on the more familiar phrases. Zia, however, seemed to think as he spoke.

'We have, I think, to be grateful for the American intervention,' he said slowly, 'because for a moment at least there is peace.'

'There is peace because the Taliban have gone?' I asked.

'No . . . The Taliban were not a trouble here. They came twice on operations to collect weapons as part of their disarmament programme . . . but after that they never visited the valley.'

'Then who caused the violence?'

'We did ourselves.'

'And the Russians,' interrupted a young man.

'Yes, during the 1980s this mosque and the castle were hit by rockets from Russian attack helicopters, but we were not

fighting each other. Things began to collapse after that time –
people rebelled against their tribal chiefs . . .'

'Sang-i-zard,' said the man on my right.

'Yes, in Sang-i-zard, where you stayed last night . . . the
Begs have lost all their land and power . . .'

'But the Begs haven't lost out here,' chimed in the young
man, and they all laughed.

Zia the Beg continued, 'But there were fights also between
different villages in this valley. We have killed thirty men from
Sang-i-zard and they have killed ten of us, so we still have a
blood vendetta with them. We have not been able to walk
from end to end of the road which you are walking for
twenty-five years because it has been too dangerous for us. It
is only safe for you because you are a stranger. We could be
killed if we went to Sang-i-zard. And the same if we walked
east. But . . . there has been no killing in two months. People
are too scared of the Americans.'

'What next?' I asked.

'We don't know,' said a villager.

'We are waiting to see whether the government will force
us to return the land and the flocks which we have stolen from
each other over the last twenty-five years,' said Zia. 'That will
be difficult. And yet without it the vendettas will continue.'

'I disagree,' said a villager. 'Are you a Muslim?'

No one worried about interrupting, teasing or contra-
dicting Zia, despite the fact that he was their feudal lord.
Everyone felt easy about starting their own conversations or
asking me a question. It seemed that even a decision to rob
another village, or kill, would happen after discussion, reasoning and disagreement. But when dinner was announced,
everyone fell silent.

Zia asked four men to go to the castle kitchen and another
to spread a cloth and bread in front of the two of us. They
moved immediately. It was clear that, despite the chatter,
Zia was respected. One man entered with a silver ewer and

platter, poured warm water over our hands and dried them with a clean white towel. Others carried in rice, a large bowl heaped with the best cuts of mutton specially selected for me, another plate with ribs and kidneys, a mound of fresh cold yoghurt and some 'Cadbury's Eclair' sweets from Iran. When I finished the yoghurt, more yoghurt was brought.

On my last six days and nights in Afghan houses, Babur and I had been fed only bread for breakfast and lunch. For supper we had occasionally had plain rice, but we had eaten no meat, vegetables or fruit. Now I was tasting the food of a great feudal chief. It was far beyond the means of the men who sat watching. I was very grateful for the generosity and for the protein. I wanted to take some meat to Babur, but meat was very precious and the villagers would have been angry to see it fed to a dog.

At dawn, the young men remained on their mattresses for an extra half hour lie-in, while the older men prayed. I stepped outside. The light, in a curving blaze of orange and lurid yellow, reached from the eastern ridge, strong and high, into a mass of grey cloud. A descending magpie swept his wings forward, so that he hovered for a moment above the snow crust before touching the ground. I had not seen a bird since Kamenj. Everyone was hungry and carried a gun and this was not beneficial for the wildlife. For breakfast, because I had mentioned that we ate eggs in Britain, fried eggs were produced laid on a bed of onions, and two men sat beside me to ensure that my tea cup was filled and to provide me with generous helpings of sugar for each cup.

*

For the fourth day in a row, Babur and I walked for eight hours on narrow paths, hammered by footsteps into a bed of ice between three-foot walls of snow. This time I was accompanied by Hussein Ali, a broad-shouldered, middle-aged man from the castle. Now that I was further from the road and deeper into the Sar Jangal valley, every feudal chief seemed to see it as his obligation to provide me with an escort to the next chief, so that I was being passed like a parcel down the line. These men were willing to walk a full day through the snow to accompany me and then a full day back in the other direction. I always insisted they took some money, but they were clear that they were doing it for me as a traveller and it was sometimes difficult to persuade them to accept.

Babur was limping. I stopped to massage his left foreleg and thereafter he moved a little better but still slowly and I was again worried for him. I too was feeling lethargic. Because the sun fell full on to the left of the ice path, melting it, the path sloped to the left-hand side: a tendency exaggerated by subsequent travellers. I slipped every few steps over the next eight hours and I didn't like it.

Hussein wore a thick, quilted coat, a blanket wrapped around his head, huge sunglasses with the manufacturer's sticker still in place in the centre of each lens and a pair of rubber galoshes which did not seem to keep out the snow. He was more tired than either of us and we had to keep stopping for him to catch up. I gave him some of the Dairy Milk, which the British soldiers had given me in Chaghcharan, and it seemed to speed him a little, though Babur didn't like it. I was pleased to have Hussein's company. But even though I was accompanied by a Hazara, children still threw stones at us in every village and called their dogs down on Babur.

The Sacred Guest

That evening we came down a cliff and across a wooden bridge to the castle of Qala-e-Nau, and Hussein Ali left. I led Babur down to drink in the Hari Rud, terrifying a woman who had crouched under the bridge to go to the loo. When I reached the courtyard of the mosque, some men and children appeared and stared at me in silence. I asked to see Haji Nasir, to whom I had a letter of introduction. None of them moved or spoke. I asked if there was somewhere I could put Babur and they replied, 'Nowhere.'

'But surely you have animal sheds . . . where are they?'
Silence.
'Where is Haji Nasir?' I asked.
'Perhaps in the mosque.'
I left Babur outside because he was considered unclean and walked into the mosque. When I had unlaced and removed my heavy boots in the hall and entered, I found Haji Nasir waiting for me. He was a slender, elderly man. I took out my letter of introduction and gave it to him.

'I am walking to Yakawlang,' I said.
Silence. I waited for him to invite me to stay in his village. He said nothing.
Finally, I asked, 'Can I stay here?'
'We shall see.'
'I have a dog, is there somewhere I can put him?'
'Nowhere.'
'Any blanket for him?'
'No.'

'Please.'

Finally, he told me to take Babur to the cellars of the castle: a catacomb of sprawling chambers, occupied by some sheep. The men who led me were too scared to approach Babur, but they indicated that I could put him in the final cellar. He lay down immediately on some straw and fell asleep.

Then I re-entered the mosque and took off my iced and soaking socks. Haji Nasir watched. He did not suggest that I could dry them before the morning on a stove; he did not offer tea. I clearly needed to persuade him that I was worth speaking to. We were nine days' walk from Kamenj and had just reached a village which had not heard of Haji Mohsin Khan, so I dropped him from my introductory speech.

'I have walked here from Chaghcharan,' I said. 'On the first night I stayed with Commandant Maududi in Badgah, on the second with Abdul Rauf Ghafuri in Daulatyar, on the third with Bushire Khan in Sang-i-zard, and last night with the nephew of Mir Ali Hussein Beg in Katlish. They have treated me very well.'

Then I took out my notebook and showed him the pictures, which I had drawn of these men.

He looked at the pictures and then said, 'You can stay here tonight and someone will bring you some tea,' then he walked into the inner room of the mosque to pray.

*

In all the countries through which I travelled I had been told with pride that, 'we [the Iranians, or the Pakistanis or Indians or Nepalis or Afghans] are famous for being the most hospitable and generous people in the world. It is a religious duty for us. Everyone will welcome you immediately into their houses. You will be treated like a God.'

But this was not my experience. Hospitality and generosity were formal religious obligations. Most communities, whether Islamic or Hindu, and Muslims, talked a great deal about their responsibility to a *mosaffer* (a traveller), or a *meman* (a guest). But in practice people often welcomed me reluctantly. This was understandable: they were often very poor, lived tough lives and were suspicious of the few strangers whom they had met. I was often disappointed by their hospitality. It was only later that I began to see how fortunate I was that they provided me almost every night with shelter and some bread to eat.

*

The following day, although the snow remained waist deep on either side of the ice track, it was so hot that I walked in my shirt. My dysentery had slowed under the impact of the antispasmodic pills, but I was still feeling weak. A couple of young men fell in with me on the path. One shouted, 'Give me some money.'

I said I didn't have any.

'What are you doing?'

'I am writing a book.'

'Give me your book.'

'I only have notebooks.'

'Give us the notebooks.'

I stepped around him off the path and sank to my waist in snow; Babur fell forward and sank out of sight.

'Take me to England with you,' the boy shouted.

'You don't have a passport.'

'Give me a passport.'

'I'm sorry.' By now I had dug Babur out and staggered past the boy on to the road.

'Give me your boots.'

I pushed ahead while they discussed what they should ask me for. They seemed to believe that, if they only guessed the right thing, I would give it to them, and they followed me for two hours. Finally, I stopped to rest Babur and they sat down beside me. I handed them my last two pieces of Cadbury's

Dairy Milk. They chewed a little before spitting it out, throwing the remains on to the snow and asking, 'Can we have your sunglasses?' They seemed to have a surprisingly developed concept of the tourist for two boys who had never left Afghanistan. Strangers had opened conversations by asking for money and a passport many times in Nepal, but this was my first such conversation in Afghanistan.

At midday they gave up and left me by a simple mud mausoleum. It was built in honour of a traveller who had died in the snow here. The villagers had found his frozen corpse and decided on the basis of his clothes and books that he was a holy man. They guessed he was a wandering Sufi, but they couldn't tell me whether he had been a Chistiyah. Pilgrims now come to the shrine to ask for children or cures and to bathe in the hot spring near the shrine, which is called 'Boiling Blood'.

Here too the villagers found statues of women's heads with exaggerated black eyebrows, like the ones that Dr Amruddin had excavated in Ghar. Although the death of the saint proved what a lonely area it could be in the winter, the heads implied that the hot spring had been inhabited for a very long time. The similarity between these heads and those one hundred kilometres west suggested that a single Neolithic culture may once have dominated all the mountains between there and Jam.

The Cave of Zarin

I was told that I was now only two or three days from Yakawlang. So far I seemed to have been much luckier than either the Emperor Babur or the saint: days of bright sun after the latest snowstorm had left the powder crust only two feet deep and the path through the snow was clear. Babur the Emperor was, like me, relying on the worn ice track as a path, but fresh snow had hidden it and he was unable to find a guide to help him as he continued up the Sar Jangal valley:

> Placing our reliance on God and sending on Sultan Pashai before us, we again advanced by that very road in which formerly we had been stopped and forced to return. In the few days that followed, many were the hardships and difficulties that we endured: indeed, such hardships and sufferings as I have scarcely undergone at any other period in my life. I wrote a poem then:
>
> > There is no violence or injury of fortune
> > That I have not experienced.
> > This broken heart has endured them all.
> > Alas, is there one left that I have not encountered?
>
> For about a week, we continued pressing down the snow without being able to advance more than a Kos (two miles) or a Kos and a half... Qasim Beg [his aged chancellor] and his two sons and two or three of his servants dismounted with me and we all worked in beating down the snow. Every step we sank up to the middle or the breast, but we still went on trampling down. As

the vigour of the person who went first was generally expended after he had advanced a few paces, he stood still, while another advanced and took his place. The ten, fifteen or twenty people who succeeded in trampling down the snow, next succeeded in dragging on a horse without a rider ... the rest of the troops, even our best men and many that bore the title Beg, without dismounting, advanced along the road that had been beaten for them, hanging down their heads. This was no time for plaguing them or employing authority. Anyone with any spirit would have worked.

Given that Babur emerged two days later at the pass to Yakawlang he must have been not far from the village in which I was standing, possibly in a parallel valley. Three hours before dusk, with the clouds closing in, we climbed steeply up from Shahi into much deeper snow. My pack often threw me off balance. Babur was less sure-footed than me and we both slipped frequently into the deep powder. We were soon climbing beyond the last houses up a long slope that led over a ridge and descended down the side of a large snow bowl. A beggar from the shrine had accompanied us up the path shouting 'Uncle' and pulling at the back of my pack. He left us by a thin line of frozen water, beneath a snow-covered rock at the bottom of the slope. This, he said, was the source of the Hari Rud River.

I had now been following the Hari Rud for nearly a month from six thousand feet below us.[53] I had seen Abdul Haq carry Aziz through it when it was in a shallow bed between canals and poppy fields. This was the river that flowed past Babur's house. I had crossed it where it was frozen in the narrow gorge, beneath the minaret of Jam. We had fallen into it through the ice below the castle of the Hazara chief Mir Ali Hussein Beg. Now we were leaving it behind.

---

53. Beyond Herat, the Hari Rud forms the border between Afghanistan and Iran and then the border with Turkmenistan.

Before he left, the beggar pointed to a cliff, the only piece of steep bare rock amongst the snow, and said that if I climbed up its face and turned north, I would reach a village after two hours. I stood for a while and watched his tiny dark figure climb up out of the bowl, pause for a moment on the ridge and drop out of sight. It was half past four in the afternoon, it had begun to snow again and Babur and I were alone. I was not certain that we would reach a village before dark and it would be an uncomfortable night outside.

With my first step towards the cliff, I found myself buried up to my chest. I swung my pack off my back, pulled myself out until I was lying flat on the snow, managed two more steps, and then sank again. Babur struggled along behind me. Since it was only two and a half feet from his shoulder to the ground, he had more difficulty struggling out and I had to haul him by his scruff. It took us twenty minutes to reach the cliff. At its base, I found there was a steep slope running up its east side. Babur began to climb ahead of me and I followed. My thigh muscles were burning so we rested by the mouth of a cave. We were at the base of the watershed between the Hari Rud and the Zarin valley. I was grateful that the snow was gentler than it had been for Babur the Emperor:

When we reached the cave of Kuti at the foot of the Zarin pass, the storm was terribly violent. The snow fell in such quantities that we all expected to meet death together. We halted at the mouth of it. The snow was deep and the path narrow, so that only one person could pass at a time. The horses too advanced with difficulty over the road which had been beaten and trampled down and the days were at their shortest. The first of the troops reached this cave while it was still daylight. About evening and night prayers the troops ceased coming in; after which every man was obliged to dismount and halt where he happened to be. Many men waited for morning on horseback.

The cave seemed to be small. I took a hoe and cleared for myself,
at the mouth of the cave, a resting place about the size of a
prayer carpet . . . some desired me to go into the cave but I
would not go. I felt that for me to be in . . . comfort, while my
men were in the midst of snow and drift . . . would be inconsist-
ent with what I owed them . . . it was right that whatever their
sufferings were . . . I should share them. There is a Persian
proverb that Death in the company of friends is a feast. I con-
tinued therefore to sit in the drift in the sort of hole which I had
cleared and dug out, to myself till bed-time prayers when the
snow fell so fast that as I had remained all the while sitting
crouching down on my feet, I now found that four inches of
snow had settled on my head, lips and ears. That night I caught
a cold in my ear . . .

About bed-time prayers a party which had surveyed the cave
reported that it was very extensive and was sufficiently large to
receive all our people . . . I sent to call in such of the people as
were at hand . . . such as had any eatables, stewed meat, pre-
served flesh or anything else in readiness, produced them; and
thus we escaped from terrible cold and snow and drift into a
wonderfully safe, warm and comfortable place where we could
refresh ourselves.

When we reached the top of the cliff, we found ourselves
after days in the valley bottom suddenly looking down on
snow-covered ridges and slopes, peppered with the marks of
miniature avalanches. There was a band of brilliant turquoise
light stretched along the crest of the eastern hills. We continued south. When the light had almost entirely gone and the
snow was falling more heavily, I began to think about digging
a snow hole for the night, but ten minutes later I saw some
lights to our right. We walked towards them and after about
half an hour, reached a small hamlet, where some men were
sitting on the roofs.

'Peace be with you,' I shouted up.

'You have a war dog?' they said, apparently uninterested in why we should have just come off the mountain at dusk.

'No, I am looking for the house of Seyyed Kerbalahi . . . I am a traveller and I need shelter.'

'How about a fight now? Our dogs against yours . . . come on . . .' and they put up the wolf-whistle.

'This dog is not a fighting dog,' I snapped. 'If you try a fight, I'll kill your dogs with my stick.' Perhaps sensing that I was tired and angry enough to fulfil my threat, the men held the dogs back. This was, it seemed, the hamlet of Siar Chesme, where I had been told that I would find a headman called Seyyed Kerbalahi. I walked up to his courtyard and stood there shivering and waving my letter of introduction. He shouted down: 'Why are you here? The village mosque is twenty minutes back down the hill. You should go there . . .'

As on many previous nights, I was anxious to get Babur fed and housed and to get into the warmth myself. I emphasized my distinguished hosts and grand introductions. Eventually he allowed me in.

Devotions

Di Muezzin shab-e-vasler
Azan pechle rat.
Hai! Kum bakht,
Kia wakht he khoda yad Aya?

– Mirza Ghalib

From the Muezzin, on the night I lay first with my girl,
The call to prayer broke night into dawn.
Hey shithead! What time is this
To remind a man of God?

Seyyed Kerbalahi's guest room was large and decorated with some of the most expensive carpets that I had seen. He said he was too busy to speak to me because he was praying. An old servant brought me some supper consisting of soup made from rotten meat, which I could not stomach, and some bread. Then Seyyed Kerbalahi sent some tea with his wife but he did not join me for the meal. I wondered if he was having a better meal next door.

This was a remote area. The servant who brought the soup had been to the nearest bazaar at Yakawlang but he had never seen Chaghcharan or any place of that size and in a later conversation Seyyed Kerbalahi's nephew had to try to explain to him what an aeroplane was. The Seyyed's wife, who brought in the tea, asked me about my journey, but she had not heard of any of the places I had walked through that day.

'Where have you been?' I asked.

'I was born in this village. I am the fifth and only surviving one of Seyyed Kerbalahi's wives and I have never been more than an hour's journey by foot from this village in the forty years that I have been alive.'

She explained that the Seyyed's father had moved to this place in the mountains from Yakawlang in the 1940s. They seemed to have prospered. All the Seyyed's brothers were senior mullahs and their son was studying in Tehran. Although she was a grandmother she was not comfortable being alone with a man and after five minutes of conversation she left me. Seyyed Kerbalahi joined me after dinner. His real name was Rasul. He was called Kerbalahi, he explained, because he had been to Kerbala in Iraq to visit the sacred Shia shrine of Imam Hussein twice in the late 1950s, once for three months and the other time for five months.[54]

I asked him why he had not completed the Haj by going on to Mecca from Kerbala.

'It would have been too expensive.'

'But Mecca is quite close by the time you have gone from Afghanistan to Iraq.'

'It would have been a seven-day trip so I came home.'

He tuned the radio to a Pakistani channel, which was broadcasting in Urdu.

'Can you understand Urdu?' I asked.

'No,' he said. 'I have put it on for your benefit.'

He then began praying. Every minute or so, he interrupted his prayer to throw a comment at me such as, 'Later I will arrange for someone to dry your socks.' Then he would start his prayers again from the beginning. I suggested gently that he should finish his prayers before we spoke.

---

54. I did not ask Seyyed Kerbalahi but I assumed that he, like the majority of people in the Sar Jangal valley, was a Shia. This was certainly implied by his pride at having visited the great Shia shrine in Kerbala.

'But a guest is ordained by God,' he said reprovingly.

'Thank you,' I replied. 'Well, there was something I wanted to ask you . . .'

'I am praying. We should talk later.'

When he had finished he picked up a large copy of the Koran and began to mumble over it and then glanced up and asked if I had any photographs.

I handed him the pictures of my family. He frowned at them briefly and handed them back.

'I have walked here from Herat,' I said.

'I'm reading the Koran and your Farsi is not good enough for a conversation,' he replied.

We sat in silence, till I decided to lie down and sleep.

At dawn he began his lengthy prayers again. By the time he had finished, a crowd of villagers had gathered in the guest room. Seyyed Kerbalahi picked up my Dari-English dictionary and began looking at it a page at a time. Usually people who want to be seen reading my dictionary know which way up to hold it. Seyyed Kerbalahi didn't.

Then he moved to another position in the room, carefully opened a sandalwood box and unwrapped a different copy of the Koran. The morning continued with rambling prayers, a little browsing of the Koran and occasional bad-tempered visits to his balcony to tell anyone who wanted to see him that he was too busy with his religious devotions to be disturbed. I imagined that this was the pattern of most of Seyyed Kerbalahi's days.

Finally I took my leave. On the guest-room wall I noticed two faded aquatint photographs.

'They are my brothers,' he said, 'martyrs . . . one was killed in Lal and one on the path to Yakawlang.' They were not dressed like most martyrs as Mujahidin but in neat Russian dress uniforms.

The Defiles of the Valley

Seyyed Kerbalahi had told two men to go with me. It was good to have them with me because another foot of snow had fallen during the night, covering all tracks. We had to break trail up the steep slope that rose behind the village. In the loose new powder we slipped back one step for every three steps we gained.

Babur enjoyed it far less than I did and I had to drag him a great deal of the way. We came onto the ridge after two hours. This was the central watershed dividing western Hazarajat from the province of Bamiyan and we could see the bare cliffs thirty kilometres east below us along the edge of the Zarin valley. This, they said, marked the entrance to Yakawlang – my destination that day. The clouds were moving quickly in a cold wind, revealing occasional glimpses of a pale sun.

Samarakot lay at the bottom of the slope. After I had taken Babur down to an ice hole below the village for a drink, Hassan Zargon came to greet us. He was a kind, welcoming and respectful host. He gave me two soft-boiled eggs and sent food out to Babur. Like Zia in Katlish, he provided a man with a white cloth and warm water to wash my hands, and he filled my tea glass and poured in sugar. Since it was snowing again, he said that I should stay the night with him. I told him that I wanted to reach Yakawlang that night. He said it would be impossible. It was two or three days' walk away. When I insisted, however, he told his seventeen-year-old son Asad and another boy to guide me over the next pass.

The next stage over the Zarin pass would have been impossible without them. The snow was falling very fast. We saw glimpses of a few black rocks and at times a ridge would disengage itself from the fog and we would see, racing across the surface, a fine, sand-like flurry of snow, caught in the southeast wind. But most of the time the white-out was total. Sensing the gradients, we picked our way up over ridges, and through deep snow bowls. We could not see the texture of the snow at our feet. Where the snow had fallen on a hard crust, it was only knee deep. Here, Asad was able to pick a route. But then he'd lose it again and then we'd be ploughing through much deeper powder, lifting our legs as high as sumo wrestlers with every step.

After an hour and a half the snow thickened, driven horizontally into our faces. We were all very cold. At every ridge Asad turned and shouted through the storm, '*Manda na Bashi.*' (May you not be tired.) We sank into a deep drift and for ten minutes Asad plunged cheerfully around in a wide circle, till he had worked out where we were. I wondered how these ridges and valleys would have looked in the summer. Finally, we were on the last slope down into the Zarin valley, which was only twenty kilometres from Yakawlang. The pass had taken us three hours and Asad and his companion were now going to walk back in the other direction through the blizzard.

I offered Asad some money but he was horrified. It seemed that a six-hour round trip through a freezing storm and chest-deep snow was the least he could do for a guest. I did not want to insult him but I was keen for him to have some money. I insisted, feeling foolish as I did so. He refused five times but finally accepted out of politeness and gave all the money to his companion. Then he wished me luck and turned back up the hill into the face of the snowstorm. I turned along the Zarin valley, towards Yakawlang.

Babur the Emperor probably spent his final night before reaching Yakawlang on the slope we had just descended:

Before we reached the bottom of the Zarin pass, the day closed in around us. We halted in the defiles of the valley. The cold was dreadful and we passed that night in great distress and misery. Many lost their hands and feet from frost. Kupek lost his feet, Siyunduk Turkoman his hands and Akhi his feet, from the cold of that night. Early next morning we moved down the glen. Although we knew this was not the usual road, yet placing our trust in God we advanced down the valley, and descended by difficult and precipitous places. It was evening prayer before we reached the other end of the valley. It was not in the memory of the oldest man that this pass had ever been descended when there was so much snow on the ground; nay it was never known that anyone even conceived the idea of passing it at such a season. Although for some days we endured much from the depth of the snow yet, in the issue, it was this very circumstance which brought us to our journey's end. For if the snow had not been so deep, how was it possible to have gone, as we did when there was no road, marching over precipices and ravines? Had it not been for the extreme depth of the snow, the whole of our horses and camels must have sunk into the first gulf that we met with:[55]

> *Every good and evil that exists*
> *If you mark it well is for a blessing.*

It was bed-time prayers when we reached Yakawlang and halted.

Five hundred years later I reached Yakawlang some hours after bed-time prayers. Asad had left me at about three in the afternoon. I knew that I had to walk fast to reach Yakawlang

---

55. The belief that fresh snow makes paths safer by covering crevasses was held also by nineteenth-century alpine climbers. They therefore insisted on crossing the *haute route* from Chamonix to Zermatt in the fresh snow of January. Today it is believed that fresh snow is dangerous and people prefer to cross snow slopes in the spring, when there is less snowfall and the crevasses are visible.

that evening. The valley floor was low and broad and Zarin was a cluster of caves dug into the sandstone wall. The entrances to the caves had often been finished with walls and it appeared from their soot-black ceilings that most of them were once inhabited. This was the first cave-dwelling culture that I had seen. From here to Bamiyan more and more of the villages had caves, now mostly used for storage and flocks. Opposite the caves was a large, ruined mud castle.

From Zarin I emerged onto a clear, broad vehicle road: the first clear road I had seen for two weeks. This was the road from Lal but I saw no vehicles on it, probably because all the passes on either side were closed. For the first time, in the late afternoon sun, I was able to see the true colour of the hills free of snow: there was a coal-black peak with slopes of sulphurous yellow, an emerald green mountain, dark purple cliffs with a white crest and in the foreground pale brown sandstone cliffs with dark eyelets of caves at the base, each stained with soot.

I climbed into this blaze of colour, but underfoot the colours of the mountains faded into sombre shades of grey, khaki and rust. We reached the stream and valley of Yakawlang at sunset and at the same moment the snow began to fall. On the valley floor the pale yellow of the corn stubble was dusted with white, the hills had turned the smoky pink of a Ching vase and the mist gathered on the peaks, in the thick waves of a classical Chinese painting. The air was alive with snowflakes.

Babur writes of his arrival:

The people of Yakawlang who had heard of us as we descended, carried us to their warm houses, brought out fat sheep for us, a superfluity of hay and grain for our horse, with abundance of wood and dried dung to kindle our fires. To pass from cold and snow into such a village and its warm houses, on escaping from want and suffering, to find such plenty of good bread and fat sheep as we did, is an enjoyment that can be conceived only by such as have suffered similar hardships or endured such heavy distress.

I entered Yakawlang, pacing fast, swathed in my blanket, with Babur behind me. It was now dark. I hammered on a number of gates but, although I could see lights within, no one opened their doors to me. At the fifth compound a man opened a shutter and when he heard I needed a bed, told me to go to the Médecins Sans Frontières office at the top of the hill. We did so. The gate of the MSF compound was opened as soon as I knocked by an Australian male nurse. He looked at me in surprise and then led me to a new clean room built into the side of the valley. There, I was welcomed. Lola, a Spanish doctor, gave me some pig fat for Babur. I was offered a hot shower and then Petr, a Czech from the People in Need Foundation, sat with me as I ate cornflakes, peanut butter, honey and Marmite, and drank hot chocolate and coffee.

The next morning I walked through the bazaar to look at the 'warm houses' that had welcomed Babur. I found only charred, empty shells. Yakawlang had been one of the largest towns in Hazarajat with a literate and politically engaged population. The Taliban attacked the town in 1998 and executed four hundred men against the clinic wall. Since then 75 per cent of the population of Yakawlang had either died or fled.

In the charred, empty shells of what had once been shops in the lower bazaar, some men had set up trestle tables with small awnings. In one there were biscuit boxes, in another the hanging carcass of a cow. But it was mostly rubble, filled with the fresh faeces of men and dogs. I walked past shop after shop without ceiling or upper walls, black with soot. The smoke from the fire must have filled the narrow valley, and the rattle of the firing squad's automatic weapons would have echoed off the steep walls.

*

The MSF house into which I had been welcomed was probably the most remote and isolated Médecins Sans Frontières operation in Afghanistan. The staff had flown to Kabul in a giant Antonov plane a month earlier and had driven into Yakawlang when the passes were still open. Before their arrival there were no medical facilities in the entire district. They had opened nine clinics, including one by the caves in Zarin. Replacement staff had arrived just before the passes had closed. Some of the staff who were due leave had been marooned for two weeks in Yakawlang, unable to get to Bamiyan.

Since it was only three or four days by foot to Bamiyan, I suggested they walk with me rather than waiting for the passes to clear, but they wanted me instead to travel by vehicle with them. The Australian male nurse had seen a horse and its rider cut in half on the path ahead, and warned me that the path was heavily mined. The Spanish doctor, Lola, warned me that to get to Bamiyan on foot I would have to cross a very large snow plateau, in which I would not see a house for thirty kilometres. She had just amputated the frostbitten leg of an Afghan soldier who had tried to cross the pass and she thought she would have to take off one of his comrades', legs that afternoon. She reminded me to take aspirin if I began to develop frostbite.

They were very generous hosts and I was sorry to leave them. So was Babur. MSF had adopted a puppy and it ran around Babur in circles, yapping at his heels, trying to make him play. He wandered ponderously around on the roof of the compound, pretending it didn't exist and occasionally giving a gruff bark if the puppy bit him too hard. Play for him, when it happened, was a solitary activity, in which he ran far ahead and rolled in the snow. But he had been very well fed. I hoped he had recovered his strength sufficiently to be able to reach Bamiyan because there the roads were open and he would be able to travel by vehicle and wait for me in Kabul.

Part Six

I am the grave of Biton, traveller:
If from Torone to Amphipolis you go
Give Nicagoras this message: his one son
Died in a storm, in early winter, before sunrise.

– Nikainetos, third century BC

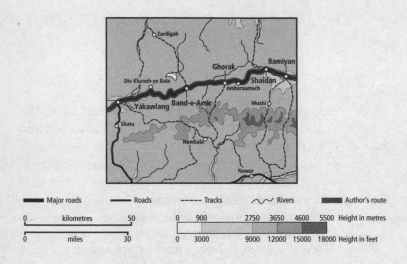

The Intermediate Stages of Death

From the ridge a mile beyond Yakawlang, I looked back. The charred houses were concealed by distance and absorbed into the shapes of the hills and the lines of poplars and willow. After the rest and meat at Yakawlang, Babur started strongly, moving more quickly than me and pulling me on his lead up the first couple of slopes. But soon he was tired again. After two hours, on the final climb from the Firuzbabar plain towards the long snow plateau, I saw my first men of the day. They were leading a donkey. On the donkey's back was a man on a stretcher. I assumed at first that they were taking a relative to the Yakawlang clinic. But as I drew level, I saw that he was beyond hospitals.

A glistening piece of pink flesh still clung to one cheek but his eyes had gone and there was only a thin tuft of grey hair on the back of his skull. Enough tendons remained to hold his grey jawbone in place. His knees were together, his arms stretched out stiff to either side, his head was slightly raised. He was wearing a tattered brown homespun jacket, his hands were well preserved and the wrinkles on his fingers suggested that he had been old. He was wearing two transparent plastic bags, tied at his wrist as gloves, to keep the cold away. They had not worked. He had frozen to death.

They did not know who he was. They had found him on the snow plateau. He had been walking from Bamiyan to Yakawlang. Because he was travelling alone on foot they assumed he was a poor man from a remote area. He might have been on his way to visit his family for the Eid festival. It was Eid that day and they had given up their own festival to take the man to the district headquarters.

I had never seen this intermediate stage of decayed death before: only the newly dead and the skeleton. I wished the two men luck, then continued on to the plateau which the man had been crossing. A cold wind rose. The footprints on the snow path were a couple of days old. After two or three hours, very conscious of the plain, which stretched unbroken to the horizon on every side, I stopped for some biscuits and water and began to shiver, aware of my wet feet and being alone. I was suddenly defeated and I felt instinctively that I did not have any energy to make it to Kabul. Yet I rose to my feet and began moving, slowly at first and then increasingly quickly, dragging Babur behind me, wondering when my muscles would stop moving.

Just at sunset, having seen no human since the corpse, we reached some large terraces of snow, so flat that I realized they were a chain of frozen lakes. The waterfall had frozen into bloated stalactites, streaked with intense copper oxide green and turquoise blue and sulphur yellow, and creamy with snow where they struck the water. The low sun sank into the straight cleft of the cliff behind me. The coloured alchemy of the ice drained into twilight.

On the other side of the lake was a village. I didn't turn towards the village but instead pressed on towards a wall, which divided the upper lake from the lower. Having wanted to stop three hours earlier, I now wanted to continue beyond the lake and keep walking across the plain. I thought of the stars over the fresh snow and the size of the plain and the peace of it. I was entranced by my forward movement. I did not want to stop. But Babur just lay down in the snow. I struggled with him and pleaded, but he would not move. Finally I gave up and followed him towards a house, which we reached just after dark.

This place was Band-e-Amir. The decayed mud room in

which we stayed had once been a guest house. Until the Soviet invasion the lakes had been a tourist destination, and thereafter Russian soldiers had come here on leave. I was the first foreign paying guest that my host had had in his guest house for twelve years. My money bought me five flat fishes which he had caught through an ice hole in the lake. He fried them and served them with bread. He said I was lucky. The Taliban had fished by dynamiting the lake and there were few fish left.

Winged Footprints

The next morning I walked over the surface of the ice and stood in the very centre of the lake, looking back at the mosque that was carved into a sheer cliff wall the colour of elm wood. A smooth layer of powder snow covered the three terraces of the lakes, broken only by a single set of footprints and a single set of paw prints.

Babur and I climbed up the facing cliff onto the snow plateau, which we had been crossing the previous day. After a few minutes, it seemed that I had never been so alone or anywhere so silent. The only sounds were the creak of my staff and my steps. Across the whole circle of the plateau, I could see nothing except our tracks in the snow and, behind them, the mountain peaks. The snow was light and ruffled under my boot and when I looked back there was a slender feather flaring out from each heel mark. As we continued, the winged footprints and the oblong grooves of the staff changed shape, freezing and melting in the sun.

I stopped, sat down, got up, walked ten more minutes and then because I felt exhausted, sat down again, half buried in deep powder. My feet were wet, my hands were cold and the wind moved in a fine white mist over the surface of the snow. I lifted my sunglasses and the sudden light consumed all the features of the place: shrinking, contorting, corroding and dissolving. There was no winged footprint or horizon in the even glare of the snow. I could not remember why I was walking.

I was sick, my muscles were stiff. The snow formed a bright clean cushion, perfectly shaped to fit my back. Lying back, I felt warm and at ease. I closed my eyes and smiled. It occurred to me that no one could criticize me for staying here. I half opened my eyes again. The sun seemed particularly brilliant, the unbroken powder stretched without end. It was a very private place and here, buried in the snow with only my head in the sun, I would not be disturbed for days. I knew there would be villages ahead but there seemed no point in trying to reach them.

Beside me, Babur was scuttling snow with his large paws. He buried his nose in the powder, emerged blinking, with a white beard on his black muzzle, then lay heavily down, craning his head to the side to lick the ice. After a few minutes, he sat up on his haunches and walked stiffly over towards where I was sitting. He sniffed carefully around my collar, so I could feel his warm breath on my neck. He pushed his nose gently against my ear. When I did not respond, he backed away, watched me, approached again and finally began to walk away, onwards across the snow plain, looking occasionally over his shoulder. When he was two hundred yards ahead he stopped, turned to me and barked once. I stood and followed in his tracks.

After about eight kilometres, we reached a small hamlet between Subzil and Kuh-I-Kinuti, where we were given some bread and tea in a house which they said was 'poor'. It was. Most houses had at least one coloured rug on the floor, some acrylic blankets and a brightly decorated box in which a bride brings her possessions, but their floor was covered in undyed goat's wool, the trunk was plain tin and the blankets were home-walked felt.[56]

*

56. The English word 'to walk' rather than being some Indo-European ur-word is in fact a late and eccentric adaptation of the Anglo-Saxon word for pressing wet felt, 'walken' – an activity usually performed with the feet.

Babur's foreleg was very stiff. Leading me off the plain seemed to have taken his strength. I walked on ahead, hoping that when he saw himself left behind in an empty waste of snow he would catch up. He didn't, however. He slowed almost to a halt, hanging his head, limping step by step towards me and finally just lying down. I walked back and talked to him a little. At ten stone he was too heavy to carry, and at this pace it would take us a month to get to Bamiyan. I tied him to the lead and set off pulling him behind me, faster than he wanted to go. I had to pull him at least as far as Bamiyan, if I was to have a chance of getting him by vehicle to Kabul and a vet.

From the hamlet we had to climb again. We were following a watercourse and I was keen to get Babur some water, but the ice must have been eighteen inches thick and however often I drove my steel-shod staff into it, I was not able to break through. Higher up, however, the ice was thinner. I called Babur, 'Come on, sweet, come on, my darling . . . come on – there's a good dog – water . . . ' and Babur simply lay on the bank with his head between his paws looking at the mountains. I tried to pull him down and he pulled back. He had refused to drink from the lake at Band-e-Amir perhaps because of the chemicals in the water. We had a whole day without water ahead.

I squatted down by the hole that I had made in the ice and again splashed the water and dribbled some on his nose. He turned away, grimacing, but something must have penetrated, because eventually he moved heavily down towards the river and drank. After a couple of minutes, he straightened up, still dribbling and looked around. I remained squatting. He lowered his head and began drinking again.

We had too far to go that day to stop for long, but we did stop when we came down from the ridge into Pasuruan. Here we had rejoined what had been the main road from

Yakawlang. No one was using it because of the mines. Pasuruan had been burned by the Taliban and so had the next village, Ghorak, which we reached at nightfall.

Blair and the Koran

Below Ghorak I was met by Ali, the headman's son. I explained that I wanted a bed for the night. He said it would be difficult.

'Travellers sleep in the mosque but you can see the mosque . . .' he pointed to the long, fire-ravaged shell among the abandoned houses. 'No one can entertain a guest here.'

I waited in silence. After a minute he said, 'We could see my father. Follow me and be careful of the mines.'

'The Taliban laid the mines?' I asked to make conversation.

'No, we laid them, but we can't remember where they all are.'

I followed him through the ruined buildings to the crest of the hill, where we entered his courtyard house. It had been burned like all the others, but the family had repaired part of one room. Smoke from the dung-fed stove filled this his father's room. I could not see how many people sat inside, but I could hear a baby screaming in the far corner. Ali's father lay on a high iron bed, swaddled in blankets. It was the first time that I had seen a bed in an Afghan village house. He looked about eighty. He asked me to sit. And then he broke into a lung-bruising staccato cough that pulled him upright with a quivering body and wet eyes, mouthing, 'In the name of Allah,' through the cackle and roar as he retched into a tin spittoon. When it subsided, he lay down and closed his eyes and said, 'I am sick. Excuse, please, my rudeness to my guest.'

'I should go . . .'

'You are our guest. You will stay for meat,' the headman

replied. 'Some rice, some meat . . . my baby son is crying. He is two and I am old and too decrepit to discipline him. Accept, please, my apologies. My elder son will tell you about the Taliban and us Hazara. They burned our Koran. Look.'

Ali lifted the lid of a carved wooden box, kissed the bundle inside, unwrapped it carefully, said a prayer and opened the book. The fire had consumed one corner, exposing thin layers of oil-blackened paper, and as Ali opened it, some ash fell from the binding.

'The Taliban did this to our holy Koran,' said Ali's brother.

'If you want to understand the Taliban, look at what they did to our holy Koran,' Ali added.

There was no electricity or television in the village. These men had never visited an Afghan city or met a journalist. I wondered why they were explaining this to me immediately and why they had chosen to focus on this Koran rather than on what the Taliban had done to their families and their village.

'Can you read the Koran?' I asked.

'No. We cannot read or write.'

'Did the Taliban take it out and burn it?'

'No. It was lying in one of the houses that the Taliban burned when they attacked the village.'

'So it was accidental.'

'Yes. You see what kind of people the Taliban are.' He meant I imagined that they were sacrilegious infidels.

'How many people did the Taliban kill in this village?' I asked.

'Five.'

'Six,' corrected another, 'Hussein, Muhammad Ali, Ghulam Nabi...'

'Six,' agreed Ali.

'From your family?'

'Yes. My brother. His father. But look at the Koran.'

There was no Fanta in this village; the only global brand was Islam. Ali thought the only thing he and I had in common was the Koran and that I would understand that anyone who burned the book, even accidentally, would be damned for sacrilege. He didn't think foreigners would be interested in deaths in his family. In a way he was right. The West paid little attention to the killing of the Hazara. What moved them was the destruction of the Bamiyan Buddhas or the fate of the lion in the Kabul zoo. Nine hundred thousand dollars had been raised for the lion in Britain and the United States. Tony Blair paid particularly close attention to the Koran, but Ali would have had difficulty understanding his view of it.

On 20 September 2001, Blair packed his Korans for his tour of the Middle East. Nine months before, he had told an interviewer that he possessed two different editions. Now, according to the *Guardian*, he had three. 'Blair', it stated, 'now carries a copy of the Koran at all times for "inspiration and courage" – a habit he picked up from President Clinton's daughter.' He had encouraged Muslims to study their holy book before September 11th, telling readers of the *Muslim News* that 'the concept of love and fellowship as the guiding spirits of humanity is so clear . . . if you read the Koran.' On 7 October, he said: 'The acts of these people are contrary to the teachings of the Koran . . . it angers me, as it angers the vast majority of Muslims.'

And a week later, he said, 'I can't understand how anybody who truly studies the teaching of Islam and the words of the message of the Koran can possibly justify the slaughter [of September 11th].' Bush joined in: 'Islam's teachings are good and peaceful, and those who commit evil in the name of Allah blaspheme the name of Allah. The terrorists are traitors to their own faith . . .'

Blair's handling and discussion of the Koran would have struck Ali as highly eccentric. In Ali's view, Blair could not have read the Koran because he could not read Arabic. Since the Koran, unlike the Bible, is the verbatim word of God, spoken through Muhammad in Arabic, a translation is not considered to be the Koran. At times, it has been considered blasphemous to translate it at all. Ali carefully wrapped his Koran, kept it in a wooden box on a high shelf and approached it only after ablutions and with a prayer. He would have been horrified to see Blair thumb through his translation on the plane or make confident statements about its meaning. The dense network of metaphor, poetry and allusion is traditionally interpreted with reference to the sayings/Hadiths of the Prophet and long traditions of legal and theological exegesis. As a result, public pronouncements on the meaning of the Koran are usually reserved for the most learned and senior of mullahs.

Blair's confidently casual handling of the text was not supposed to be patronizing or presumptuous. It was intended to display his sensitivity to Islamic culture. Perhaps he mistakenly assumed that the Koran resembled his Protestant vision of the Bible, which can be translated without problem; easily understood; free of apocrypha; open to interpretation by lay people and physically to be handled much like any other book. This may also be true of other Protestant Christian commentators such as Bush. In November 2001, there was a photograph of Bush casually dragging a Koran across the table with his unclean left hand, while the mullah who presented it struggled to smile.

Much of the British media followed Blair in defining Islam almost exclusively in terms of the Koran, without referring to the text's cultural context. They might not have been as quick to discuss the Catholic Church merely in terms of the gospels. But perhaps they were more interested in changing Islam than in describing it. On 16 September 2001, the *Guardian* remarked that the houris promised to the faithful in the Koran were purely innocent symbols, rather than virgins provided for sexual services, and that therefore, by implication, the suicide bombers had been misled. A month later, the *Observer* wrote of one version of the faith that 'this is not Islam any more than the Ku Klux Klan is Christianity'. Commentators rarely described the variety of Islamic beliefs and practices. This may have been because their comments were primarily intended to calm anti-Muslim sentiment in

Britain (and perhaps in the case of Tony Blair appeal to Muslim coalition partners). Anti-Muslims also approached the Koran without considering its context. They did so in support of a different agenda. In November, the Chairman of the British National Party wrote:

> [We] began by looking for the piece [in the Koran] which has been quoted again and again since September 11th, including by George Bush, Tony Blair, Iain Duncan-Smith and an endless string of journalists: 'Whoever kills a soul is like one who has killed the whole of Mankind.' This sentence is at the heart of the Politically Correct campaign to ensure that the war fever against Islamic terrorists doesn't lead to an explosion of hostility against Muslims per se. After all, isn't it clear evidence that Islam is at root a peaceful, loving religion; Christianity with a towel on its head?
>
> Indeed it would be, if it were genuine. But the problem is that this quotation is a Politically Correct fabrication. Just look at what Surah 5, Ayat 32 actually says:
>
> '. . . whoever kills a soul, not in retaliation for a soul or corruption in the land, is like one who has killed the whole of mankind.'

He then went on to cite twenty-three verses as 'evidence' that Muslims are 'a threat to British life'.[57]

---

57. The response of British intellectuals was more sophisticated. After September 11th they, unlike the mainstream media, did engage with the motivations of the hijackers, the symbolism of their action, its historical context and the difficulties inherent in any response. But even intellectuals sometimes wrote pieces that would have surprised many Muslims with their confident pronouncements on Islamic orthodoxy, or with their reluctance to admit any differences between very distant cultures. Thus Terry Eagleton wrote in the *London Review of Books* that 'It's Islamic fundamentalism, not *The Satanic Verses*, that represents a blasphemous version of the Koran', while Mary Beard suggested 'that full-blown martyrs are a rare community, much more numerous in the imagination than on the ground' on the basis of her study of early Christianity.

Salt Ground and Spikenard

The next day, I fell in with two boys from Ghorak who were driving a donkey to Bamiyan to buy salt. We walked the first five hours, perhaps twenty-five kilometres, without stopping for a break. I noticed very little of the landscape. We climbed over some ridges and I saw how very difficult it was to move a donkey through deep snow.

Like many villagers they were tough on their donkey: I saw them break a bamboo stick on her back and then strike her with a sharp stone. But, in the snow, the boys beat a path for her and whenever she lay down, returned to patiently lift her again. She would then take a couple of floundering steps and lie down while they beat more of the path and returned to stroke, encourage and lift her once more. In the Qarganatu valley, the boys pointed out a number of mines, some only two feet from the edge of the path. I tightened Babur's lead.

In the early afternoon, we came over the Shibartu pass. This had been one of the Hazara resistance centres. Khalili, the Hazara commander, had run an airstrip here, where supplies were dropped from Iran. All that remained of the village was a single crowded room. All the other buildings had been burned by the Taliban and abandoned. But this valley had not only suffered under the Taliban: Babur reached it in mid-February, 1507:

> *We descended by the hill-pass of Shibartu. The Turkoman Hazara had taken up their quarters in the line of my march, with their families and property and had not the smallest*

intimation of my approach. Next morning on our march we came among their huts, close by their sheep folds, two or three of which we plundered; whereupon the whole of the Hazara taking alarm, abandoned their huts and fled away to the hills with their children.

Soon afterwards, there was information that a body of them had stopped our people in a narrow defile and were assailing them with arrows ... our men were all rather perplexed and halted. I came up alone. I attempted to encourage them. Not one of them listened to me or advanced on the enemy, but they stood scattered about in separate places. Although I had not put on my helmet, my horse's mail or my armour, and had only my bow and quiver, I called out that servants were kept that they might be serviceable and, in time of need, prove their loyalty to their master; not for the purpose of looking on while their master marched up against the foe; after which I spurred on and advanced ... [He inserts a Turki poem about the events ...]

> My men, on seeing me advance, advanced also,
> Leaving their terror behind.
> We gained the top of the hill, and drove the Hazara
>   before us,
> We skipped over the heights and hollows like deer;
> We plundered them and divided their property and
>   sheep;
> We slew the Turkoman Hazara,
> And made captives of their men and women;
> Those who were far off too we followed and made
>   prisoners
> We took their wives and children.

Fourteen or fifteen of the most noted insurgents and robber chiefs of the Hazara had fallen into our hands. It was my intention to put them to death with torture at our halting ground, as an example and terror to all rebels and robbers; but Qasim Beg happening to meet them, was filled with unseason-

able commiseration and let them go: (As Saadi, the Persian poet, writes . . .)

> To do good to the bad is the same thing
> As to do evil to the good;
> Salt ground does not produce Spikenard;
> Do not throw away good seed on it.

Pale Circles In Walls

We continued up on to the Shaidan pass. I moved in slow steps like the donkey. My pack seemed to force me into the ground and the struggle of movement made me aware of little except my breathing. My head came down to watch the path, my thoughts settled, burrowing into the movement. Babur's head was sunk right down, his tongue was lolling out of his mouth and I knew that if I let him off the lead he'd stop entirely.

On the Shaidan ridge we stopped on a path littered with anti-aircraft shells. The Taliban had used this position to fire on the Hazara planes at Shibartu. The village of Shaidan looked beautiful as we descended. Its fields were broad beside the river. The ornate octagonal towers of the castle stood above a mud bazaar of eighty shops that led to the courtyards of a seminary. Ancient poplars lined the landlords' orchards. The old caves in the cliff were set with wooden windows and above them a fifteen-thousand-foot snow peak rose against a dark blue sky.

But when I reached the first building, I realized that this was a ghost town. All the shops were smoothly rendered in dark soot. In Kabul, where machine guns and high explosive had struck concrete, there were pockmarks or craters. Here there were none. The fire had consumed the lintels and rafters and left crisp shells of baked mud. In some the charred stumps of roof beams remained, in others there were pale circles in walls, as black as the poplars in the landlords' gardens and the empty window frames of the caves. All the buildings were abandoned. The Turquoise Mountain must have looked like this after the attack of Genghis Khan.

Six years before, there had been two thousand families in Shaidan. Three years ago the Taliban had killed eighty men in the bazaar. A year ago, fresh from dynamiting the giant Buddhas thirty-five kilometres away, they killed one hundred and twenty. Seven months before my arrival, they found the village abandoned and torched it. Most of the population had fled to refugee camps. Shaidan was still empty.

In Herat many of the war reporters[58] predicted that the Afghans would hate the American-led attack on the Taliban. They said that the Taliban treatment of women, their use of Sharia law and their demolition of the Bamiyan Buddhas, had not been unpopular in the villages. They stressed that the Taliban were 'no crueller' than the Northern Alliance and had improved security in rural areas. They suggested that intervention would simply replace one group of crooks with another and anger Afghans in the process.

But the Hazara I met were delighted the Taliban had gone and they did not resent the Americans for expelling them. Nowhere in Afghanistan did the cruelty of the Taliban seem so comprehensive or have such an ethnic focus. In a three-day walk from Yakawlang, where the Taliban had executed four hundred, to here in Shaidan, where the seventy shop fronts were reduced to blackened shells, every Hazara village which I had seen had been burned. In each settlement, people had been murdered, the flocks driven off and the orchards razed. Most of the villages were still abandoned.

Earlier in my journey, I had found Tajik and Aimaq communities were not entirely opposed to the Taliban. They agreed that security had been better under the Taliban. Tajik women now wore head scarves in the village and only put on

---

58. This may have been because many of them had been in the Balkans and remembered the fury of anti-Milosevic Serbs over the Kosovo bombing.

the full-face *burqas* to visit town, but no one objected to the
lack of female education under the Taliban or the imposition
of Islamic Sharia law. Seyyed Umar, who had complained the
most about them ('they stole donkeys from me'), turned out
to have been a Taliban commander. But these Hazara had
lost their houses, their livelihood and often their lives. They
knew little and cared less about the World Trade Center. But
they were not angry with the coalition for getting rid of the
Taliban. In the short term things had improved for them, they
were freer and more secure, they had some power again and
they were pleased with their own provincial governor, Khalili.

@afghangov.org

I doubted that the new policy makers in Kabul understood
much of this. For the last three months, whenever I reached
a Nepali town with an Internet cafe, I had received an email
from someone who had gone to govern Afghanistan. They
started passing the UN application forms around in October
2001, and then the circulars appeared: 'Please don't expect
to write to this email – there is no Internet connection in
Kabul.' Finally, there were messages from new addresses
'@pak.id', '@afghangov.org', '@worldbank.org', '@un.org,'
talking about the sun in the mountains. I now had half a
dozen friends in Afghanistan, working in embassies, think-
tanks, international development agencies, the United
Nations and the Afghan government, controlling projects
worth millions of dollars. A year before, they had been in
Kosovo or East Timor and a year later they would have
moved on to Iraq or to offices in New York and Washington.

Their objective was (to quote the United Nations Assistance Mission for Afghanistan) 'the creation of a centralized,
broad-based, multi-ethnic government committed to
democracy, human rights and the rule of law'. They worked
twelve- or fourteen-hour days drafting documents for
heavily funded initiatives on 'democratization', 'enhancing
capacity', 'gender', 'sustainable development', 'skills train-
ing' or 'protection issues'. They were mostly in their late
twenties or early thirties, with at least two degrees – often
in international law, economics or development. They came
from middle-class backgrounds in Western countries, and

in the evenings, they dined with each other and swapped anecdotes about corruption in the government and the incompetence of the United Nations. They rarely drove their 4WDs outside Kabul because they were forbidden to do so by their security advisors.

There were people, such as the two political officers in Chaghcharan, who were experienced and well informed about conditions in the rural areas of Afghanistan. But such people were barely fifty individuals out of many thousands. Most of the policy makers knew next to nothing about the villages where 90 per cent of the population of Afghanistan lived. They came from post-modern, secular, globalized states with liberal traditions in law and government. It was natural for them to initiate projects on urban design, women's rights and fibre-optic cable networks, to talk about transparent, clean and accountable processes, tolerance and civil society and to speak of a people 'who desire peace at any cost and understand the need for a centralized multi-ethnic government'.

But what did they understand of the thought processes of Seyyed Kerbalahi's wife, who had not moved more than five kilometres from her home in forty years? Or Dr Habibullah the vet, who carried an automatic weapon in the way they carried a briefcase? The villagers whom I had met were mostly illiterate, far from electricity or television, knew very little about the outside world and had very distinctive attitudes towards politics, Islam and ethnicity. The people of Kamenj understood political power in terms of their feudal lord Haji Mohsin Khan. Ismail Khan in Herat wanted a social order based on Iranian political Islam. Hazara such as Ali hated the idea of centralized government because they associated it with the domination of other ethnic groups and with their suffering under the Taliban. These differences between groups were deep, elusive and very difficult to overcome. Village democracy, gender issues and centralization would be difficult concepts to sell in some areas.

Their policy makers did not have the time, structures or resources for a serious study of an alien culture. They justified their lack of knowledge and experience by focusing on poverty and implying that dramatic cultural differences did not exist. They acted as though villagers were interested in all the priorities of international organizations, even when they were mutually contradictory.

In a seminar in Kabul, I first heard Mary Robinson, the UN Human Rights Commissioner, say, 'Afghans have been fighting for their human rights for twenty-five years. We don't need to tell them what their rights are.' Then the head of a major food agency added privately, 'Villagers are not interested in human rights. They are like poor people all over the world. All they think about is where their next meal is coming from.' To which the head of an Afghan NGO providing counselling responded, 'The only thing to know about these people is that they are suffering from post-traumatic stress disorder.'

The differences between the policy makers and a Hazara such as Ali went much deeper than his lack of food. Ali rarely worried about where his next meal was coming from. If he defined himself it was chiefly as a Muslim and a Hazara, not as a hungry Afghan. Particular versions of Islam, distinctive views of ethnicity, government, the proper methods of dispute resolution (including armed conflict) and the experience of twenty-five years of war differed from region to region. Even within a week's walk I had come across areas where the local *begs* had been toppled by Iranian-funded social revolution and others where feudal structures were still in place, areas where the violence had been inflicted by the Taliban and areas where the villagers were inflicting it on each other. Policy makers were unable to devote the time, imagination and persistence needed to understand these diverse experiences.[59] It was therefore almost impossible for them to change Afghan society in the way they wished to change it.

*

In Ghorak, I asked Ali who should be the President of Afghanistan.

'Governor Khalili,' the room replied in unison.

'But the Pashtun and the Tajik don't want your Hazara

---

59. Critics have accused this new breed of administrators of neo-colonialism. But in fact their approach is not that of a nineteenth-century colonial officer. Colonial administrations may have been racist and exploitative but they did at least work seriously at the business of understanding the people they were governing. They recruited people prepared to spend their entire careers in dangerous provinces of a single alien nation. They invested in teaching administrators and military officers the local language. They established effective departments of state, trained a local elite and continued the countless academic studies of their subjects through institutes and museums, royal geographical societies and royal botanical gardens. They balanced the local budget and generated fiscal revenue because if they didn't their home government would rarely bail them out. If they failed to govern fairly, the population would mutiny.

Post-conflict experts have got the prestige without the effort or stigma of imperialism. Their implicit denial of the difference between cultures is the new mass brand of international intervention. Their policy fails but no one notices. There are no credible monitoring bodies and there is no one to take formal responsibility. Individual officers are never in any one place and rarely in any one organization long enough to be adequately assessed. The colonial enterprise could be judged by the security or revenue it delivered, but neo-colonialists have no such performance criteria. In fact their very uselessness benefits them. By avoiding any serious action or judgement they, unlike their colonial predecessors, are able to escape accusations of racism, exploitation and oppression.

Perhaps it is because no one requires more than a charming illusion of action in the developing world. If the policy makers know little about the Afghans, the public knows even less, and few care about policy failure when the effects are felt only in Afghanistan.

leader as President of Afghanistan,' I said. Other Afghans blame Khalili for atrocities in Kabul.

'Ahmed Shah Masud,' coughed the headman, 'is the only national figure.'

They all nodded.

'But he is dead,' I muttered.

They nodded again.

'Well, then, who? Hamid Karzai, your current leader?'

'Definitely not . . . no . . . a Pashtun American puppet...' the headman said.

'Well, then, who?'

Silence. It seemed that they had never considered the issue. Perhaps they thought it wasn't up to them to choose the President or that Kabul didn't matter.

'Please eat your meat,' said the headman, half-seeing the tray of plain rice and stale bread. There was no meat because the Taliban had taken most of their flocks. But it was too dark and the headman was too ill to notice.

'Come on,' I said, 'who should be your leader?'

'The king . . .' someone suggested eventually. The others looked a bit uncertain.

'But he's eighty-five.'

They all nodded.

'If God was willing there would be no war,' added Ali, 'but we will in the future fight for many things against other people.'

While the Note Lasts

On the outskirts of Shaidan we stopped for the night at a large house which had been converted into a military barracks. Babur got his own room in the wrecked compound of an old landlord. I slept surrounded by thirty soldiers on a small floor and most of them snored. The room was not wide or long enough for us to sleep lengthways, so we slept with our legs tucked up, curled around the person beside us, and we couldn't turn over.

They were Hazara troops and they were mostly sleeping in American-issue sleeping bags. The bags were thin and marked 'for moderate cold'. I wondered whether the American officer from Logistics (Covert Operations) had known that the temperature could sink to minus forty and whether he or she cared. Some slept in little wool commando caps, or pieces of green webbing, from which hung empty new water bottles. Many were wearing brown all-in-one felt jumpsuits, presumably designed as undergarments, outside their clothes and Norwegian zip-top polo shirts.

I was woken by a migraine and bad diarrhoea. I went outside a couple of times to relieve myself, barely conscious either of the daylight brightness of the full moon, redoubled on the snow, or the cold. I noticed that the waistband of my trousers was now very loose. Back in the room I tried to record what it was that had once seemed so wonderful about the walk in Afghanistan. I wrote: 'a culmination of all walking – the desert – the night sky – the feudal castles standing back

– the single lance of the Jam minaret in its narrow valley – the international dimensions of the war – the snow.'

Then I wrote out over three pages every meal I had eaten in the previous month, lingering over days when I had boiled eggs. Dawn broke hardly brighter than the full-moon night, with a pale lemon line across the mountains to the east. The others woke complaining about the cold. Despite the press of bodies, ice had formed on our wet clothes. Some pushed through to the kitchen to smoke themselves by the dung-fed fire, leaving the rest of us a little space to stretch out.

Then to my delight they served tiny, sweet, curled pastries, which they call *basraq* or *haju*. I ate fifteen of them and everyone laughed because it is usually children's food. As we ate, our host, Khalife Amir, played a tambara lute made of a small, yellow plastic oil bottle, a table leg and two wooden awls. He fingered only one string: the lower one. I had not heard music for a month. My days had passed in silences with flurries of thought in a landscape that changed slowly. The music brought a sense of time back to me, note by note. Each pause was charged with the anticipation of the next note and the slow revelation of a tune. He measured silence, dividing each minute into a succession of clear notes from the string and binding it with his voice. The others, who had not been able to hear music performed in public during the four years of the Taliban regime, were quiet. I did not understand the words and did not need to. The sadness was clear in the tune and in the singer's tone and in the expression of the listeners, and so too was the beauty shared between us.

*

At midday, I stopped at Baraqi, sat on a platform above the road and ordered tea and biscuits. The teashop showed that we were getting closer to Bamiyan and the road head to Kabul. Every three metres along the drystone wall facing us, one of the stones was painted bright red to indicate the presence of a mine on the path. They were anti-vehicle mines and we were light enough not to trigger them so we walked over them. The anti-personnel mines seemed to be laid just off the sides of the road. A month ago a horse had been frightened on this road, bolted a few steps into the desert and killed itself and its rider.

Babur was lying at the base of the wall, in the shade. He roused himself for a moment, barked at his own echo with a gruff, leisurely roar, licked his private parts and then lay down to sleep again. The weather was very warm and, for once, the blue sky was not a sign of cold. Behind a row of poplars was the river. I remembered the sweet pastries for breakfast and enjoyed the warm sun.

In the early afternoon we left a narrow gorge, passed a hot spring which, like so many in Afghanistan, was only lukewarm, and emerged into the broad, level fields of the Bamiyan valley. As the day became hotter, Babur began to lunge for every narrow strip of shade he could find to lie down. I had to keep dragging him to his feet again.

At the edge of the valley, we were absorbed into a rolling sequence of donkey caravans going to the market. Two small boys in bright blue gumboots and sparkling prayer caps sat on top of bundles of thorn brush kindling, piled on donkeys. Beside them was a young cow, her dull hide draped loosely from sharp hip bones. The cow was a speculation: the family had bought her in a mountain bazaar three days before and thought that they could double their money by selling her. But they could not afford to feed her. A lone man on a mule, slowed from a fast trot, forced his way between the donkeys and then cantered ahead of us down the valley road. Behind him were some hard-faced men who carried nothing on their donkeys and had come to buy oil and salt.

We drew level with four donkeys ridden by women wearing faded sky-blue *burqas*, which they had pulled out of cupboards in honour of their trip to town. In the villages they didn't cover their faces. They had lifted up the skirts of their *burqas* to ride and I could see a baby peering out from the folds of mauve, scarlet and purple underclothes. Their men walked beside them, wielding Buzkashi whips. The donkeys didn't travel straight but jibbed from side to side, easily distracted, heading up off slopes towards village houses and bumping into each other, so that the drivers were at a continual trot around their flanks, shoving and pushing them back on to the path. Old men and young women mounted on the donkeys crashed into each other from different angles. One man on foot with a dark face, brown corduroy *shalwar kemis* and an orange hat perched on his curly ginger hair was perpetually sprinting off to capture a donkey that wanted to carry his wife and baby into the neighbouring fields.

The silk and Buddhist scriptures carried into Bamiyan thirteen hundred years earlier must have arrived amidst similar billows of sand and screams of muleteers. The dust must have prevented earlier travellers, such as Babur or Marco Polo, who travelled in long columns of horses and pack-animals, from seeing the landscape. I was grateful to be generally travelling alone.

The caravans dispersed around the shattered remnants of the bazaar, which was a new kind of ruin: not with solid walls and blackened rafters but with the craters and shattered silhouettes that marked an aerial bombardment. A pale brown sandstone cliff hundreds of feet high rose sheer from the northern edge of a valley, broader and more fertile than any I had seen since Herat. Cut into the cliffs to my left were two empty niches, each two hundred feet tall, with rubble at their bases. For one thousand four hundred years, two large Buddhas had stood in the niches. But seven months before I reached them the Taliban had dynamited the figures. This valley of Bamiyan at eight thousand feet was once the western frontier of the Buddhist world.

Part Seven

The Wurduk [tribe of the Pashtun] are all agricultural. They are a quiet sober people.

– Mountstuart Elphinstone,
The Kingdom of Kaubul and its Dependencies, 1815

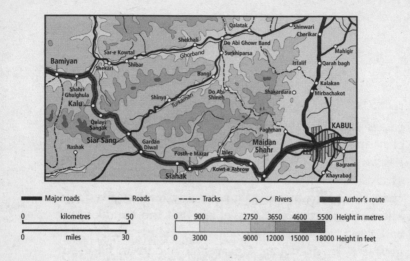

Days 31 & 32 – Bamiyan to Kalu

Day 33 – Kalu to Siar Sang

Day 34 – Siar Sang to Siahak

Day 35 – Siahak to Maidan Shahr

Day 36 – Maidan Shahr to Kabul

Footprints on the Ceiling

Religions, like camel caravans, seem to avoid mountain passes. Buddhism spread quickly south from Buddha's birthplace in southern Nepal across the flat Gangetic plain to Sri Lanka. But it took a millennium to reach China and instead of crossing the Himalayas to get there it followed a parabolic curve one and a half thousand kilometres east, five hundred kilometres north and then two and half thousand kilometres east again.[60] The religious belt stretched eventually to Mongolia and Japan, but in Afghanistan Buddhism filled only a narrow belt that left pagans among the valleys to the east and west in Kailash and in Ghor.

As Buddhism moved it changed. In Tibet it incorporated the previous Bon-Po religion and spawned new demonologies. In eighth-century northern India, it became scholastic; among the forest monks of Sri Lanka, pragmatic; in Newar, Nepal, married monks practised inverted tantra and in Japanese Zen devotees contemplated the most minimalist of paradoxes. Afghanistan was where Buddhism met the art of Alexander's Greece. There, in the Gandharan style, it first developed the most distinctive artistic expression of the religion: the portrayal of the Buddha in human form. The giant statues of Bamiyan were the most monumental legacy of this innovation.

From the base of the eastern Buddha niche, I climbed up a

---

60. A piece of silk could do the journey in nine months. Buddhism took nearly a thousand years.

sloping mud staircase and emerged about forty feet above the ground, into a long, open corridor lined with empty rooms. I followed more steps upwards. The walls of the cliff on either side were carved with balconies, circular staircases and octagonal rooms with vaulted ceilings, rising storey after storey up the rock. I continued, two hundred feet above the valley floor, over fragile sections of mud, and emerged where the head of the Buddha had once been.

This was distinctive mountain architecture. Gandharan Buddhist sculpture of Afghanistan is generally renowned for its grace and balance. But the Bamiyan Buddhas were ungainly and inflated. Their central function seems to have been to dominate the mountain landscape. It was impossible to achieve detail or elegance of form in the loose crumbling rock. Everything had been sacrificed to allow the figures to climb up the face of the sandstone cliff.

Descending towards the other Buddha, I turned into a side passage, where I found a room still decorated with traces of dark blue and gold paint depicting the heads and traceries of figures in a procession. The last Buddhists probably lived in Bamiyan at about the turn of the first millennium. Their religion, initially weakened by a Hindu revival, was extinguished by Islam. By the time the Ghorids captured the valley in the twelfth century, there was hardly a Buddhist left between Bamiyan and Bangladesh. We now know little about what kind of Buddhism was once practised in Bamiyan. From tens of thousands of monasteries, stretched over a thousand kilometres, only fragments of stupas, sculpture, inscriptions and manuscripts, and the records of Chinese travellers, remain.

At the end of another passage, I saw that the Taliban had scorched the whole interior of a room, presumably to remove a fresco, and then stamped white boot-prints over the ceiling. This must have taken some effort, since the ceiling was twenty feet high.

The Ghorids, who chose this valley as their second capital alongside the Turquoise Mountain, had perhaps felt some affinity for this alternative mountain architecture because they had left the cliff Buddhas untouched. The Taliban, however, had dynamited them because they disapproved of idolatry. Many Hazara seemed to have difficulty believing this. 'Perhaps they were looking for gold underneath,' suggested one of the men in the donkey caravan, when I asked him. But they didn't seem very worried about it. It must have been strange to find the giant statues absent, when they had been visible from every side of the valley for a millennium and a half. But as the man said, 'There are things which matter much more to us.'[61]

I emerged into a monk's meditation cell, set back from a long open veranda. I sat in the cell and looked out over the broad green valley, a hundred feet below, to the white snow peaks behind. The scene might once have resembled a miniature version of Lhasa before the Chinese invasion: the whole edifice around the Buddhas painted in bright colours, prayer-flags on the peaks and the valley filled on holy days by the chanting from processions of monks in saffron robes. The dynamited niches, without their Buddhas, now echoed the earliest forms of pre-Gandharan representation, in which the Buddha is depicted only by an empty seat, showing where he had once been.

---

61. Babur passed through Bamiyan on his journey but although he can't have missed the Buddhas, he never mentioned them. He had no interest, it seems, in a pre-Islamic past. The lack of interest may reflect the Islamic opposition to pagan idols. In the nineteenth century, the locals apparently had no idea what the statues represented and it took the study of Chinese chronicles and related statues for a British team to establish that they had been Buddhas.

I Am the Zoom

Bamiyan was now a garrison town. The northern passes were clear of snow and it was possible to drive to Kabul in eleven hours. A few vehicles were coming in every day. There was a major airstrip, some foreign military personnel and the offices of a number of relief agencies. Most of the people whom I saw, however, were uniformed soldiers of the new governor Khalili: clean-shaven teenagers in camouflage jackets and new CIA-supplied combat boots, mostly too large and unlaced. The tails of their double-breasted shirts stretched to their ankles. Many of the boys had used black eyeliner to make themselves look beautiful. They had filled the street, shouting at acquaintances, peering into shop fronts, fiddling with the Kalashnikovs on their backs and interrogating strangers. Land Cruisers rolled past, containing the personnel of aid agencies and American Special Forces. An Afghan commander's pick-up stopped, with a cold man holding the heavy machine gun mounted on its open back. There were no women to be seen.

I wanted to get transport to Kabul for Babur because he was too sick to be able to walk the last hundred miles with me. I spent the afternoon in the bazaar talking to truck drivers but no one was prepared to take a dog. At dusk, I began to look for accommodation. Most travellers would have slept on the floor of one of the restaurants in the bazaar, but I was tired and didn't want to leave Babur in the street, so I resorted again to the international staff. I tried not to bother MSF again because I thought they had been generous enough in Yakawlang, but when none of the other agencies were prepared to take me in I fell back on MSF and was again warmly welcomed.

I had two days' rest and I spent much of my time with a French photographer, Didier Le Fèvre, who was also staying in the MSF house. Didier had travelled across Afghanistan with the Mujahidin in the early 1980s and he was back to photograph the war. Most of the war photographers carried large digital cameras; Didier was using black-and-white film and two old Leicas. In a war zone most photographers prefer to use a zoom. Didier didn't have one. 'I am the zoom,' he said. Whereas most photographers were chasing news stories by car and helicopter in different Afghan cities, Didier had been in Bamiyan for a month without moving, photographing Hazara refugees. Didier was returning to Kabul in an MSF vehicle, and they and he kindly agreed to take Babur with them and drop him at a friend's house in Kabul.

Karaman

The next day I went down to watch the Buzkashi game, taking place on a series of fields, some fallow, some ploughed and planted, just to the east of where the Buddha statues had been. Buzkashi is a form of polo played with a dead goat instead of a ball. As I arrived, horses were cantering in through the dust, snorting into the cold air; white-bearded elders, in suit jackets, were talking in low voices at the edge of the arena; young grooms were walking the horses to limber them up, and riders with turbans tightly tied beneath their chins strutted back and forth, tapping their whips nervously against their boots. No one was interested in talking to a foreigner.

This was one of the very first games since the Taliban had banned the sport. The crowd was discussing some of the men who had gathered to play: the feudal landlords Nasir and Shushuri, and Karaman, a famous player from Dang-e-Safilak in a tall woollen hat. Commander Yawari from Yakawlang, it was said, had come three days along the mined road to be here on a horse valued at ten million Afghanis.

Some of the horses were village ponies with plain blankets, canvas girths and reins made from string, but most were elaborately decorated. Abdul Qoudus from Shaidan was preparing his white stallion again. He had already dressed and undressed the animal twice. The horse was turning nervously on its halter and dribbling over its tight double bit. First Qoudus spread the *julum* blanket on its back, which he said his wife had taken a month to weave. It was a two-metre-long kilim with thirty bands of woven design, alternating between black, white and red, and fringed with a line of quivering coloured tassels. He laid a separate saddlecloth over the *julum* and tied a band of bright orange and green, called a *taule*, around the horse's neck. He smoothed the tassels on the nose and neck and flicked the glinting metal discs on the bridle and made them ring. He took a bright patchwork neck quilt with a diamond borderline and tassels, and pulled it over the horse's tall, blue-veined ears and stretched it to the broad shoulders. In the centre of the horse's forehead hung a brass disc set with green glass. Finally he lifted on the saddle, with its high-rearing pommel. It was covered with burgundy carpet worked with black, orange and white flowers and tassels of electric green and pink.

Khalili's soldiers stood in a line along the steep ridges, above the monks' cells and silhouetted against the bright sky. Overweight security officials with radios and Russian hats were wandering through the thousands of spectators who had now gathered up the slopes and along the cliff walls to the north. On the south side of the arena was a team of foreign soldiers in civilian clothes carrying large guns, and above them, on the hospital roof, chairs were being arranged for Khalili.

Abdul Qoudus, like many of the jockeys, was wearing the new American brown all-in-one thermal combat suit as his jodhpurs. He had wrapped grey felt bandages around his calves and, before jumping into his saddle, he swapped shoes with his groom – taking off his white, battered baseball boots and slipping into a pair of highly polished, brown tasselled loafers.

The ground was more suitable for a steeplechase than polo. Qoudus joined the other riders, who were exercising their horses at full gallop, clearing ditches, furrows, field boundaries, rocky ground and drystone walls, their bodies leaning almost horizontal, swept back into their saddles.

More of Khalili's security forces stepped down from pick-up trucks. There were rumours that BHL, Bernard Henri-Lévi, the celebrity French philosopher and now the French prime minister's special representative for Afghanistan, was to arrive by helicopter from Kabul and watch the match. But he never made it.

The game began with the teams converging on the body of a goat. The pack leader leaned out of his saddle at the gallop till his right hand was almost touching the ground, grabbed the goat by its hindquarters, lifted himself back into the saddle and, wrapping his leg around the carcass for extra grip, turned his pony on its back legs and spurred for the opposition's goal. He had it for only a few seconds before a man from Nayak tore it from his hand and raced off in the other direction. The mass of horseflesh plunged after him, spectators running from the flailing hooves, till the pack turned fast towards the other side of the pitch.

Commandant Yawari, who was not playing but circling the pitch on his grey, called out for his jockey to swap. This was against the rules. The man cantered up to the edge of the crowd on Yawari's prize horse. The slash of a Buzkashi whip had opened his face from ear to point of chin. He stumbled off, another jockey vaulted into the saddle and some soldiers ran in holding their rifles to stop the horseman re-entering the pitch. The jockey did not look at their weapons. He acknowledged neither their threats nor the crowd's cheers, but frowned in concentration, his eyes fixed between the ears of his horse. He spurred towards the soldiers, driving them back on either side, and when he was through, he held his hands still above the saddle pommel as though in prayer, touched his heels to the horse's flanks, leaned back in the saddle, cast his eyes up to the ridge line and released his horse into the gallop. Beneath him, the legs of the horse pounded towards the sand-cloud and the screaming pack.

As the north wind moved the dust, I could see the quivering hindquarters of Abdul Qoudus's white horse backing out of the knot and then being squeezed in again with the thighs of its roaring jockey. Just as Yawari's jockey reached the tumult, Karaman emerged, at the canter and then the gallop, pressed against a man from Shaidan. They were both clutching a leg of the goat. The loudspeakers shouted, 'Karaman, Karaman' and the crowd shouted, 'Karaman, Karaman,' because no one knew the name of the other man and, to justify their cries, Karaman broke away with the goat and dropped it neatly for a goal.

*

The next morning, I got a letter of introduction from Aziz, a friendly and intelligent official in Governor Khalili's office. I took Babur for a final walk. After a day's rest, he was again curious and active. We walked onto the plateau beside the remains of the great Ghorid fort and he trotted beside me marking tree after tree along the small canal. When he ran in front, I called him back. He ignored me and kept going; I chased him. As he reached an old tank, he slowed enough for me to catch him by the scruff and to see what had excited him. Tied to a track was a young Asian wolf, about half Babur's side. His ribcage was visible and he was turning desperately from side to side. A group of young soldiers sat near him, smiling at his exhausted struggle. They said they had trapped the wolf as a cub and would sell him to a general.

I turned and walked away, pulling Babur with me. Babur looked up at me warily with his yellow wolf's eyes. He was only half a domestic animal. Although he had chosen to follow me and trusted me to touch him and feed him, I never felt I owned him. He was autonomous. Nothing would induce him to chase a stick or sit on command or come when called. He never begged or tried to endear himself. I released him. He ran ahead and rolled in the dust and as I approached him he ran ahead again. This was a game he enjoyed. When

I reached him, breathless, for the fourth time, he rolled over on his back for me to tickle his stomach.

I wondered whether he might not be strong enough to do the last four days to Kabul, but I wasn't prepared to risk it so I scratched him one more time and then led him back to the MSF compound, checked his water and confirmed with Didier that he was willing to take him to the capital. Then I tied Babur to a post, pulled some dried mud out of his dusty coat, put my pack on my back and walked out.

Khalili's Troops

I was now entirely alone for the first time since I had met Babur at Dahan Rezak. As I entered the bazaar, the snow was falling past the empty niches where the Buddhas had once stood. At three check-posts on the road out of town, Khalili's soldiers stopped and questioned me.[62] They were mostly boys from distant villages, with new uniforms from America and salaries from Iran. They didn't care who they stopped. My pack was heavy, I had forty-five kilometres to walk that day and I was frustrated by having to stop and answer their questions. On the outskirts of town, an older man ran out of another guard post.

'Who are you?' he shouted.

'I am Rory from Scotland.'

'Where are you going?'

'To Kabul.'

'Why are you alone? Why are you not in a vehicle? Come here.' Twenty other men with rifles had appeared behind him.

---

62. In the eleven weeks since the Taliban had left, the Hazara district had been peaceful and Khalili, the governor (a Hazara mullah from a poor family), had no plausible rival. The new commanders, whatever their social origins, were acting like the old feudal lords. They administered justice, distributed development aid and represented their districts to the governor. They were not all educated or even literate, and they often helped themselves to foreign money, but their districts were surprisingly calm and most people said they supported Khalili. He even seemed to be relatively popular with the new government in Kabul.

'I'm sorry, I've been stopped by four check posts already – I don't have time for this. I have letters from Khalili and I have permission to walk on this road.'

'I said, "Come here". Now boy!' shouted the commander.

'Goodbye.' I turned and walked on.

I had gone about twenty yards when I heard people running behind me; my sleeve was grabbed; I turned to shake the man off and he punched me in the face: the knuckles striking the side of my cheekbone just below the eye. I stumbled and then turned around with my own fists-ready. He stepped back and we circled around each other, with me feeling clumsy under my pack.

About twenty Hazara had now run up and were gathering in a circle around us. I was only just aware of the others. I did not meet their eyes or look in their faces. All my attention was now on the man who had punched me and who was looking for a chance to punch me again.

'What are you doing?' I shouted. 'I am a *mehman* in your country, a *mosaffer*.' I was using Koranic words to remind them that Muslims are supposed to be hospitable to travellers.

As I spoke the man lunged for my walking stick and grabbed it. We struggled for a second and then he ripped it out of my hands. I couldn't believe this was happening. My reactions seemed stupidly slow. I felt like a baited bear. The man swung the stick at me, slowly enough for me to move back. He was taking his time and the crowd was watching to see how he was going to hurt me. My cheek stung from his punch and I was very angry. He wasn't. He seemed excited instead, turning the stick in his hand, thinking about how and where to strike me next. He looked at the older man in the crowd, who nodded at him. Then he announced, 'I'm going to knock you down.'

'Stop.' I said. 'This is wrong. I'm a Briton. I am a guest of your Governor Khalili. You have just punched me in the face.

I'm a very important man; you can't do this to me. What is your name?'

The man wasn't listening. He feinted with the stick. I stepped back. He feinted once more, slowly enough for me to duck. He was just warming up and getting the feel of my stick. His pupils were unnaturally enlarged, his mouth was fixed into something between a grimace and a smile and his hands were trembling slightly. There was something very practised, even graceful, about the way he moved the stick from hand to hand. He'd done this many times before and the crowd had watched it before.

I glanced at the crowd and saw the interpreter whom I had met in the MSF house. 'This man,' I shouted. 'He knows me, he'll explain.'

The older man, apparently the commander, interrupted, 'Do you know him?'

There was a pause, the man with the stick turned to look at his commander and then the interpreter said, very distinctly, 'Yes, he is the foreigner who has walked here from Herat.'

'Why is he walking? Foreigners drive Land Cruisers.'

While they were talking, I swung my pack off, opened the top compartment and drew out the letter from Khalili's representative introducing me to his commanders. I handed it to the interpreter to read because I assumed the men were illiterate. 'Listen to this,' I shouted at the commander, 'Khalili asks you to help me. Not punch me in the face.'

The interpreter read the letter in a calm, neutral voice: 'The governor requests his commanders to assist and protect the historian of the Hazara people, Rory Stewart.'

'Why didn't you show us the letter earlier?' The commander demanded.

'I told you about it,' I shouted back, 'and you wouldn't listen. You're coming with me to the palace to tell Khalili why you assaulted his guest. You will lose your job.'

'I advise you to forget this,' interjected the interpreter firmly, 'they didn't realize you were a foreigner.'

'The fact that I'm a foreigner is irrelevant. They shouldn't do this to anyone.' The soldiers laughed. Hitting people was their job. 'What are you all laughing at? You are evil men . . . thugs.'

'You're the evil man,' shouted the commander. 'What do you expect? You can't just walk around alone . . .'

To my relief, the MSF administrator had now appeared as well. I told him the story. He seemed a little embarrassed. I could see how I must have looked – a dirty foreigner sweating and shouting after a brawl with some soldiers. 'Who exactly punched you?' he asked.

I looked down the row of men. My stick had been dropped. I was certain that it was the tall man, but I was unsettled by his calm, martyred expression as he stared at the ground. 'This man . . .' I said, and then I was fed up with the whole thing. 'Forget it . . .' I muttered, picked up my stick and walked off. I was so angry that I could think about little else for the next two hours. I had insulted the commander in front of his men, threatened to report him to the governor and was now setting off alone down an empty road. There was nothing to stop the commander sending his men after me or radioing the check posts ahead to deal with me.

For the next ten kilometres, I turned around at every noise and wondered what chance I might have of cutting sideways into the hills. But two hours passed and nothing happened and I concluded that he couldn't be bothered with me. In India and Pakistan, security forces had seemed worried about hitting foreigners, being reported to their superiors and losing their jobs. But these men didn't appear to care. They probably thought the governor wouldn't mind their assaulting a traveller. His main priority (encouraged by millions of CIA dollars) was catching Taliban and Al-Qaeda escapees, of whom I might be one. Nevertheless they hadn't killed me and

I wondered whether that was because I had showed them the letter from the governor. The incident seemed to show that despite the traumas of the last twenty-four years, Hazarajat was still in some ways an orderly society. If you had a letter and weren't a direct threat, people largely left you alone.

I saw three more check posts over the next twenty kilo-metres and I held out the letter before I reached them. The first one snapped that I was an infidel but let me pass. The second check post did the same. The third one was at the base of the red fort of Zorak. This had been a large Ghorid fortress. Here Genghis Khan's favourite grandson was killed by an arrow, redirecting Genghis's fury against the mountain kingdoms. The check post read the letter, questioned me, let me go, called me back, read it again and then when I was on my way, called me back again. Their commander announced that he was going to drive me to the headquarters in Bamiyan for further questioning, fifteen kilometres back down the road, which I had been walking on for three hours. Despite having resolved, only three hours earlier, never to defy a policeman again, I lost my patience.

'No, I refuse.' I replied. 'I am a guest, I am a close friend of the governor. I stayed in his guest house. He has given me permission.' None of this was true. I walked on ignoring the angry shouts behind me, and to my relief there were no footsteps following me and the shouts faded. I turned up a narrow gorge towards the snow peaks, and saw no one for four hours.

And I Have Mine

Then, at dusk, I came to the Hazara village of Lower Kalu. I was nearing the edge of the Hazara district and in a couple of days I would reach Pashtun territory. I began to climb the steep mud slope towards the castle, past the very recent crater made by a coalition bomb. I was aware of the familiar smell of human faeces outside the houses. I hammered on the gate, making the iron chain rattle on the dark wood. After a minute, an old man appeared.

'Peace be with you,' I said.

'And also with you,' he replied. He looked at the purple bruise on my cheek and then said, 'Come in.'

I followed him through the courtyard to the guest room. Unusually for a Hazara he did not suggest that I should sleep in the mosque. He put a cushion under me, gathered some twigs, fed the fire and blew on it till it flamed fiercely. Then he asked if I would give him my socks so he could dry them. I gave them to him gratefully. Then he left, and returned with a pot of sugared tea and sat cross-legged in silence watching me drink. When I had finished, he brought some plates of rice and spinach and said, 'We are still the commandants in the valley, but the Taliban killed our flocks, so I am sorry that I can't give you meat. This food has been given by foreigners.'

Only when he saw that I was warm and had finished eating did he lean forward and ask, 'And who are you? And where are you from?'

I answered and then asked him about his family. Nasir-i-Yazdani said that he was one of the chiefs of the Besut tribe of the Hazara, related to the great Begs whom I had met in the Sar Jangal valley two hundred kilometres away: the Sangizart chiefs of the Blackfoot and Zia, the young Katlish chief of the Nauruz Beg. They were almost all descendants or relations of the great Hazara leader, Mir Yazdan Baksh, and called themselves *Mir Bache-ha* (Children of the Mir). Mir Yazdan Baksh had been executed on the orders of the Afghan king beneath the Buddhas at Bamiyan at the end of the nineteenth century.

After dinner Nasir-i-Yazdani's grandsons perched on his lap and his nephew sat beside him, while he discussed his grandfather's pilgrimage to Mecca in the 1930s and I told him a little about my walk.

'You're walking alone?' said Nasir-i-Yazdani. 'What has happened to Hazara hospitality? A guest cannot walk alone. My nephew here will accompany you tomorrow over the pass to Besut and my cousin there will see you to Maidan Shahr.'

While Nasir-i-Yazdani was talking, I sketched him. I have the picture beside me now. With his thin beard, narrow eyes and lined face he looks like a solemn Mongol emperor. I have failed to capture his smile or his kindness.

After dinner we went outside into the snow. I had been walking through the Hazara district for weeks. I had seen the feudal grandeur of Sar Jangal, the destruction at Yakawlang, the aggression of Khalili's soldiers and now this gentle welcome. But I realized I knew very little about the Hazara.

A half moon lit the valley and the Kalu River was heavy with melt-water. The river moved down the narrow gorge, and vanished into the darkness, skirting the red castle that Genghis burnt, towards the colossal Buddha niches. It flowed seventy kilometres to the charred beam that suggested a balcony in the Shaidan bazaar where, pressing into the parched fields, it drowned the winter wheat.

Nasir-i-Yazdani said that he'd hit a Russian vehicle with a rocket, near the crater where the coalition had blown up four Taliban in a car. Then he led me inside because it was cold and

he thought I was tired. I told him how I had hoped to understand the Hazara but had only gathered disconnected and
puzzling anecdotes. I asked what could explain the Hazara to
me. He smiled and put clean blankets on the floor. And when
I lay down he removed a bundle from a carved wooden box,
kissed it, said a prayer, unwrapped it and opening the Koran,
read:

> And what can explain the steep path to you?
> It is the freeing of a slave,
> Or the giving of food in a day of starvation . . .

And as I lay wondering who he was, he continued gently:

> Unbeliever, I do not worship what you worship,
> Nor do you worship what I worship.
> I shall never worship what you worship,
> Nor will you ever worship what I worship.
> You have your religion and I have mine.

The Scheme of Generation

The next morning his nephews walked with me. We passed a bazaar where seventy men had been killed by the Russians and from which one hundred and fifty people had been taken by the Taliban. Three months earlier, a small group of Arabs had been stationed in the bazaar, fighting on behalf of the Taliban. Then we began the long climb over gentle snow slopes to the thirteen-thousand-foot Hajigak pass. Nasir-i-Yazdani's ancestor Mir Yazdan Baksh had crossed this pass. So had Genghis's army and the Afghan King Abdul Rahman Khan on his great campaign to conquer the Hazara, a hundred years ago.

On the other side of the pass, we reached a chain of men clearing snow off the road. They were supervised by an old man who swung a long rosary bead while the men swung their spades. He was a cousin of the local chief.[63] He led me into the side valley in which the castle of Harzard is hidden from the road and fed me dehydrated milk, which is called Makse. The son of the chief then entered. I asked him about his family. He replied,

Mir Waiz Hotak begat Shah Ashrafi Hotak; and Shah Ashrafi Hotak begat Shah Hussein Hotak, who was given the government of Kandahar by Nadir, the Shah of Iran;

And Shah Hussein Hotak begat Malik Waisi Hotak; and Malik Waisi Hotak begat Abdul Rehman who left Kandahar and

---

63. Ahmadi of Dewali Ghulakesh.

built the castle of Besut; and Abdul Rehman begat Nur
Muhammad, who built this castle of Harzard, and Amir
Muhammad, from whom is descended Mir Yazdan Baksh;

. And Nur Muhammad begat Daulat Muhammad; and Daulat
Muhammad begat Isfand Wakil; and Isfand Wakil begat Lal
Wakil; and Lala Wakil begat Saifullah Wakil; and Saifullah
Wakil begat Aladad Wakil; and Aladad Wakil begat Khan
Ali Wakil;

And Khan Ali Wakil begat Haji Hussein Ahmed Khan; and Haji
Hussein Ahmad Khan begat Haji Assan Jan Khan, of whom
was born Muhammad Hakim, who is me.

He had just recited fifteen generations from memory. This
was more than the fourteen that separated Christ from the
exile in Babylon or David from Abraham, or the ten that separated Abraham from Noah and Noah from Adam. And he
could, and did, go sideways as well, showing how Mir Yazdan
Baksh was descended from Abdul Rahman and how he in
turn was related to Mir Zafr of Kalu, with whose great-great-
grandson, Nasir-i-Yazdani, I had stayed the previous night.
Although this man was young he was a traditional Hazara
chief. Like his relative Nasir, he had started in 'Shura-e-tafaq',
the party of the Hazara landlords after the Russian invasion,
but like Nasir his family had quickly realized their error and
allied with Khalili. This had allowed them to be relatively well
supplied with weapons from Peshawar and to retain both
their power and their land. Those landlords who had not
joined Khalili had largely been toppled by Iranian-sponsored
village revolutions.[64]

---

64. The Russian invasion of Afghanistan coincided with the Islamic revolution in Iran. The Iranian government, which was Shia, was particularly
interested in the Shia Hazara and, as well as supporting them against the
Russians, encouraged them to stage an Iranian-style revolution. A funda-
mental ingredient of this there, as in Iran, was the confiscation of land
from feudal landlords.

I was quicker without Babur and I covered seventy-seven kilometres in those two days. I entered Dahan-e-Siar Sang that night an hour after dark, under a light snowfall with no moon to light the way and the ice cracking frequently under my feet. My stomach had gone and I had a hacking cough. The zip on my jacket had jammed, one of my bootlaces had snapped and the rice bag, which covered my backpack, had fallen to pieces. I had bed-bug bites and prickly heat, my nails were long and my hair had not been cut in four months. At the door of the commander's house in Dahan-e-Siar Sang, I ran my filthy hands over my failure of a beard, black eye, blistered lips and peeling nose and looked at my clothes, which had not been washed for three weeks. I could understand why the commander was not immediately keen for me to sleep on his floor.

The Source of the Kabul River

On the next day I climbed to fourteen thousand feet, through bright snow, to cross the last pass, the Unai and then descended for two hours from the ridge. In the late afternoon, I reached a half-crumbled fortress with six octagonal towers and arrow slits in the shapes of long-tailed clubs and diamonds. An Afghan king had built this Siahak fort to protect Kabul and Ghazni from the Hazara and had appointed a Persian to command it. It had still been the frontier with the Hazara in 1998, when the Taliban finally broke through Siahak, killing one hundred and fifty people on their way to Bamiyan. It was the frontier again now, manned by a garrison of Besuti Hazara under the solemn-looking commander of the marches, Commander Muhammad Hussein Fahimi.

Beyond the fortress were four sacred springs, the source of the Kabul River, which I would follow now out of Afghanistan. I had seen the river before on previous journeys, some years earlier. I had watched it flow through the narrow Sarobi Gorge, where the journalists were executed, and past the olive trees of Jalalabad, where Dr Brydon staggered to safety. I had looked at it tumbling beneath the foliage of the Shisham and the Kikul trees and the tumult of mynah birds, beyond Peshawar in Pakistan. I had sat beside it at Attock, where its brown torrent ran into the green water of the Indus, and where the last Khwarezmian overlord of the Ghorids spurred his horse over the cliff to escape from Genghis Khan, prompting Genghis to say, 'Leave him. There is a father that a son must have.' Here at the source, the stream was a narrow bubbling slurry of grey effluent, lined with eggshells, potato peelings, onions and engine oil, which were signs of Siahak's prosperity and proximity to Kabul. The willows on the banks were bare.

That evening, the commander of the Hazara marches showed his status by laying out pills labelled Drotravine, Metanemic Acid and Rowatex. He ate one of each before offering them around and everyone, except me, took a handful. Then he drank from a bottle, which had a picture of a brain on one side and an oxen plough team on the other. It looked veterinary.

At breakfast, he reminded me that I had reached the frontier of the Hazara state. 'Now you are in the flatlands of Wardak. Beyond are the Tajik and the Pashtun-Taliban-Al-Qaeda. This is the first place where the roads are clear all the way to Kabul. The difficulties you must have met so far were problems of snow and mountains. Now the landscape is flat. It is only seventy-one kilometres to Kabul. But the people are much more dangerous. Get in a car. You will be in Kabul in two hours not two days. Do not walk.'

I said that I had to finish the journey to Kabul on foot. I couldn't explain why I was determined to walk every step of the way. I agreed with him that it would be stupid to be killed on the last night of nineteen months of walking. But I did not feel that I could stop so close to my goal.

'Is the problem money? We can give you money for a jeep . . .'

Eventually and very reluctantly, he said goodbye and ordered two of his soldiers to accompany me to Maidan Shahr. They were young and new to their jobs, and far from their home villages. The older boy, Nasir, was seventeen and had just returned from six weeks in Tehran. His clean-shaven chin and his yellow-tinted aviator sunglasses were the legacy of this trip. Just outside Siahak we passed a girl who looked

fourteen. She glanced at us as she was drawing water. 'Shall
we catch her and fuck her?' he asked. His friend laughed
loudly. Then Nasir asked, 'How do you say "fuck" in English?'
and repeated my answer over and over again, laughing more
each time. In Iran, people had often wanted to talk about the
beauty of Persian girls but Afghans, like Pakistani villagers,
never discussed women with me.

They led me to a small shrine to the Prophet's uncle,
where I admired twenty black carp in a slender pool of the
Kabul River. Now that we had crossed the final mountain
pass, the land was immediately and obviously richer. There
was no snow on the ground and the day was very hot. In the
fields were Tajik men with beards, much longer and thicker
than any Hazara's. Their houses had long balconies and their
irrigation ditches were lined with double avenues of poplar
and willow. The bazaar of Takana was filled with birdsong
from cages slung on all the eaves, above crates of oranges, jars
of eggs, onions and open sacks of grain. For the first time
since Kamenj I saw orchards.

Beyond Takana, ten kilometres into our walk, we were
stopped by a local commander who recognized my young
escort as Hazara. He told them that they were beyond their
frontier, had no right to walk there and should turn back.
I intervened. After an argument he waved us through, but I
could see the young men were worried. Every ten minutes
thereafter they asked me why we couldn't get a car; they were
walking more and more slowly, and at this pace we would
never make it to Maidan Shahr before dark. Finally Nasir, the
seventeen-year-old, said, 'We were told to deliver you to Haji
Ghulam Ahmed but he is not in Maidan Shahr at all . . . he is
in Bamiyan. We can't continue.'

That they could not continue had been clear for some
time. I sat them on the track beneath some plum trees, gave
them some money and some Kendal Mint Cake, which a soldier had given me in Bamiyan, wrote a reference for them

praising them to their commander for their courageous work and sent them home. There were twenty-five kilometres left to Maidan Shahr.

Taliban

Wardak had been an early Taliban stronghold. It was still commanded by an ex-minister of the Taliban.[65] In the Tajik and Hazara areas where I had spent the last month, most people seemed to support the coalition bombardment. Here in Wardak, which was a Pushtun area, most people probably opposed it. I hardly noticed the landscape during the next half an hour, although I should have found it beautiful. I was very conscious of being alone. The sunlight, much softer here than in the high mountains, fell through clouds on to russet hills, uneven terraces and close-packed orchards.

At the next small bazaar, I entered the first Pashtun village. A group of young men who were standing outside a shop called me over. As I approached, they turned to face me, squaring their shoulders. One had his weapon in his hand. I felt to my surprise a change in the pattern of my breathing.

I greeted them formally, '*Salaam Aleikum*'. (Peace be with you.) '*Manda na Bashi*'. (May you not be tired.)

They did not reply to my greeting. A fat, bearded man in the centre snapped in Dari, 'Where are you going?'

'Do you speak Dari?' I replied.

'Yes,' he said, confused.

'Well then, perhaps you did not hear me,' I said. 'Let me repeat myself, *Salaam Aleikum*.'

Pause.

---

65. In 2002, five girls' schools were burned down in Wardak, by people who have kept firmly to their Taliban views.

'*Waleikum Salaam.*' (And also with you.) he replied.

'Is your house well? Is your body strong? *Manda na Bashi.* May your family prosper. May you live long.'

He replied immediately this time, 'My house is well. Is your house well? My body is strong. Is your body strong? *Manda na Bashi.* Long life to you.'

I smiled and shook his hand solemnly.

But when I tried to withdraw my hand, he would not let go. One of the other men took a step back as though he was uncertain what was going to happen.

'What is this?' I asked sharply. 'Why are you holding my hand?'

'Because I wanted to bring you to my shop . . .' he replied.

'Release it.'

He did so. I turned to the others, explaining that I was writing a history book and that I had walked here from Herat. As they were discussing this amongst themselves, I said a crisp goodbye and set off down the path, waiting all the time for the whistle, or shout or shot, which would call me back to the group, but which in this case did not come.

Ten minutes later, I heard someone running up behind me. He was a young man with a black turban and a rifle. I stopped. 'I am a hafiz of the Koran,' said the man by way of introduction.

'I am a teacher of history,' I said.

The man looked at me and then said, 'Show me your gun.'

'I said I am a teacher . . . do you understand . . . not a soldier . . . I carry books not a weapon.' I tried to keep my voice slow, businesslike and a little weary. Two of his friends came running up to join us, one of whom was carrying a rifle. I realized I could not understand what they were saying to each other – I had just moved from the Dari-speaking area, where I had been for the last six weeks, into a Pashto-speaking area, and I could not speak Pashto. But they spoke to me in Dari.

'Where are you from?'

'I am from Indonesia,' I said. I chose Indonesia because it was a large Muslim country that they would have nothing against and know little about. I suspected they did not like the British.

One of them laughed. 'That is a lie . . . where is your passport?'

'In the passport office in Kabul . . . I don't carry it because I don't want to lose it.' It was in a money belt around my waist.

'Speak some Indonesian.'

'*Salamat Sore. Apa Kabar? Baik-baik saja? Ada masalah di sini?*'

'Say, "I am an Indonesian professor of history."'

'*Saya bekarja sebagai . . .*'

'Are you a Muslim?'

'We have one God, the same God,' I replied. 'I am a follower of Hazrat Jesus, we have three books, you have four . . . you fast at Ramadan, we fast at Lent.' I didn't want to say I was a Muslim because I thought I'd be caught out. But I presented myself as a very Muslim Christian.[66]

'Do you speak English?'

'Yes.'

'How?'

'Because I am a professor.'

We walked side by side for a while and then one of the new men said, 'Give me four hundred dollars . . .'

'Is this a request for *zakat*?' I asked, referring to the obligatory Muslim donation to the poor.

'No,' he said confused. 'No, I don't need *zakat*.'

'Well then I will keep my money for a more deserving cause.'

---

66. Muslims are enjoined to be kind to children of the book (Christians and Jews). To say that one is an atheist or a Hindu would be provocative and dangerous.

We were silent again until we reached a large group of young mullahs who were standing in the middle of the street. I stopped, introduced myself to them, and invited them to walk with us. I felt safer the more people I met. When I said I had been in Pakistan, one gave me an impromptu Urdu examination.

'Do women uncover their heads or wear trousers in Indonesia?'

'I am afraid to say that a few women occasionally uncover their heads in the villages,' I replied. Very few women cover their heads in Indonesia.

Another young mullah joined us.

'This man,' they said, 'was the Taliban head of this village.'

'Peace be with you,' I said.

He nodded gravely. 'And also with you.' He shook my hand, enquired if I was a Muslim and, as I was going through the same lengthy answer, asked, 'What do you think of the Taliban? Who do you support, America or the Taliban?'

'I am a guest in your country. I am not an American or a Taliban. I cannot answer you.'

'Who do you think is better: Usama Bin Laden or George Bush?'

'I am an Indonesian professor of history; I am a guest in your country. I know nothing about either of these men. My speciality is Genghis Khan ... I could tell you about him. Who do you want to be president?'

'Mullah Mohammed Umar,' they shouted in unison.

'Who do you think is better, Usama Bin Laden or George Bush?' the mullah asked again.

'I know who you think is better,' I replied, 'but I know nothing about the subject.'

'Do you know how many civilians the Americans and British have killed in this country? Thousands,' said a man with a rifle, 'tens of thousands.'

'Have they killed them in your village?'

'No, not in this village. We have not seen an American or a British. They would not dare to come to our village because they are afraid to die and we would kill them at once. They are afraid to die because they have no God. They are pathetic and decadent and corrupt. Why are they afraid of their deaths? They have nothing to live for. But I am ready to die now. We are all ready to die now because we know that we will go to God. That is why they can never defeat us. That is why their civilization will be destroyed. This is *jihad.*' Everyone around nodded earnestly.

'In any case we can all hope,' I said. 'God willing, peace will come.'

'Peace will only come when all the foreigners have left this country,' snapped a new arrival. 'Are you a Muslim?'

I began to explain again. He spat on the ground, turned his back and walked off followed by five others. The Taliban head, however, took his leave gracefully, embracing me and wishing me luck. I embraced him with a show of respect and affection which I did not feel.

I was left with the three original men.

'Why don't you go down to the river there and examine the spring,' suggested the one who had asked me for money.

'No, thank you,' I said, 'I am in a hurry . . . I have to get to Maidan Shahr before dark . . . I must keep going.'

'Go on.'

'No, thank you,' I said seriously. 'I must keep going.'

They all laughed.

'Why are you laughing?' I asked.

'Because if you had gone down there, you would have been killed,' they replied.

We walked side by side in silence for a while until we reached another village. A convoy of pick-up trucks drove up behind us and an older man shouted something from one of the trucks.

'That is our Commander Haji Ghulam Ahmed. He wants us. We must go now and speak to him. We will catch you up.'

They didn't.

I quickened my pace, aware of tiredness and a slight tension in my muscles. My focus during the previous hour had been immediate and practical. I had wanted to get to the next village. The men struck me as ignorant bullies with a strangled and dangerous view of God and a stupid obsession with death. It occurred to me that they could have killed me. I did not envy the government, which was going to have to deal with them.

But I wasn't sure whether they had wanted to kill me or whether they had just been winding me up; nor whether I had handled them correctly. Perhaps I had just been lucky that the commander appeared. I hardly took in any of the scenery over the next hour. My emotions seemed muted. It occurred to me that being threatened by the Taliban made an exciting anecdote but mostly I thought about the conversation with distaste and frustration.

Toes

I turned out of the Jalrez valley, crossed a gentle ridge and descended. At dusk, I reached the mud compound that served as the barracks of Maidan Shahr and banged at the gate. It opened and rifles were levelled at me. I could not tell much about the men from their camouflage waistcoats, *shalwar kemis*, gym shoes and Soviet belts. Their Chitrali caps, however, suggested that their sympathies were with the new government, not the Taliban, who usually wore turbans. They shouted questions, I muttered answers, a commander was sent for. I pulled at the straps of my pack to take some of the weight off my shoulders and looked at my feet. More questions. Finally I was invited in.

They led me into a government office built during the Russian era. There had once been glass in the windows and there were a number of small empty rooms off the main corridor. We all sat in one room on the mud floor. There were twelve of us, and it was too small for us all to lean against the walls, but they pushed me to the head of the room. They asked me questions about the journey and about my family. There was a petrol stove and I began to warm up. I asked them about their families and, perhaps because they were men away from home, they replied at length. Many of them had been refugees.

A young man with well-groomed, bouffant hair was sent to the outbuildings to cook. He returned with two large platters of rice, which we all shared. They were amused to see how much I ate and kept encouraging me to eat more.

'Sorry if we were rough,' said the commander when we had finished. 'You are wearing local clothes. You don't quite look like an Afghan – your face, your boots. We thought you were an Arab or Pakistani. There were many Al-Qaeda looking like you here, exhausted, underfed, with a backpack on their back . . . they even had your stare. There were thousands of them in the valley from Jalrez to Maidan Shahr only a few months ago . . . We are Tajik. They were our enemy.'

'And now?'

'They have gone. But this is not a comfortable area for us – we are a garrison surrounded by hostile people.'

Some of the men were playing cards with a pack of forty-four. I felt tired but relaxed, cradling the hot glass of tea in my hands, leaning against the wall, joining in the chat. We heard some firing in the street and the men interrupted their game to rush outside. They returned ten minutes later to say that it was nothing important.

I told them about my conversation with the Taliban on the road.

'Did you meet Haji Ghulam Ahmed?' asked a young man.

I said I had glimpsed him. 'Why?' I asked.

'He was the Taliban Deputy Minister of Planning,' said the young man who had done the cooking. I had noticed him because he was the only man who hadn't so far said anything and because he had tucked his *shalwar* trousers into his socks. 'He is still the commander of this area. It was dangerous for you to walk that road. You were lucky to make it. These people are all against the American invasion.'

'And you?'

'The Taliban cut off my toes.' He pointed to his feet. Despite his socks, it was clear that both feet ended at the first joint. He smiled slightly when he saw my expression.

'Why did they cut them?'

'Because I had not grown a beard.'

He had grown one now. It was thin and scrawny, like mine, so he was called 'Hazara boy'.

We went to sleep as usual in a tight huddle. Various people clambered over me to go outside and squat in the courtyard during the night, someone kept his radio on and we woke at dawn. But I slept well. I was glad to be indoors and I felt safe. The bread for breakfast was warm and the tea was sweet. I drew a picture of the commander and gave the men the emergency rations which I had kept in my pack since Herat and had not touched. It was 'Menu 22: Vegetarian Pasta Al Fredo'. I took out the sheet of paper, which explained to US servicemen how many calories were required to remain fit for fighting, and showed them the powder which would heat the food if combined with water. They didn't understand. I was worried that they might try to eat the powder, so I added the water, slipped in the pasta and heated it for them. They all tried a little but they found the rich cheese sauce revolting.

They gave me presents for my family: a sachet of shampoo, a packet of cream biscuits and some henna with which to decorate my mother's hands. I put them in my pack. Finally, I finished my drawing of the commander and said goodbye. One of the men walked the first kilometre with me to see me safely onto the road, and said how pleased they had been to have me to stay.

There was a cold wind as I turned from Maidan Shahr onto the main Ghazni–Kabul road. The sky was overcast. Drab gravel and earth stretched on either side and the road was lined with numbers and letters in scarlet paint marking minefields. Every ten minutes or so I was passed by a truck.

That night in the barracks had been a moment of transformation. I had often been uncomfortable in villages: the filthy, crowded cold rooms, the illiterate men, the limited conversation. The more tired and bruised I was the more I wanted to get away from such places. But that night had felt like a homecoming. There was nothing pompous in the way they had spoken to me. I had savoured the hot rice, the firm floor, the shelter from the wind and the companionship. I felt how proud the men were of what they could provide and how lucky I was to share their space. They treated me as though I belonged with them and I felt that I did.

Perhaps also I felt that I was at last entitled to sit alongside them and share their food. It was not that my journey had earned me any privileges. Whatever I experienced when walking would never approach the hardiness of daily life in a village. But I felt I no longer needed to explain myself to my hosts and I loved that night and them for it.

As I kept moving, I was not conscious of the black gravel or the faint smell of diesel, but of something revealing itself within and beyond those things. Almost every morning, regrets and anxieties ran around my mind like a cheap tune: often repeated, revealing nothing. I waited for this to happen again. But no thoughts came. Instead I became aware of the landscape as I had once been in the Indian Himalayas. Every element around me seemed sharper, the colours more intense. I stared, expecting this to fade, but the objects only developed in reality and presence. I thought that this vision could not continue and I was suddenly afraid. It continued to intensify till I was not certain that I could sustain it.

This moment was new to me. I had not dreamed or imagined it before. Yet I recognized it. I felt that I was as I was, in this place, and that I had known it before. It was the last day of my walk. To feel in these final hours, after months of frustration, an unexplained completion, seemed too neat. But the recognition was immediate and incontrovertible. I had to accept that I had found something in the hills, which my hosts that night and most people already had. Beyond that I couldn't go. I had no words for it and I was reluctant to put words to it. Now, writing, I am tempted to say that I felt that the world had been given as a gift uniquely to me and also equally to each person alone. I had completed walking and could go home.

Marble

Crossing a ridge, I saw a large plain, a row of concrete apartment blocks and on another ridge, eight kilometres away, the Kabul Intercontinental Hotel. I descended into the Campanie Plain. In the main streets were stalls lined with postcards of buxom Hindi actresses; telephone booths; cyclists manoeuvring between ancient buses; taxi-drivers and policemen in peaked caps. A man shouted at me. I turned and he ran to join me.

'Get off the road,' he whispered, 'this is much too dangerous for you. There are British and American soldiers ahead. You can't just walk into Kabul, they will arrest you. Come with me. You can stay in the mosque.'

'They won't hurt me, thank you.'

He looked at me perplexed. 'But you're an Arab aren't you . . . ?'

'No,' I smiled. 'British.'

I turned off the main road. For nearly an hour I walked through blocks of modern concrete villas with the curving balconies of Art Deco ocean liners. They were mostly three stories high and must once have belonged to prosperous people. Where mortar rounds had opened up the walls of the houses and courtyards I could see plaster mouldings and the stumps of mature trees in large gardens. The flat roofs, where the snipers had lain, had been chipped by small-arms fire, but the scalloped decoration was still visible. The line of pockmarks, which ran in a line across every wall rising from left to right and reflecting the direction in which an automatic weapon moves in the hand, touched bands of green and rose-coloured marble. The broad avenues lined with scorched plane trees were mostly deserted. But I heard the voices of children. There were mud bricks sealing generous windows and plastic sheeting stretched across some of the ceilings, suggesting that life continued in single rooms.

I climbed the ridge into a wind that drove the dust into my eyes and passed the Intercontinental Hotel. I remembered the last time I had been there watching the Usama expert of a British newspaper sitting at a corner table, beneath the terracotta frieze: a piece of mystifying abstract art that before the Taliban period had been a row of Buddhas. He had been reaching under the filthy tablecloth to pour Pakistani whisky into his glass of Fanta and three waiters and three stringers were standing around the table. The stringers hadn't been eating any more than the waiters. You needed an expense account to spend fifteen dollars on a bad kebab and five French fries. The stringers had hoped someone would lend them a satellite phone and the waiters had waited for a chance to clear away a glass with a drop of whisky.

I came down off the ridge into the centre of town and passed a traffic jam, composed of seven stationary white Land Cruisers. The older ones said UN on their sides and contained young foreign men and women with Afghan drivers. The newer, sleeker models with one-digit number plates and a picture of the martyred leader Ahmed Shah Masud stuck to their darkened windscreens belonged to the senior Tajik military commanders. The cars had been stopped because there was a parade.

Fifty Afghan men of varying ages with dirty bearded faces beneath gleaming white helmets and wearing dress uniforms two sizes too large, were marching in a single, shambling lope, giggling a little and glancing from side to side to see how the passers-by were taking it. Four pairs of soldiers were holding hands. This was the new Afghan army established by the United States.

In the next street was a platoon of armed British para-troopers in berets. One patrol was examining the Hobnob biscuits and Minibix cereal packets in the supermarket, and another was buying some antiques. While the corporal dithered between a Ghorid coin and a terracotta Huma bird, a beggar in a full sky-blue *burqa* was trying to make him put a banknote into her cracked brown palm.

Turning into a side lane past the Indian embassy, I picked up a sheet of paper from the street, belonging to one of the foreigners who lived there. It was a draft proposal for the Afghan government written in English:

> There is a consensus in Afghan society: violence must end, respect for human rights will form the path to a last-ing peace and stability across the country. The people's aspirations must be represented in an accountable, broad-based, gender sensitive, multi-ethnic, representative gov-ernment that delivers daily value.[67]

To my right I could see the hill that hid the Emperor Babur's tomb. His grave lay on a terrace below a black mountain wall that rose as clean as the back of a marble throne. It faced a gentle slope, a broad valley and the snow peaks of Hazarajat. Beside it were the shattered stumps of two ancient plane trees, which by their girth may have been those that Babur describes placing in the garden. Babur planted the trees when he was nearly forty, fifteen years after his walk. The cousins who had patronized him in Herat were dead and so was Qasim. Herat itself had been invaded by the Uzbek warlord and was never to recover. There was no one left to prevent his drinking:

---

67. 'Afghanistan: Rebuilding a Nation: 6 national priority sub-programs'. Afghanistan's National Program for Reconstruction.

> On Thursday, 21st [April 1519] I directed that an enclosure
> should be made on the hill, on the brow of which I had planned
> out a garden. On Saturday 23rd I planted shoots of the plane
> and of the sycamore within the enclosure. At noon-day prayers
> we had a drinking party. At daybreak the next morning, we had
> an early drinking party within the newly enclosed ground. After
> midday, we mounted and returned towards Kabul. Reaching
> Khwajeh Hassan, completely drunk, we slept there.

A decade later, Babur, who by now had conquered India,
heard that his son Humayun was dangerously ill. He ordered
Humayun to be brought by water to Agra but the doctors
were unable to cure him. A courtier said that God sometimes
allowed a man to live if his friend offered his most valuable
possession. Babur replied that his own life was the dearest
thing to Humayun as Humayun's was to him. He would give
his life to God in sacrifice for his son's. The courtier begged
him to retract and instead to offer the Koh-i-Noor diamond.
But Babur replied that even that stone was not worth a life.
According to a contemporary: 'He walked three times round
the dying prince and retiring, prayed to God. After some time
he was heard to exclaim, "I have borne it away, I have borne it
away."'

As Humayun recovered, Babur began to sicken. He died
on Boxing Day, 1530. He had asked to be buried on this
particular hill in Kabul, with his grave open to the sky. His
great-grandson built a marble mosque beside the tomb with
an inscription, which reads in Peter Levi's translation:

> Only this mosque of beauty, this temple of nobility, con-
> structed for the prayers of saints and the epiphany of the
> cherubs, was fit to stand in so venerable a sanctuary as
> this highway of archangels, this theatre of heaven, the
> light garden of the godforgiven Angel King whose rest is
> in the garden of heaven, Zahiruddin Muhammad Babur
> the Conqueror.

The side palace, built by later Afghan kings, was wrecked; the sunken floors of the water tanks were smashed; the plaster was crumbling and there were bullet holes in the embossed leather ceiling. The holes made by mortar shells reflected those in the abandoned Soviet apartment blocks across the road.

The afternoon sun threw the long shadows of saplings up the gentle slopes over the traces of four-fold paths and fountains. Babur had founded an Indian empire and his descendants incorporated scalloped Indian Mughal arches into the mosque. But the hill of his tomb climbed north towards the snow peaks of Central Asia, which he had crossed on his way from Herat, and beyond them to his homeland, and Samarkand.

Turning into a side lane, I opened the gate of what had once been Usama Bin Laden's third wife's house. On the doorstep was my Babur asleep. I put my pack down and at the familiar sound he woke at once, trotting over, stumpy tail wagging, and rolled on his back for me to scratch his stomach. It was a fine stomach. I'd never seen him look so healthy, rested or alive.

Epilogue

Usama's house was now rented by my friend Peter. It was filled with British men and women working in Afghanistan, who had been feeding Babur shepherd's pie for a week. One of them, Mel, had become particularly devoted to him and spent much of each day stroking him, grooming him or feeding him. Having never eaten meat in his life, Babur was now eating it three times a day. He spent most of his time asleep in the garden, shaded by the vines or the mulberry trees. For an almost wild dog, he seemed to be adjusting quickly to domestic life.

Babur and I left by car two days later, following the Kabul River through the Khyber Pass to Pakistan. The car was small and Babur and I shared the front passenger seat, his hindquarters between my legs, his paws on my shoulder and his dribble on my jumper. He was terrified of cars, having never seen them in his village, and he dribbled a great deal.

In Pakistan, I arranged Babur's injections, his vet's certificates, his enormous kennel and his seat on the plane to Britain. The Pakistani summer was starting and Babur, who was most happy rolling in snow, was hot. But I wasn't too worried. He seemed entranced by the lush grass and the trees filled with birds. He was going to my home in Perthshire, where it would be cool beneath the oak trees.

Finally, everything seemed finished. I was booked to fly to London and he was supposed to follow the next day. I went out into the garden and he woke, looked up and rolled lazily on his back for his stomach to be scratched. I didn't scratch him for as long as I would have liked because I didn't want to worry him. But I suppose he guessed something was up because when I had got in the car, he came trotting around the back of the house, with his white-muzzled wrinkled face in the air. He stopped at the gate, watching me as the car backed down the drive.

After twenty months of walking, I flew from Islamabad and stopped at Dubai airport, where I was served at McDonalds by a Filipino from Luzon. I landed at London and noticed its glass shop fronts and posters of half-naked women. Where I had been in Asia the tarmac roads petered out at the edges into bare patches of littered earth. Here the concrete ran clean from the roads over the kerbs and up the walls of the houses, so that the whole city seemed rendered as a single room. Middle-aged men in suits stood in the streets at midday, looking lost and soft.

I took the sleeper up to Dunblane and walked the last twenty kilometres home. It was first light and the short halogen lights were still lit along the road. Rabbits stood beneath single trees. The sheep were spread thinly across a grass plain that could have supported a flock fifty times that size. Under a close, small sky, the river was still and broad and labelled 'Private, No fishing'. A line of daffodils had been planted for two kilometres along the verge, in front of an avenue of bare beech trees.

Clean metallic signs announced a school and a forty-mile-an-hour speed limit. A domestic cat leapt over the wall of a petrol station. The cars were parked in front of the houses with their noses thrust over the close-mown lawns. There were conservatories, dark green ironware tables behind thigh-high walls and bird tables with hanging seed. I imagined knocking and saying, 'Where is the headman? I would like to stay.'

I reached a bridge, which was built in the eighteenth

century, just wide enough for a single horse. A smart silver sign beside it announced that it had been restored in 1990, twelve years earlier, with European Union funding and opened by a general. It was overgrown with nettles and a fallen log blocked one end.

I climbed into the hills. Two overfed ponies, with long manes and hair over their eyes, trotted full bellied through the rough gorse and the mist towards me. It was a Scottish mist, damp on my hand and cheeks, though it was not raining. At Muthill I stopped in the pub for breakfast. The landlady asked, 'Why are you walking?' I remembered the reasons I had given Afghans. She added, 'Are you doing it for charity or are you on holiday?'

I crossed the old stone bridge at the south end of Crieff and the gravel sank into the damp earth beneath my boots as I turned up the drive. A sycamore had fallen, revealing the caravan site. The heavy oaks strained forward, two years thicker. The dark, stiff, torn bark had been forced further apart, revealing more smooth underflesh. Someone, my father I assumed, had moved six large box trees from the woods. I could see the yew ahead and then the grey columns of the house, dark with damp. I strode towards the steps. If I had been in a car someone would have heard me arrive, but no one was in the hall to greet me.

*

Much later, when I had kissed my mother and gone up to my room, I thought again of the telephone call which I had received in London. It was Edward from Pakistan to say that Babur had died the day before he was meant to get on the plane. Someone had given him rack of lamb. He had eaten bread all his life and had neither the teeth nor the experience to handle a bone. The shards cut up his stomach and killed him. That line of smells by unmarked boulders, stretching to a snow-ridge horizon, with ice holes for drinking, would, I thought, finish with good meat, oak trees, rabbits and a warm house. But it ended with his death.

I don't imagine Babur would have been very impressed to see me crying now, trying to bring back five weeks walking alone together, with my hand on a grizzled golden head, which is Babur, beside me and alive.

Acknowledgements

This book was written at home in Perthshire. I was lucky in the many friends who read it in draft form. I owe particular thanks to Patrick Mackie, Stephen Brown, Edward Skidelsky, Minna Jarvenpaa and Rachel Aspden for giving the book more life and all its commas.

To Clare Alexander for her imagination and energy; Mary-Kay Wilmers for first publishing me; Jason Cooper for understanding the journey and editing it skilfully and Peter Straus and Andrew Kidd for editorial support.

I am indebted to J D-B for much that I will never be able to communicate, Peter Jouvenal for his encouragement and Diana Livesey, Felix Martin, Andrew Greenstock, Will Adamsdale, Oliver Akers-Douglas, Luke Ponte, Palash Dave, Tommaso Nelli, Peregrine Hodson, Honor Fraser, Nico Schwarz, Mani Boni, Nick Crane, Fiona, Annie, Heather, Gordon, Gillie and Richard for their friendship and advice during the journey and the writing.

Throughout the walk I was inspired by the courage and determination of Mohammed Oraz, who walked for three months beside me across Iran. I had hoped to finish the journey beside him. He was killed in an avalanche on the summit of Gasherbrum 1, his sixth eight-thousand-metre peak, in September 2003.

Finally, it is to my parents that I owe the most, in this as in so much else.

OTHER PICADOR BOOKS
AVAILABLE FROM PAN MACMILLAN

ALEXANDER FRATER
TALES FROM THE TORRID ZONE   0 330 37529 6   £7.99
CHASING THE MONSOON   0 330 43313 X   £7.99
BEYOND THE BLUE HORIZON   0 330 43312 1   £7.99

JASON ELLIOT
AN UNEXPECTED LIGHT   0 330 37162 2   £8.99

WILLIAM FIENNES
THE SNOW GEESE   0 330 37578 4   £7.99

All Pan Macmillan titles can be ordered from our website,
www.panmacmillan.com, or from your local bookshop
and are also available by post from:

Bookpost, PO Box 29, Douglas, Isle of Man IM99 1BQ
Credit cards accepted. For details:
Telephone: +44 (0)1624 677237
Fax: +44 (0)1624 670923
E-mail: bookshop@enterprise.net
www.bookpost.co.uk

Free postage and packing in the United Kingdom

Prices shown above were correct at the time of going to press.
Pan Macmillan reserve the right to show new retail prices on covers
which may differ from those previously advertised in the text
or elsewhere.